HAWAII

ON-THE-ROAD HISTORIES

HAWAII

John H. Chambers

Interlink Books

For my families who with their loving encouragement of my work over many years have made this book and all the others possible, and especially for three writers, Maria G. Figueroa, Joy Chambers, and Coral Chambers. They first learned to love Hawaii long ago.

First published in 2006 by

INTERLINK BOOKS
An imprint of Interlink Publishing Group, Inc.
46 Crosby Street, Northampton, Massachusetts 01060
www.interlinkbooks.com

Text copyright © John H. Chambers, 2006
Design copyright © Interlink Publishing, 2006
Maps by Charles Higgins

Library of Congress Cataloging-in-Publication Data
Chambers, John H.
 Hawaii / by John Chambers.
    p. cm. — (On-the-road histories)
 Includes bibliographical references (p.   ).
 ISBN 1-56656-615-0 (pbk.)
 1. Hawaii—History. 2. Hawaii—Description and travel. 3.
Hawaii—History, Local. I. Title. II. Series.
 DU625.C47 2005
 996.9—dc22
                                        2005013188

Printed and bound in China

Quotation p. 240 from Rodney T. West, *Honolulu Prepares for Japan's Attack*. © 1993 Rodney T. West.
Quotation pp. 228–231 from Peggy Hicock Hodge, *Growing Up Barefoot in Hawaii*. © 1997 Mutual Publishing.
Quotation p. 278 from Ben R. Finney, *Hokule'a: The Way to Tahiti*. © Ben R. Finney.

CONTENTS

Na Pali Coast Wai'ale'ale **Kauai**
Waimea Canyon

Niihau

Koʻola

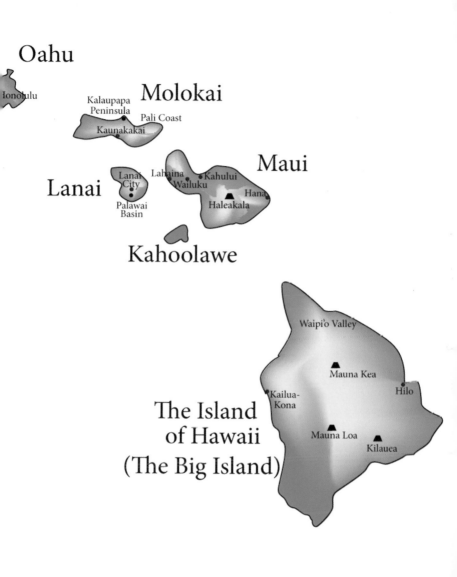

Introduction

This is a story of discovery: of intrepid anonymous Polynesian sailors who around 350 CE steered by the stars and ocean swells and first found these islands; and of daring European navigators who in the later 1700s landed and linked Hawaii to the rest of the world.

It is a description of society and politics: of the draconian control over commoners by Hawaii's hereditary aristocrats; and of the later nearly eighty-year tussle for political supremacy between native Hawaiians and American settlers.

It is a tale of religious belief: of native ideas of mana and *kapu* and human sacrifice; and of the arrival of self-assured Western Christians who brought new beliefs.

It is a report of disasters: of tsunamis that can sweep away a town's commercial center; and of a single bomb that entombed nearly 1,200 seamen in a sunken battleship.

It is an account of economies: of self-sufficient villagers' subsistence growing and gathering in their wedge-shaped parcels of land; and of immigrants sweating for a pittance in sugar and pineapple plantations producing for the market.

It is a picture of people taking their pleasures: of ancient Hawaiians dancing and playing stone castanets, nose flutes, and tiny knee drums; and of modern tourists seeking a surfeit of sights, sun, sand, surf, and sensuality.

It is the story of the links between the land and the lives of the people in the most famous chain of volcanic islands in the world—and the most various and dramatically beautiful.

Notes on Usage and Spelling

The Word "Hawaii"

Geographically and historically, the word "Hawaii" has referred to several different entities. To avoid confusion, the single word "Hawaii" is always used here to refer to the whole, to the archipelago of islands, the unified kingdom, the Territory of Hawaii, or the state of Hawaii. Following local usage, the words "Big Island" or "the Island of Hawaii" are used when referring to the island at the southeast end of the chain, the largest of the archipelago, and never the single word "Hawaii" by itself.

Written Hawaiian Language

The Hawaiian alphabet, devised by Protestant missionaries in the 1820s, uses 12 letters (a, e, h, i, k, l, m, n, o, p, u, and w) plus two diacritical marks for the glottal stop and for a stressed vowel, though these marks were not introduced until 130 years after the letters were decided on.

The 'okina or glottal stop is a sound similar to the break between "uh" and "oh" when we say "uh-oh!"—a hesitation that separates the two sounds. It is used only between vowels, e.g., in the proper nouns Ke'anae Peninsula, Ho'okipa Beach, or before a vowel at the beginning of a word, such as the Hawaiian common nouns 'ohana (extended family) and 'ili (narrow strip of land worked by an 'ohana).

The other diacritical sign, the macron, is not used in this book; it is a straight line over the stressed vowel.

It is inappropriate to use diacritical marks when a Hawaiian word has been anglicized. The word "Hawaiian" in the previous sentence is an example. This is an English word. So to mark the Hawaiian language glottal stop and write "Hawai'ian" in that sentence would be incorrect.

English and Hawaiian Words

In English, we write and say "Florence" not "Firenze," "Munich" not "München," "Moscow" not "Moskva," and so on. This is a book in English, not in Hawaiian, so in this book, Hawaii itself and the names of its eight main islands of Niihau, Kauai, Oahu, Maui, Molokai, Lanai, Kahoolawe, and the Island of Hawaii are treated as words in English, and so appear without Hawaiian diacritical marks.

Again, just as French words such as "sabotage" and "cuisine" and Spanish words such as "guerilla" and "salsa" have been absorbed by English speakers and become words in the English language, by now originally Hawaiian (or generally Polynesian) words such as "hula," "lei," "mana," "taro," and "ukulele" have also been absorbed. They are used in this book as English words and are not italicized.

In this book Hawaiian common nouns that have not been absorbed are italicized, e.g., *kapu* (taboo) and *heiau* (temple).

Fishing, scuba diving, and sight-seeing boats frolic under a glorious blue sky, just offshore from the now tourist-filled 1800s whaling port of Lahaina, with mountains of West Maui in the distance.
Maria G. Figueroa

It would have been simpler to ignore the glottal stop, but to help visitors with pronunciation, other than with the islands just mentioned, the text gives Hawaiian spelling to place names and the names of historical Hawaiians, e.g., Koʻolau Range, Waipiʻo Valley, Queen Liliʻuokalani.

Hawaiian language plurals do not add an "s." It has become common for English-speaking residents of Hawaii to follow this rule when using Hawaiian words. For the sake of consistency, the text applies that usage here with italicized Hawaiian words, thus one *heiau* and several *heiau*.

ACKNOWLEDGMENTS

Discussions with Hawaiians of various ethnicities during many visits to the islands; sessions in the library of the University of Hawaii at Manoa and in public libraries in Oahu, Maui, and Lanai; the publications of the University of Hawaii Press and other Hawaiian publishers; Honolulu newspapers and those from other islands, and many other Hawaiian publications have all helped in the writing of this book. Several Hawaiian organizations and institutions, such as Bishop Museum, Hawaii Visitors and Convention

Bureau, Maui Visitors Bureau, Oahu Visitors Bureau, and Molokai Visitors Association, have proved most helpful.

Dr. Howard Van Treaze of the University of Hawaii at Hilo gave his historical expertise, though he is not responsible for my judgments or for any opinions I may express. My wife, Maria G. Figueroa, read and commented on the manuscript and shared many of my visits to Hawaii, and in both cases contributed her own unique insights. Beatriz Llenin Figueroa helped with interlibrary loans and commented on some of the contents. Historical novelist Joy Chambers read and discussed several key chapters.

For help of various kinds, from advice, to factual corrections, to supply of or help in securing photographs and illustrations, and several other functions, I must thank Dr. Ben R. Finney of the University of Hawaii, Allen W. Hoof, archivist at the Hawaii State Archives, DeSoto Brown and Shaun Chillingworth of Bishop Museum, Marc Miranda and Carol Philips of the Hawaii Governor's Office of Information, Keith De Mello and Nicole La Berge of McNeil Wilson Communications Inc., Rebecca Pang of Styker Weiner and Yakota Public Relations Inc., Professor Ron Crocombe of the University of the South Pacific, Pat and Graham Muller, Hector L. Torres, Catherine Metz, Dr. Reg Grundy, Dr. Roger Hayward, Haydee Figueroa Torres, Andrea DiRuscio of Sheila Donnelly and Associates LLC, Diane Nicols, and Gabriela S. Llenin Figueroa. The seminal writings of Professor I. C. Campbell, now of the University of the South Pacific, helped me understand Hawaii in its wider Pacific context. Gavan Daws's book *Shoal of Time* and Michael Dougherty's *To Steal a Kingdom* have proved extremely helpful in their references to original sources.

I should also thank publisher Michel Moushabeck for readily agreeing to my proposal to write this book.

CREATION AND ORIGINS

CREATION OF THE HAWAIIAN ISLANDS

The surface of our planet, the solid outer layer of crust, or lithosphere, consists of about a dozen major rigid "plates" and many smaller ones. These plates move with respect to one another, sliding over the more fluid layer of the asthenosphere typically about 6.36 inches (21.2 cm) a year in the North Pacific. According to one theory, heat-driven circulation of huge convection cells in the asthenosphere provides the force that moves the plates. The lighter continents, embedded in the surface of the much larger plates, are carried along with their movement.

Hot Spots and High Oceanic Islands

The plate that helps give existence to the Hawaiian Islands is the mighty Pacific Plate, the world's largest. The Pacific Plate rides generally northwest and in so doing passes over a large, long-lived "hot spot" in the asthenosphere—so-called because of the molten volcanic material continually being ejected at that "spot." Hot spots are a subject of much current research and there is limited consensus about them among today's scientists. The theory that was until recently predominant asserts that the hot spot remains in the same place, relatively, beneath the plate. Over the eons in countless thousands of eruptions, volcanic material from the hot spot thrusts its way through local fissures in the Pacific Plate itself and gradually builds a volcano on top. In time, such a volcano continues to grow and rise far above sea level to form a high oceanic island. As the Pacific Plate continues to move northwest, it carries this newly formed volcanic island away from the hot spot, and from then on the volcano cannot grow anymore and becomes extinct. Another volcanic island then begins to form over the hot spot, and when it has been carried away, a third volcanic island begins, and so on. So, during tens of millions of years, a 1,500 mi long (2,400 km) "production line" or chain of islands forms. We call this chain the Hawaiian Islands, and it is the largest, most striking, and best known of all such island chains in the Pacific Ocean.

Hawaii also featured in geologists' first awareness of the existence of hot spots. The idea of a "hot spot" was conceptualized by the Canadian geophysicist J. Tuzo Wilson. Wilson recalls that in 1960:

> I was impressed by the idea of island arcs [and was trying to work out how they might form]. On the way back [from research in Antarctica] we stopped in Hawaii and visited the Upper Atmosphere Observatory on Mauna Loa at about 12,000 feet. We were sitting on a volcano and I thought about this... all the Hawaiian Islands had the same geology: the ABC pattern was repeated... but [the As, Bs, and Cs] had not necessarily occurred at the same time....

Wilson melded his thoughts with other new geological knowledge evolving at that time, such as the idea that the ocean floor was moving, and the data from new techniques for dating volcanic rocks. The explanation for a repeated geological pattern on a long chain of islands of increasing age such as Hawaii was that each island had formed in turn over a stationary volcanic source.

From northwest to southeast, moving from older to younger, the list of the eight main Hawaiian islands is Niihau, Kauai, Oahu, Molokai, Maui, Lanai, Kahoolawe, and the Island of Hawaii (the Big Island). These eight islands have a combined area of 6,423 sq mi (16,636 sq km). But in reality, they are merely the tops of huge volcanoes that rest thousands of feet down on the ocean floor. (Measured from the ocean floor, from which it rises uninterruptedly, Mauna Kea would be the world's highest mountain at about 32,000 ft/9,753 m.)

The oldest rocks on Niihau and Kauai are from five to seven million years old; those on Maui are about two million; those on the island of Hawaii, the most southeasterly and the geologically youngest of all, are about one million years old. As the plate moved, the merging of five volcanoes formed the Island of Hawaii. It is still growing because its two active volcanoes, Mauna Loa and Kilauea, still sit over the hot spot.

The woman at the bottom of this picture is viewing the end of the lava flow of Kilauea volcano in the evening, when the lava looks most spectacular. There are guided tours, and even greater caution must be shown than during the day.
Hawaii Visitors and Convention Bureau and Kirk Lee Aeder

Haleakala on Maui, Mauna Loa, and Mauna Kea are vast "shield" volcanoes and have been prodigious producers of lava. Haleakala, for instance, the largest dormant volcano on earth, would contain about a hundred so-called composite volcanoes like Fujiyama in Japan or Mt. Vesuvius in Italy. The sides of composite volcanoes become steeper toward the top, and the climber on the summit experiences the elation of being isolated at a giddy height. But with the gently convex shape of the great shield volcanoes of Hawaii, the experience on the summit is very different. There is a feeling of standing atop a vast mass of the mountain whose height is difficult to judge and easily underestimated. There seems little chance of falling off. No visit to Hawaii is complete without a trip to the top of one of these mega-mountains.

Climate

Visitors consider the climate of Hawaii idyllic, perhaps the most desirable in the world. As two characters in a Jack London short story describe the western Kona Coast of the Big Island:

"A lotus land," I said.
"Where each day is like every day, and every day is a paradise of days," he answered… "It is not too hot. It is not too cold. It is always just right. Have you noticed how the land and the sea breathe turn and turn about?"

Although there is little seasonal variation, there can be great variation from one place to another. While the sun is shining in endless balmy, palmy days in Kona, in Hilo on the east coast there can be huge floods.

In the populated coastal areas, the ocean moderates humidity and there are continual caressing sea breezes. Windward slopes of islands receive more rainfall from the prevailing northeast trade winds than do leeward sides. The 18-mile-long small island of Niihau off southwest Kauai lies in that island's rain shadow and is the driest of all.

Average temperatures in downtown Honolulu are 72°F (22°C) in the cool month, 78°F (26°C) in the warmest. Average water temperatures on Waikiki Beach are 75°F (24°C) in late February and 79°F (26°C) in late September. With the exception of some areas on their leeward sides and within the active or dormant volcanic regions, all the islands are marvelously fertile with ample and, in places, enormous amounts of rainfall. Mt. Wai'ale'ale in Kauai receives about 440 inches of rain a year (11,280 mm). The driest region, in leeward Big Island, Kawaiehae, has 8.7 inches (220 mm); Honolulu gets 23 inches, Hilo 129 inches.

Though all the inhabited islands lie in the tropics, there is a noticeable difference in time of winter and summer sunset and sunrise. From the summit of Mauna Kea, Mark Twain wrote on the climate for the *New York Tribune* in 1873:

You cannot find as much climate bunched together anywhere in the world as you can in the Sandwich Islands [Hawaii]. You may stand on the summit of Mauna Kea, in the midst of snowbanks that were there before Capt. Cook was born, maybe, and while you shiver in your furs you may cast your eye down the sweep of the mountain side and tell exactly where the frigid zone ends and vegetable life begins; a stunted and tormented growth of trees shades down into a taller and freer species, and that in turn, into the full foliage and varied tints of the temperate zone; further down, the mere ordinary green tone of a forest washes over the edges of a broad bar of orange trees that embraces the mountain like a belt, and is so deep and dark a green that distance makes it black; and still further down, your eye rests upon the levels of the seashore, where the sugar-cane is scorching in the sun, and the feathery cocoa-palm glassing itself in the tropical waves; and where you know the sinful natives are lolling about in utter nakedness and never knowing or caring that you and your snow and your chattering teeth are so close by. So you perceive, you can look down upon all the climates of the earth, and note the kinds and colors of all the vegetations, just with a glance of the eye—and this glance only travels about three miles as the bird flies, too.

The most active of the world's volcanoes, Kilauea on the southern end of the Island of Hawaii, continues to expel huge volumes of lava onto the island and into the ocean along the island's southeastern shore. Irreplaceable ancient petroglyphs, *heiau*, and historic landmarks, churches, roads, villages, and occasional people, all become food for the insatiable appetite of this monster.

Though they have the same chemical composition with varying physical conditions, two different-looking kinds of lava are produced by Kilauea. There is "a'a" and "pahoehoe." A'a is rough and chunky. Pahoehoe looks like monstrous fields of solidified black mashed potatoes. Though these are Hawaiian words, they are now used by all geologists.

Twenty miles out to sea, a new seamount known as Lo'ihi, also over an arm of the hot spot, is growing too. Though it is still about 3,000 ft (900 m) below the surface, in time Lo'ihi may merge with the Island of Hawaii, making it even larger. However, Lo'ihi cannot be seen

The Big Island volcano Kilauea has been in continual eruption since 1983. The fate facing anything that lies in the path of its lava is shown by this section of the Chain of Craters Road on the Big Island, covered in 2003. Hector L. Torres & Catherine Metz

except via technology because water is such a wonderful absorber of light and heat.

Life and Death of Islands

Like the people who live upon them, the Hawaiian Islands are born, live, and perish. For after their volcanoes become extinct, all Hawaiian islands become smaller under a combination of four "W's" and two "E's." The erosion of water (rain and streams), wind, and pounding ocean waves wear them down. They also begin sinking under their own massive weight, which presses on the crust beneath them. Earthquakes too play a part. The windward Kohala Coast of Hawaii, the north shore of Molokai, and the western Na Pali coast of Kauai, which now present sheer faces to the sea, are dramatic examples. Here earthquakes have shaken

Halfway between southwest Maui and Kahoolawe Island, this small crescent-shaped islet, Molokini, is the projecting top of a submerged volcanic tuff cone. Its 19 ac rise to about 165 ft (51 m) above the ocean. Black coral was harvested here until the 1970s. A marine reserve, its coral and waters teem with open ocean fish, making it ideal for snorkeling and scuba diving.

Hawaii Visitors and Convention Bureau and Ron Dahlquist

Lava Man: Thomas A. Jaggar, Jr.

Thomas Augustus Jaggar, Jr. (1871–1953) lived among the jagged lava rock of Kilauea Volcano. He loved volcanoes, delighting in the danger. Breakfast taken, Jaggar would climb down a rope ladder dangling on the cliff face of the caldera and march to bubbling Halema'uma'u Crater to observe and measure. Sometimes he cooked his eggs in the volcanic heat. He began the now famous Hawaiian Volcano Observatory (HVO).

Jaggar travelled the world to watch volcanoes and volcanic action, from St. Pierre in Martinique, destroyed by Mt. Pele in 1902; to Vesuvius and Pompeii, destroyed in 69 CE; to underwater eruptions in Japan. But nowhere matched Kilauea, because the slow-moving continual eruption that makes it so inviting for tourism also makes it ideal for scientific study. Originally from the Massachusetts Institute of Technology (MIT), Jaggar thought that the normal practice of observing volcanoes only when they were erupting was ridiculous. He realized that the often-active Kilauea Volcano would be the best site in the world to make continual observations.

So in 1912 he had a hole dug in the lava in the north rim surrounding the caldera, a few minutes' walk from his house. The diggers were prisoners of the territory of Hawaii who had been sentenced to hard labor. They hacked through nearly six feet of volcanic ash and pumice to a layer of hard pahoehoe lava to provide a firm floor for the concrete poles on which Jaggar would anchor his seismometers.

Jaggar continually designed new instruments. He even developed a rugged portable seismograph that could be operated in outlying areas by amateur assistants. For exploration around the coasts, he designed an amphibious vehicle.

Jaggar worked endlessly for financial support to construct and man his observatory. Lorrin A. Thurston—lawyer, businessman, and leader of the coup that removed Queen Lili'uokalani—was a continuing help into 1930. Several "Big Five" companies supported the project, and MIT gave funds, as did the University of Hawaii. The Observatory was later successively sponsored by the US Weather Bureau (1919–24), the US Geological Survey (1924–35), the National Park Service (1935–47), and (since 1947) again the US Geological Survey.

From the early 1940s, HVO occupied a new building 600 ft (185 m) in from the caldera rim. In 1948 HVO moved to another headquarters at the top of Uwekahuna Bluff on the northwest rim of Kilauea Caldera. All this occurred under Jaggar's direction. But he had died by the time the new and larger present building in a similar location was completed in 1986.

Studies of tsunamis reflected Jaggar's concern for life and property. In 1933 HVO seismograms predicted the arrival of a tsunami from a distant earthquake, and for the first time in history people in low-lying areas were warned.

When Jaggar died, his wife Isabel had his body cremated and spread his ashes in the fiery red lake of Halema'uma'u Crater in Kilauea Caldera—the home of Volcano Goddess Pele. Pele must have been pleased.

For more information, visit HVO's website at hvo.wr.usgs.gov.

and shaved off mighty chunks in huge landslides to sculpt some of the highest sheer sea cliffs on the planet—around 3,000 ft (900 m).

Given Hawaii's reputation for a balmy climate, it comes as a surprise to some tourists that Mauna Kea (13,796 ft/4,205 m) and Mauna Loa (13,679 ft/4,169 m) are high enough to have snow fields in winter, where people ski. So snow has also helped erosion, and ice too, because Mauna Kea had a summit glacier during the last ice age. The terminal moraine left by the retreating glacier can be seen just above the State Recreation Area between Mauna Kea and Mauna Loa.

Once the volcano ceases to grow, the growth of coral reefs becomes crucial in the island's life. Coral reefs are created by the accumulation of billions of limestone skeletons left by millions of generations of tiny coral polyps, most no larger than a pinhead. Coral thrives in clear salt water where the temperature remains at 65°F (18°C) or above. The solid base for polyp growth must not be more than about 160 ft (49 m) below the surface. The colony of coral polyps grows slowly upward, building upon the skeletons of earlier generations, until it reaches low tide mark. What are called fringing reefs begin to form around the island's circumference

The growth of the fringing reef keeps pace with the island's sinking. The reef also acquires sand, driftwood, vegetation, and debris. As the island continues to sink, the coral reef detaches, and slowly an ever-widening and deepening lagoon forms between the island and what has now become a barrier reef. There are reefs and slowly widening lagoons along the coasts of the middle-aged islands of Kauai, Oahu, Molokai, Maui, and Lanai, and such a reef is beginning to form in places around the island of Hawaii too.

After millions of years the island disappears from sight to leave an approximately circular lagoon, surrounded by what is now a coral atoll that marks the circumference of where the original volcanic island used to be. Such lagoons may be many miles wide, as wide as the original island, but the land of the ring-shaped atoll is normally only about 200–400 yd/m across. The beaches of such atolls are formed by the powerful Pacific surf, which pounds the coral, shells, and further assorted debris into tiny fragments—the pristine white of the Hawaii travel posters. For such reasons, the geologically oldest islands in the Hawaiian chain, transported by the Pacific Plate far to the northwest of Kauai and Niihau, have now sunk and eroded away, leaving only coral atolls showing above the ocean.

Low and flat Kure Island and French Frigate shoals are scarcely above high tide mark. The most famous of these coral atolls is Midway, site of the Second World War Battle of Midway. However, several hundred feet below the surface, the base of every coral atoll sits atop the eroded and sunken summits of former volcanic mountains, once as majestic as Mauna Kea.

The most northerly island in the Hawaiian archipelago passed over the hot spot around 70 million years ago. All these northwest islands are uninhabited, part of the Hawaiian Islands National Wildlife Refuge. Whereas the depth of coral reefs is relatively shallow around Hawaii's occupied islands, like Oahu, the depth of coral reef increases dramatically (proving their age and evolution) as one travels northwest into the region of atolls. At Midway, deep-core drillings have been made. These show there is a minimum of 820 ft (253 m) of coral deposits, and coral limestone shows to depths of about 1,066 ft (325 m).

Travel in time to Oahu, Maui, and the other main Hawaiian islands in 20 million years and only circular coral atolls enclosing lagoons will remain. By that time, Midway, Kure, and the French Frigate shoals will long have eroded entirely away and be far underwater.

In most countries, people run as quickly as possible from a volcanic eruption, but not in Hawaii. In Hawaii people usually rush toward the eruption. Why? Though most of the world's volcanoes erupt violently, as is often the case with Hawaiian volcanoes, Kilauea Volcano at present erupts gently and can be viewed safely from short (but still hot) distances.

Each year some 2.5 million visitors travel to observe this astonishing growth at the end of Chain of Craters Road in the Hawaii Volcanoes National Park. The fortunate travellers arrive just when spectacular lava fountains spew forth, lakes of molten rock form, or red and yellow-hot rivers of lava flow. It is of course necessary to carefully follow the instructions of the park rangers and the trails they strictly line with yellow markers.

Tsunamis

People used to call tsunamis "tidal waves"—a misleading name. A tsunami (pronounced tsoo-nah-mee) is a series of waves generated in the ocean by a disturbance that moves the ocean water column up and then down. Earthquakes, landslides, volcanic eruptions, explosions, and even at times the impact of cosmic bodies such as meteorites cause tsunamis. The potential energy that results from pushing water above normal sea level is then changed into kinetic energy to propagate the tsunami horizontally. From the area of the disturbance, the energy waves travel outward in all directions, much like gargantuan versions of the ripples caused by throwing a rock into a pond. The time between wave crests may be anything from 5 to 90 minutes, but is generally about 10 to 45 minutes.

A Tsunami Warning System (TWS) has been set up, consisting of 26 participating countries monitoring seismological and tidal stations throughout the Pacific Basin, evaluating earthquakes that may generate a tsunami and sending out warnings. The Pacific Tsunami Warning Center (PTWC) near Honolulu is the operational headquarters of the Pacific TWS.

Pacific Ocean tsunamis are almost always caused by earthquakes, which can occur near to where they come ashore or thousands of miles away. Some tsunamis become monstrous. Close to a coast, their height reaches 30 ft and upwards (about 100 ft in the worst cases) and they can rush inland hundreds of yards at a speed faster than an Olympic sprinter can run. In 1946 a tsunami with waves of 20 to 32 ft smashed into Hilo on the Big Island, destroying the downtown area and killing 159 people.

Many tsunamis generate "edge waves" that churn back and forth parallel to shore, resulting in many waves at a particular point on the coast. Often the first wave is not the largest, so the danger lasts for hours. Water near the shore may recede for long periods, temporarily exposing the ocean floor. At Hilo and other places on the east coast of the Big Island when the ocean receded during the smaller tsunamis, local people walked out onto the bare ocean floor with buckets to gather stranded fish such as moi, papio, and mullet—a potentially fatal practice when the tsunami's waves return.

The speed at which a tsunami travels varies as the square of the depth of the water. So in the deep ocean, a tsunami will be only a yard or so high (though it can be tens or even hundreds of miles wide), but soon it is travelling extraordinarily fast. In the open ocean, many average an amazing 450 mi per hour. Wave speed and wavelength (distance between wave crests) decrease as the tsunami reaches shallower water, so the energy per unit area has to increase. This forces the wave to rise to a great height.

Most populated areas in Hawaii near the coast have considerable heights behind them to which people can escape. Fortunately, greater Honolulu, with a disproportionate three-quarters share of the state's population, lies on a coast that rarely experiences tsunamis. Hawaii's tsunami warning system carries out periodic drills. Visit www.geophys.washington.edu/tsunami/intro.html and walrus.wr.usgs.gov/tsunami for more about these phenomena.

Honopu Valley, Na Pali Coast, Kauai. Access is by boat, kayak, helicopter, or via the rugged and dangerous Kalalau Trail. In the 1980s the US Geological Survey, using sonar, discovered some 70 major landslides covering about half of the underwater flanks of the Hawaiian chain. Several of these probably helped sculpt the sheer cliffs of the Na Pali coast (and caused tsunamis). In a few million years, landslides, erosion, and sinking will have destroyed this coast and reduced Kauai to a small island with a mountainous interior, about the size of Nihoa, the next island, about 150 mi to the northwest.
Hawaii Visitors and Convention Bureau and Robert Coello

In 2003 a member of a group of travel operators received first, second, and third degree burns over eight percent of his body. He must have entered an area that had been closed, because the Park Rangers reported that "no trail was open that would let visitors get close enough to lava to burn themselves." In 2002 a Florida woman was found dead about 50 yards from a lava flow, apparently from exposure. Too many tourists ignore warnings to carry water, wear hats, use proper footwear, bring high energy snacks, and be sufficiently fit to hike half a mile or more across hard, rough, dried, rolling black lava fields. Here the heat rises well above 100 degrees. In the year 2000, two hikers from Hawaii and Washington DC died, probably from pulmonary edema caused by inhaling steam. They were only 100 yd/m from where the lava was entering the ocean and creating huge volumes of dangerous gases and steam—too close for safety.

ORIGINS OF POLYNESIANS AND HAWAIIANS

The Polynesian islands of New Zealand, Samoa, Tahiti, Easter Island, Hawaii, and all the others lie thousands of miles from the settled continents of Australia, Asia, and the Americas. The Hawaiian Islands, for example, are over 2,000 mi from California. Yet with simple sailing vessels, the Polynesians colonized them all. Moreover, Polynesian culture, including language, remained fascinatingly similar. This means that colonization must have been achieved relatively quickly, historically speaking. Otherwise, with such far-flung archipelagoes, greater cultural differences would have had time to evolve.

In 1959 the anthropologist Kenneth P. Emory of the splendid Bernice P. Bishop Museum in Honolulu—which every tourist to Honolulu should visit—first proposed the now-accepted view of the origins of the Polynesians and thus of the Hawaiians. His predecessors debated where Polynesians had come from. Emory drew together conceptions from his own ethnological, linguistic, and archaeological work in many parts of Polynesia (he was once stranded on a remote atoll for two months), along with the data of other researchers, and produced a stunning new explanation of Polynesian origins. The Polynesians, and thus the Hawaiians, did not come from Southeast Asia or through Micronesia or from South or North America. In fact they did not come *from* anywhere other than Polynesia itself.

The Polynesians evolved in the western Polynesian region of Samoa and Tonga from a small population of mixed Southeast Asian origins. Their ancestors had come by way of

Flora and Fauna

The seeds of now endemic plant species were brought to the originally completely barren Hawaiian islands by winds, currents, tides, and birds, which caused the growth of extensive forests, shrubs, and grasslands over everything except for the relatively recent volcanic lava lands and the summits and calderas of the great volcanoes.

Extreme isolation limited the arrival of species, as seen from the fewer than 300 flowering plant species, for instance. The same species evolved into new varieties to fill the many different ecological niches from tropical beach to alpine summit. For instance, the delicate silversword or *'ahinahina*, which grows only on top of Haleakala, Maui, and Mauna Kea and Mauna Loa on the Big Island, is closely related to the greensword, which is found in the summit bogs of lower mountains and other mid-elevations, and to a liana in mid-level forests. They and some 24 other trees and shrubs all descended from the same original.

There are no defensive adaptations of Hawaiian plants either, because thorns and plant poisons were unnecessary in a land where there were no natural predators. Some plants such as the Hawaiian raspberry (*'akala*) lost the thorns formerly attached to their continental ancestors. Extreme isolation also ensured that most native flora are unique.

Since the first Polynesians arrived, a vast variety of food and ornamental plant life from many parts of the world has been introduced together with trees—from Indian banyans to Australian eucalypts. Food plants grown both commercially and in backyards for home use have long included a cornucopia of coconuts, sugarcane, pineapples, papayas, bananas, mangoes, guavas, lichee, avocados, breadfruit, macadamia nuts, limes, passion fruit, taros, and tamarinds. Most varieties of garden vegetables are raised in the islands, and flowers abound all year.

Native birds, long isolated from other similar species, have evolved certain characteristics of their own—for example the *nene* (Hawaiian goose), the Hawaiian stilt, and a variety of small forest birds. Some species have become extremely rare, but action has been taken to preserve them. Vast numbers of sea-birds nest on the northwestern atolls and to a lesser extent among the inhabited islands. Tiny golden plovers make an astonishing nonstop 3,000 mi (4,800 km) journey from Alaska to Hawaii where they pass the winter, as do ducks from Alaska, Canada, and the northwestern United States. Quantities of non-native mynas, sparrows, cardinals, and doves live in the trees in both town and country.

Pigs and chickens came with the original Polynesian settlers. Cattle were introduced in the later 1700s by the English naval captain George Vancouver, and horses in the early 1800s by Kamehameha's English advisor, John Young.

Introduced wild animals include mongooses, rats, frogs, and toads. The most recent uninvited guest is the Puerto Rican coqui, a small frog with a loud, shrill voice that had reached plague proportions by 2005. In the more remote regions of some of the islands, there are sheep, pigs, and goats. Marine life abounds. About 5,000 humpback whales migrate to Hawaiian waters every year between November and May—up from about a thousand in the mid-1960s when regulation of commercial whaling began. They winter there, mate, gestate, give birth, and nurture their calves before returning to northern waters for the spring.

temporary settlement along the north coast of New Guinea, and the Melanesian islands such as the Solomons and Vanuatu to the east. Over a period of perhaps a thousand years or more, they evolved their unique Polynesian physical type and culture. With few exceptions, Emory's account is now accepted by all scholars of the Pacific peoples, historians, anthropologists, sociologists, archaeologists, linguists, and geneticists. New evidence and discoveries continually add to and confirm the story.

Voyages of Colonization

A phase of colonization of the far Pacific by Samoans, now clearly Polynesian, began around 1 CE. In deliberate expeditions, they carried food, tools, seeds, plants, and domesticated animals. They appear to have settled the Marquesas first and were well established there by the 300s. From the Marquesas, they returned southwest to the Society Islands (Tahiti, etc.).

Polynesians from the Marquesas seem to have sailed north to Hawaii about 350 CE. Their numbers were small, travelling in perhaps only two or three great double canoes. Wooden crossbeams that held platforms and huts joined the canoes, everything being tied with sennit (coconut-fiber lashings). Because these vessels were far from watertight, their passengers had to continually bail the seawater that seeped in.

Polynesians were superb voyagers, and they developed nautical traditions different from those of Europeans, navigating by nature and not by mathematics. Through trial and error and without a system of writing, they lost and rediscovered knowledge as they went. Navigating by the sun and stars, they constructed mental star-maps of the constellations that they followed. They read the winds and currents, observing the different patterns of waves which form near islands and in the deep ocean as well as the flight of seabirds and landbirds. They could judge the distance from an island over the horizon by noting the species of bird— boobies can fly about 40 mi from home, frigate birds as far as 75. The regular patterns of migrating birds that fly north or south would have pointed to land in those directions.

Like any good modern yachtsman, they could detect reefs from the color of the water above them and recognize the presence of land by the shape, color, and movement of clouds. Clouds above land appear to be more stationary. Because of light reflection off their lagoons, clouds above atolls also often have a green tinge. Off-shore breezes bring the smell of vegetation.

It was such techniques that allowed some Marquesan Polynesians to sail across an astonishing 2,400 mi of open ocean and to become the first human residents of the Hawaiian islands—perhaps many others perished trying. And if they had luck, the red glow in the night sky of mighty erupting volcanoes might have directed those very first daring voyagers while far out to sea.

They brought with them items essential to their survival: *pua'a* (pigs), *'ilio* (dogs), and *moa* (chickens); the roots of *kalo* (taro) and *'uala* (sweet potato); the seeds and saplings of *niu* (coconut), *mai'a* (banana), *ko* (sugarcane), and other edible and medicinal plants.

Given the prevailing winds and currents, it would have been almost impossible for these people to make return voyages to the Marquesas. Within a few hundred years, they were well established.

There was a second colonization of Hawaii by people from the Society Islands around the year 1200 CE, and as this route was more easily navigable, there seems to have begun regular back and forth contact between the Society Islands and Tahiti during the next few centuries. Claiming descent from the greatest gods, the newcomers, who may have been larger in stature, took control. As in other places and times in world history, the invaders became the new rulers of Hawaii and developed a strict class-based social structure. Then for some reason, contact with southern Polynesia ceased. During the 400 or so years of isolation that followed, a unique Hawaiian culture developed and knowledge of deep ocean navigation was lost. In recent decades, however, these navigational traditions have been resurrected, and ancient voyaging techniques are once again well understood.

2

Early Hawaiian Culture

Because like all Pacific Islanders Hawaiians were non-literate, there are no written records of early Hawaiian life. Historians, however, have gained a good idea of former times by deduction from both the customs observed by the first European explorers and naturalists and those Hawaiians themselves have related. Careful critical analysis of preserved oral chants, songs, traditions, and genealogies has also been helpful. And the modern sciences of archaeology and linguistics have revealed much.

Many Gods

As with other Polynesians, the Hawaiians had a complex religious culture that involved respect for nature and ancestors and gave meaning to everything they did. Like the Ancient Greeks, they had many "departmental" gods whose power and presence kept them in awe. Kane, Ku, Kanaloa, and Lono were the most significant of these gods.

Kane was the most important, with responsibility for much of creation and the sustainer of life and took dozens of forms. Ku instantiated the male generating force. He too had multiple forms. Today one can view splendid red and yellow feathered images of him with a mouth of sharp dogs' teeth in Honolulu's Bishop Museum. As the fearsome war god, Ku's *heiau* had to be the most elaborate. Lono controlled agriculture and harvests and kept soils fertile. Kanaloa was the sea god the people had to placate to keep sea voyages safe and hurricanes and tsunamis at bay.

There were also many local gods and spirits. Some of these were special incarnations of the supreme four. Thus Kane as Kanehekili threw lightning bolts and Ku as Kumokuhali'i was the god of mountain forests that supplied timber for large canoes—builders of trading and war canoes worshipped him.

Kahili Room, Bishop Museum. Symbols of Hawaiian royalty and similar in function to the orb and scepter of European monarchs, tall, feather-topped poles or kahili, *were carried by young noblemen, relations of the chiefs. This room has splendid examples, together with cases and pictures displaying royal memorabilia and describing the various reigns. On the wall to the left are portraits of Kings Kamehameha III, IV, and V.* Bishop Museum

The great demigod Maui, like Prometheus, supposedly brought fire to human beings and lifted many islands out of the ocean with his fish-hook. Peleaihona (Pele, who eats the land), the goddess of volcanoes, created and destroyed. She threw molten red fountains into the air, controlled the great flows of lava, and now and then showed herself in Halemaʻumaʻu, the fiery red crater heart of Kilauea Volcano on the Big Island, where to believers she still resides. These gods created and controlled the life of the world.

Each family also venerated its ancestral minor god or spirit, the *aumakua*, some creature of special and personal meaning, such as the shark or the crab, and families took care to honor them and do them no harm. Various rituals and observances of supplication to the gods punctuated the calendar, such as the extended period of Makahiki devoted to Lono, so significant during Captain James Cook's last visit. What we today call religious thought and belief were so inseparable from everything else that the Hawaiians had no word for religion.

Highly regarded and feared, the *kahuna* (priests/professionals) were experts on religious ritual and conducted complicated ceremonies that required correct sequence word-perfect *mele* (songs) and *oli* (chants), often of great length. Traditional songs and chants preserved the mystical pantheistic conceptions of the religion.

This feather image of the fearsome Ku stands in Bishop Museum. Together with Kane, Lono, and Kanaloa, Ku, representing the male generating power, was one of the four major gods. Its mouth is lined with sharp dogs' teeth. Ku took several dozen forms.
Maria G. Figueroa

As in all animist systems, the words themselves held the power. A *kahuna* could be sacrificed for neutralizing the power of a chant or angering a god. *Kahuna* might also be specialists in some art, such as canoe-building or herbal medicine.

The greatest structures on the islands were the stone platforms or *heiau*, temples to the gods at which the *kahuna* officiated. Many *heiau* were about 12 ft high and 80 by 40 or 50 ft in area, some much larger, constructed of vast numbers of stones. Human hands had to heft these stones because there were no beasts of burden on the islands. Upon the *heiau* rested carved images of the gods, a tower for offerings, and often a small structure for the *kahuna* and *ali'i* (ah-lee-ee) or chiefs. A *heiau* dedicated to Ku as war god would require human sacrifices, ideally some high *ali'i* from an enemy tribe.

Modern Hawaiian Food

As a result of history, Hawaiian menus have long looked like something from the UN.

First were the native Hawaiians with their coconuts, berries, sweet potatoes, yams, turmeric, ginger, pork, fish, taro (pounded to make poi), and tropical fruits like mangoes and papayas. They held enormous feasts based on pork cooked slowly in huge *imu* (underground ovens) and surrounded by gargantuan amounts of everything else.

Captain Vancouver left his cattle, and some decades later came the American missionaries with their hearty New England cooking and enterprising Americans and Europeans who introduced coffee bushes, pineapples and citrus fruits, and macadamia nuts (from Australia).

Next were the Chinese who showed locals that rice goes with everything and versatile lychees can finish it and who introduced many regional dishes. The Japanese arrived with their *shoyu* (soy sauce), the crucial ingredient in much modern Hawaiian cooking. There were *tempura* (deep-fried vegetables and meats in batter), *sashimi* (thin, sliced raw fish), and today Honolulu swims in sushi bars and saki.

The Koreans brought garlic, *kalbi* (marinated short-ribs), *jun* (foods fried in egg batter), *bi bim bap* (rice with vegetables, egg, and sweet sauce), and *kim chee* (pickled vegetables). The Portuguese had *pao dolce* (sweet bread), *chorizo* (spiced sausage), marinated meats, and thick bean soup. The Puerto Ricans brought *mofongo* (mashed fried or boiled green plantain with pork, garlic, etc.) and rice and beans, and from the Philippines came fried spring rolls, *pancit* (noodles, vegetables, pork), pork rump, fish sauce, and *bitsu bitsu* (scones of sweet potato). Later, the Thais and Vietnamese introduced noodle salads and broths of sliced beef and chicken.

The mixing and mingling of traditions took place on the plantations, and vegetables were grown in backyards. Blending has continued. As the owner of the Oahu restaurant that often wins Hawaii's best restaurant award says, "When I was growing up, my grandfather cooked Chinese and my mother Japanese, but she mingled in Filipino, Chinese, and Hawaiian."

Tourist hotels, resorts, and leading restaurants have introduced top chefs from the United States and Europe who have brought their own foods and developed a unique blend called Hawaiian Regional Cuisine. Farmers grow special crops to supply restaurants and hotels; large hotels produce their own herbs; resorts have tropical fruits and organic vegetables.

As popular as ever is the luau, or large open-air feast, based on feasts of ancient times. The centerpiece is still large slices of moist, smoky pork cut from the whole pig, cooked underground, and heaped on a large platter. Accompanying are onions and sweet potatoes, tomatoes, a large container of poi, fish steamed in *ti* leaves or seasoned raw, chicken, yams, seafood, and *laulau* (small bundles of green taro leaf steamed with pork or fish). Nowadays there are often dishes from non-Hawaiian traditions as well.

There exist many hotel and commercial luau. But the best are still the private, family, birthday, wedding, anniversary, organization, or fund-raising ones. Though they may vary in authenticity, all luau are part of the rich blend of tradition.

Many *heiau* still stand. Several are of deep interest, such as the specially restored Pu'ukohola Heiau built by Kamehameha the Great in 1791 on the Big Island.

SOCIAL AND POLITICAL CONTROL

Over the centuries, but particularly after the arrival of the Tahitians, the Hawaiians developed tribes with wide social distinctions and caste-based hierarchies ruled by aristocratic families. The highest chiefs, the great *ali'i*, claiming descent from the gods, topped the social pyramid and held despotic power. They marked their status by wearing marvelous capes of bright red and yellow tail feathers plucked from tens of thousands of birds and tall, curved "helmets" of the same materials. The *ali'i* made the items themselves, tying small bunches of feathers with fiber, the supporting "fabric" being similar to a fine-mesh fishing net. The largest could contain hundreds of thousands of feathers and took many years to produce.

The *ali'i* caught the birds and allowed them to escape after plucking. Since European contact, *o'o* birds, the source of the yellow feathers, seem to have died out, though it is still possible some may be living in the vast soggy mountaintop Alaka'i Swamp in northwest Kauai. There are several fine specimens of cloaks in the Bishop Museum. Museums around the world, from Oxford, England, to St. Petersburg, Russia, and Christchurch, New Zealand, hold many others—for they were bartered for or given as gifts to European voyagers during several decades in the early 1800s.

Incest kept the purity of these highest bloodlines—the ideal marriage for a great chief was to his sister or half-sister. This way the chiefs could merge and preserve the mana of the family, believing that powerful offspring would result. But because the biological facts of incest are the exact opposite of these unscientific beliefs, such actions brought about babies with deformities and defects, and these were immediately destroyed. Still, because great *ali'i* took more than one husband or wife, genes mixed, and deformed offspring were less common than might be supposed.

Children inherited political power from the father and social status from the mother, though a man could improve his standing with a carefully selected marriage. Conflicts over succession and land became common, similar though smaller in scale to dynastic struggles in feudal Europe or medieval India. Islands, tribes, and clans fought one another in battles and wars, thereby deciding issues of chief and clan succession. For though inheritance was crucial, a ruling chief still needed to be able to hold his position by force of arms against ambitious young usurpers.

Like the rising and setting of the sun, a person was born irrevocably into a status or class. A system of laws known as *kanawai* enforced the strict social order, based upon belief in interrelated mana and *kapu* (a form of taboo as Westerners refer to it). Mana was the active and positive form of control, and *kapu* exerted a restricting "thou shalt not" control. Each was enormously complex. Serious, mysterious, and amazingly effective, they at one time or another might influence every aspect of social, political, and economic life, from eating to fighting and sex. Deriving significance from the gods and the great chiefs, special places, things, and times also acquired mana and were sacred—in various degrees and ways they were also *kapu* or forbidden.

Possessing immense mana, the *ali'i* were themselves variously *kapu*. They expected absolute obedience from commoners. This could include *kapu moe* to the greatest chiefs, which involved avoiding looking upon them, falling down in prostration before them, and remaining there until the chief had passed by. In this small population, such class distinction was perhaps as great as any in world history.

Thomas Manby, master's mate to Captain George Vancouver, during his 1793 visit to the Big Island describes the following example of *kapu moe*, entertaining and enlivening to the sailors, but deadly serious to the Hawaiians:

> In the evening shortly after dark a double canoe came alongside, which threw our female visitors into the greatest confusion. An elderly woman came on board whom we found to be a captive queen taken prisoner in the island of Mowee [Maui] about three years ago.... No woman can stand in her presence—which created a droll scene, as our decks were full of girls at the time of her unexpected coming aboard. They went about on their hands and knees flying from every place the captive approached, scrambling up and down the ladders of the vessel to the great diversion of our sailors....

David Malo, Early Hawaiian Writer

In 1837 David Malo prophetically wrote:

> If a big wave comes in, large and unfamiliar fishes will come
> from the dark ocean, and when they see the small fishes of
> the shallows they will eat them up.... The white men's ships
> have arrived with clever men from the big countries. They
> know our people are few in number and our country small;
> they will devour us.... Such has always been the case with
> large countries, the small ones have been eaten up.

Born on the Big Island during the period when Kamehameha was
campaigning to control the country, David Malo passed his boyhood
and youth in the court of the chief, Kuakini. Here he acquired
knowledge of Hawaiian oral history, practices, and traditions. He
became an important advisor to chiefs and later to kings, his sharp
perceptive comments always acknowledged though not always
valued. At various periods Malo taught school, became a public
servant, was made the first superintendent of public schools of the
kingdom, was elected to the legislature, was appointed a minister in
the government, and wrote history in his spare time.

One of the early converts to Christianity who completely
rejected the truth of the old beliefs and practices, he nevertheless
remained all his life a powerful opponent of foreign domination.

As King Kamehameha III in his long reign (1825–1854)
allowed more foreigners in government positions, Malo grew
increasingly disillusioned and despairing. Reporting the opinion
of many native people, he wrote to the king, "If the Kingdom is to
be ours, what is the good of filling the land with foreigners? What
will be the end of these numerous cases of the oath of allegiance
being taken?" It was obvious to him that this would be no
temporary phenomenon, but the beginning of the Hawaiians' loss
of their country. He was equally and for the same reason opposed
to allowing land to be sold to foreigners and wanted a ten-year
moratorium during which to educate native Hawaiians about land
ownership. Malo died a year before the king, when his worst fears
were already being manifested.

His most famous work is *Hawaiian Antiquities*, which
discusses genealogies, traditions, and beliefs. Malo designated the
place for his burial high up a mountain, where, he hoped, "no
white man will ever build a house."

According to the gods and conveniently for the men, women were inferior in rank and many *kapu* suppressed them. One *kapu* forced women to eat apart from men; another forbade them from eating turtle flesh, roasted pork, coconuts, bananas, and a variety of other nutritious foods. When they were menstruating, women could not sleep in the same house as men but in a special women's house.

A system of *kapu* regulated fishing, planting, and the harvesting of other resources (and, as a side effect, could help preserve them from overuse). A *kapu* might apply to a section of beach specially good for surfing and reserved for the use of *ali'i* only. Thomas Manby describes another fish *kapu*:

> … we learnt that a general Tabooroora now existed through the island. It had been in force eight days and would not expire till two more were past…. The present Tabooroora is an invocation to the god who presides over fish: it is annually observed at this time of year, as a notion prevails that were this ceremony neglected, the [fish] would immediately quit the shores of Owhyee [Hawaii].

Every infringement of *kapu* was believed to disturb the stability of or endanger the wellbeing of society, so the chiefs and the *kahuna* enforced *kapu* rigorously, indeed from a modern point of view neurotically, and the punishment for both women and men often ended in death—silent strangling, beating into a bloody pulp, the slow torture of broken arms and legs. Many lives ended as a sacrifice on a *heiau*. Punishment for disobeying the menstruation *kapu* was death. An early 1800s missionary reported that a five-year-old girl had her eye pressed from its socket because she ate a banana.

Accidental violation usually had the same result, because no distinctions were allowed for intention. If disaster struck, such as a tsunami, it was immediately assumed that someone had secretly broken a *kapu* and angered the god or gods, so culprits had to be found and punished. In the history of the world, political freedom for the common people has never existed where their right to own land has been absent, and old Hawaii was a good example of the lack of both. An ancient Hawaiian proverb revealingly puts the point: Chiefs are sharks who walk on land.

Building the Double Canoe, Hokule'a, 1974-75

Anthropologist Ben Finney wanted to replicate the long early voyages of the Hawaiians. In 1973 at his instigation, residents of Hawaii formed the Polynesian Voyaging Society in order to raise money to construct and sail a large double-hulled voyaging canoe similar to those used in ancient navigation. There were no excavated specimens to use as a model, other than sections recovered from swamps and caves. There were, however, many illustrations and descriptions made by early European explorers and artists that the builders could consult.

Though they could not use the old techniques and tools because that would have delayed the construction for years, they tried to make the craft as accurate as possible so it would perform at sea just as its ancestors had. Thus constant suggestions to "improve" the craft, from unwanted "advisors" and even some members of the Board of the Voyaging Society who should have known better, had to be resisted—suggestions that would have turned the canoe into a modern sailing vessel. These included widening the space between hulls, adding keel fins, and even using a modern sail shape.

The builders also encountered the darker side of Hawaiian character, the opposite of aloha. *Kahuna* (native priests) continually interfered. In accordance with the best modern ideas about safety at sea, yellow life rings and yellow bad weather suits had been purchased. But the builders were warned that they were breaking *kapu*: "You cannot have anything yellow or black on the canoe. They are *kapu* colors." The *kahuna* also claimed, "No women can sail. It was *kapu* in ancient times for women to sail on double canoes." But there must have been some women in the first canoes otherwise there would have been no Hawaiians. And so on. A number of native Hawaiians working on the project complained of strange illnesses that they believed to be spiritually caused. Some even left the project because it had become, they said, spiritually "too dangerous." There were also warnings that *haoles* (Caucasians/ foreigners) should not sail on the boat.

Fortunately, all this and much more were surmounted and on March 8, 1975, at the north end of Kane'ohe Bay, windward Oahu (a site chosen for its importance to voyaging traditions), the double canoe slid down a ramp of coconut logs and floated serenely in the ocean. Named *Hokule'a* (Hawaiian for Arcturus, the shining star that sails right over the Big Island), the canoe was 62 ft (19 m) long with eight crossbeams, a deck, railings, and two masts. She had two Polynesian-style sprit sails and two long steering oars at the stern. Sea trials showed her to be seaworthy, doing 10 knots when propelled by the trade winds. The builders were confident that *Hokule'a* could make the more than 6,000 mi (10,000 km) voyage to Tahiti and back as ancient voyagers were believed to have done, and they were in time proved correct.

Social and Economic Life

Typical island terrain consisted of high central mountains, from which radiated ridges and valleys that led out to flat coastal plains and beaches and in places to lagoons and coral reefs. Such facts of geography probably helped shape the political units. In time *ali'i* came to control an area of land called an *ahupua'a*.

An *ahupua'a* was ideally, though not always in reality, a long wedge—a pie-shaped piece that ran from the shore and coastal plain to the top of a mountain. Passing from the fishing area of the coast through different altitudes and soils, such an *ahupua'a* provided a full range of vegetation and foodstuffs.

Within an *ahupua'a* would be a number of large extended families or *'ohana*. An *'ohana* was controlled by a senior male, the various roles and duties of the *'ohana* being allocated according to age and sex.

Hawaiians fished in coastal waters and collected shellfish, seaweed, and salt along the shore. They had fish ponds circled with stone walls in conveniently shaped parts of the coast for trapping and harvesting fish—a process we now call aquaculture. They made fishhooks from bone, stone, and shell and made fine knives from sharks' teeth. For containers, they used coconuts and shells; for bowls and bottles, gourds. Vegetation fibers provided string for many purposes. Chisels and gouges came from human and animal bone. Their adzes and rasps were the rough skins of stingrays and sharks, and they used coral sand for polishing. With such basic tools, they made houses and double canoes, the largest 100 ft (30 m), with masts and woven mats for sails.

Inland and in middle altitudes they raised pigs, dogs, and chickens and harvested sweet potatoes, taro, and other crops. They cut food with sharpened bone knives and made elaborate irrigation channels and terraces held by retaining walls of stone. To plant, they used digging sticks cut from hardwood such as koa.

In the forested uplands, they cut koa trees with stone axes to form hewn-out wooden bowls and house posts and to build canoes—tough work. Here also they caught birds.

In time there evolved the idea that each *'ohana* should also occupy a narrow strip of the *ahupua'a* called an *'ili*. The *'ili* was land allocated to a specific family (*'ohana*) to farm, subject to taxes by their chief. The family shared everything produced by its various members who lived at different elevations. Most of the family would, however, live along or near the coast where the largest family house was situated, for it was there that most social and food-producing activities took place. Archibald Menzies, naturalist to Captain George Vancouver, described the farming in Waikiki, nowadays the famous beach and tourist area of Honolulu. What he writes would have been typical of farming during earlier centuries as well:

> The verge was planted with a large grove of coconut palms, affording a delightful shade to the scattered habitations of the natives.... We pursued a path back to the plantation, which was nearly level and very extensive and laid out with great neatness into little fields planted with taro, yams, sweet potatoes, and the cloth plant... divided by little banks on which grew the sugar cane... and the whole was watered in a most ingenious manner by dividing the general stream into little aqueducts leading in various directions so as to supply the most distant fields at pleasure...

Everyone helped to build the houses. With heavy, shaped stones, men pounded taro to make the gray, porridge-like *poi* (staple food of Hawaiians, eaten with the fingers) and cooked in underground pits called *imu*. The women looked after the young children, beat the inner bark of *wauke* (paper mulberry) to make *kapa* (bark cloth), wove matting from coconut palms and banana leaves, or produced garlands of flowers or leaves called *lei* (a custom that has continued). Life was rich and varied: there was little time to become bored or frustrated, and everybody contributed, from children to old people. In places there also existed the *kauwa*, members of a lowest class of outcasts used as sacrifices. Commoners paid taxes in kind (food and goods) to their *ali'i*.

Hawaiian attitudes toward sex were uncomplicated. It was perfectly normal for young people to engage in much spontaneous sexual experimentation with many different partners prior to the forming of a permanent union. Even after such unions, various ritualistic games, such as the famous night gathering called *ume*, allowed sexual activity

Hula

Ancient Hawaiians loved dancing. The origins of hula are lost in the mists of early Hawaii, but there exist many different accounts of its evolution.

Though simple to the uninitiated, hula has always been a combination of choreography married to poetry, especially in past times to the epic poetry of chants and *mele* (songs). Strict discipline was involved in its learning and *kapu* applied. As a significant form of art, hula was often taught in an enclosed thatched structure, the *halau hula* (hula school).

Hula addressed many aspects of the human condition and human emotions. One form was a deeply spiritual exercise, a manner of worship and a way to pay homage to the gods. Another honored the *ali'i* (chiefs) whose genealogies linked them to the gods. Hula could be used to greet visitors, celebrate events or individuals, or to entertain or entice someone of the opposite sex.

Whatever its purpose, hula was danced and enjoyed with a deep sense of meaning by both performers and audiences. Never superficial, there was always a dimension of awe or homage. The accompanying music involved many different instruments. Varying with the particular hula, dancers wore appropriate head, neck, wrist, and ankle adornments of leaves, grass, and flowers.

Upon their arrival in 1820, the Calvinist missionaries, unwilling or unable to regard Hawaiian culture in its own terms, rejected hula. They missed the depths of meaning and saw only the sensual dimension, which they considered something unnatural to be prohibited. To Hiram Bingham it was "that depraved native dance." As soon as they could, the missionaries banned it.

But hidden from their inquisition in secret, isolated places, a sort of underground hula always survived and the skills were passed down through the generations. Hula was for a time restored by King Kamehameha III, "re-restored" by King Kamehameha IV, and ostentatiously promoted by King Kalakaua, who pointedly engaged the best dancers for his coronation celebrations. So, despite discouragement and persecution, hula has never been entirely absent from Hawaiian culture. During the latter nineteenth century, hula began to absorb some of the rhythms, music, and musical instruments of the newcomers of different ethnicities.

In the most common form, the body of the dancer remains relatively stable, the feet mark the time, and the arms and hands show or interpret the meanings. In the more energetic forms the dancer moves gracefully, using the whole body as well as the feet and hands. Facial expressions are also employed.

Modern hula are usually danced to songs rather than to the chants of old. Lyrics are in Hawaiian, English, or in combination, and it is such hula that are usually performed for visitors. From the 1910s, Tin Pan Alley commandeered hula, producing a very popular ersatz form that at times even involved gibberish rather than Hawaiian words and that native Hawaiians derogate as *hapa haole hula* (half foreign).

Its origins lost in the mists of history, hula is the quintessential Hawaiian art form. These keki *(children) perform at a Honolulu festival.*
Hawaii Visitors and Convention Bureau and Jo Solem

More recently there has been a revival of traditional hula forms as part of the Hawaiian renaissance. Today in Hawaii the dance is enormously popular and can be enjoyed at the following sites and events and many others:

Merrie Monarch Festival
Bishop Museum
Kodak Hula Show Waikiki Shell—Kapiolani Park, Honolulu
Prince Lot Hula Festival
Na Mele O Maui—Ka'anapali, Maui (first week in December)
Molokai Ka Hula Piko—Papohaku Beach County Park, Molokai (third Saturday in May)
Polynesian Cultural Center—La'ie, Oahu
Hotels and public areas such as Kuhio Beach, Aloha Tower Marketplace, Ala Moana Shopping Center, and many malls hosting performances by hula schools.

with other "spouses." For the privilege, unlike in Christian or Islamic tradition, no man was forced to do penance or was challenged to a duel, and no woman was disgraced or ostracized. In Hawaii, as throughout Polynesia, dancing was common. Much was erotic. The hula attained a high degree of artistic elegance.

Hawaiians, like all Polynesians, were non-literate, but had a spectacular oral tradition of memorized myth and storytelling. Some also committed to memory immensely long genealogies and chronicled their cultural history through *oli* (chant), *mele* (song), *hula* (dance), and *mo'olelo* (storytelling). Children played memory games and adults passed on myths and legends to their children. Among the most intriguing were stories of the *menehune*, the mythical little people. The island of Kauai was supposed to be a stronghold of *menehune*. There, many *heiau*, tracks, fishponds, and watercourses such as the "Menehune Ditch" near Waimea, are supposedly their work (see sidebar, page 44).

Though the commoners and outcasts worked hard and life was not a matter of sitting in the sun, there was also ample time for leisure. Hawaiians integrated Polynesian arts into their way of life, including elaborate wood carving, weaving of mats and clothing, ceremonial drinks such as *kava*, and the art of tattoo.

Surfing developed early. Hawaiians loved water and water sports and both sexes learned to swim as babies. *Ali'i* had their own favorite surf breaks banned to commoners. As with other Polynesians, Hawaiians seemed amphibious to the early European and American seamen —as they do to visitors today. Handling canoes was both a sport and a life-skill. In fact the official sport of the modern state of Hawaii is outrigger canoe racing.

Percussion and wind instruments created most of the music. (There was also a stringed instrument, the musical bow or *'ukeke*.) The people made rattles from seed-filled gourds with hard leaf handles, and also whistles. As with other Polynesian peoples, the Hawaiians also had fascinating bamboo nose flutes. From 10 to 22 inches long, they were played by closing the left nostril with the left thumb and concentrating the blast of air through the right nostril into a specially shaped hole in the flute. The forefinger and thumb of the right hand held the flute and the middle and fourth right-hand fingers played the two finger holes. Today Hawaiians are again playing these instruments in a reaffirmation of their culture.

Some dancers used stone castanets in the hula, two in each hand clicking in time to the steps. They crafted some castanets from heavy stone to produce a louder click.

The most unique instrument was the knee drum, made from a coconut cut across at just above its greatest diameter. The makers of these drums smoothed the upper edge of the coconut and stretched a piece of sharkskin across the opening, held by taut multiple side strings, the bottom ends of which they fixed to a circle of woven cord at the base of the drum. Attached to the base cord they fitted a second cord around the leg just above the knee. They then beat this tiny drum with a thick two-ply twist of coir fiber knotted at the end. The knee-drum appeared nowhere else in Polynesia. It accompanied a standing wooden hula drum, with the musician playing both drums at the same time.

War

Hawaiians were just as aggressive as the rest of the world, and once tribes formed, war became a well-known part of Hawaiian life.

Warrior skill was considerable. From the late 1780s, the English traveller Nathaniel Porlock reports that two chiefs came aboard his ship and provided a demonstration. One stood at a distance of about 8 to 10 yards away and hurled five spears. The other chief dodged and caught the first spear by the shaft and then used it to ward off the other spears. The second chief then hurled the five spears once more and this time the first parried these with his dagger. Athletic contests, wrestling, and mock battles encouraged warrior skills and values, at times leading to death.

Most battles and warfare took place along traditional lines. Often it was necessary to placate the war god Ku by constructing a *heiau* to gain his support. Then the chief had to consult the *kahuna* to find the best time for attack. The two armies would meet and first indulge in various formalities. Sometimes only the *ali'i* of both sides would do the fighting and much was hand to hand. The beautiful feather cloaks mentioned above became battle prizes, so a successful chief might possess a number of them.

Menehune, *the Little People of Hawaii*

Some of the most popular Hawaiian myths and legends relate to the activities of the *menehune*, mysterious, leprechaun-like little people, the equivalent of the dwarfs, pixies, and trolls of other folklores.

Today *menehune* are used to advertise everything from candy and automobiles to luggage carrying at the airport. Commercial artists portray them as wide-eyed, ingenuous, happy, miniature people entirely absorbed in their present task, whether pounding poi or paddling a canoe. The University of Hawaii in upper Manoa Valley, a supposed former residential area of *menehune*, uses a *menehune* as mascot for its football team. Young grade-school children say that their greatest fears are of goats, tsunamis, and *menehune*.

Described as experts in stonework, *menehune* are often credited with having constructed what are now the ruins of ancient *heiau* (temple platforms), unusual rock formations, and fishponds. Several dozens of such sites are spread around the Honolulu area and through all the other main islands. *Menehune* are said to hasten construction by forming a double row of hundreds of workers to pass stones from hand to hand from the distant quarry to the build site.

They average two or three feet in height and are solid, squat, strong, and muscular. Sometimes they are described as being very hairy. Descriptions of their heads remind one of Cro Magnons or Neanderthals.

Many people prefer mystery to fact. Perhaps the best explanation for the origin of the *menehune* myth in the Hawaiian psyche is this: When the arrogant newcomers from Tahiti arrived and took control, the original inhabitants, descendants of voyagers from the Marquesas and perhaps smaller in stature than the Tahitians, had already developed a flourishing culture of beliefs and practices, of stone *heiau*, and stone-walled fishponds. The Tahitians, reluctant to acknowledge the quality of the culture and people they were suppressing, consciously and unconsciously relegated their achievements to the status of myth. (The supposed hand to hand passing of stone is a clear reflection of actual building practices. The squat stature of the *menehune* may be a distorted depiction of the perhaps smaller Marquesan-Hawaiians.)

Not all *ali'i* were formally scrupulous in war. They sometimes used ambush or destroyed food resources, and one chief cunningly ruined his opponents' water supply.

The limited subsistence economy restricted fighting, which tended to be limited to sporadic raids and occasional larger-scale battles rather than extended warfare. Political expansion was therefore also restricted. By the time of Cook's arrival, most islands still had more than one political entity. The largest, the Big Island, had four. Had there been no contact with the West and its military and naval technology, this state of affairs might have extended indefinitely. As we shall see, it was partly because of his acquisition of western weapons that Kamehameha was able to unify the islands in a relatively short time.

Captain James Cook was the first to report on the many weapons possessed by the natives and their excellent condition—a fact that suggested frequent use.

Spears were by far the favorite weapon. Made of hard wood, the shorter spears of 6 to 8 ft (2 to 2.5 m) were used as throwing spears, the much longer spears of 9 to 18 ft (3 to 6 m) as pikes for thrusting. Some spear points were barbed.

Hawaiians seem to have been the only Polynesians to use daggers. Some were double pointed. Others had a wide blunt end for bashing. Many had a loop of sennet midway, allowing the user in close combat to slip his hand to either end to stab or bludgeon as he chose. There were also long blades (some even from swordfishes) and curved blades and several kinds of clubs of heavy wood for breaking limbs and smashing in heads. Some may have been as long as 6 ft (2 m), though most existing clubs are short, from 10 to 15 in (0.25 to 0.4 m). Clubs had smooth or rough heads—natural lumps at the ends of roots or branches trimmed to a usable shape. There were also stone club heads, grooved at the top so they could be lashed securely to wooden handles. Most clubs had a string loop at the end to slip over the warrior's hand. They also used stone hand clubs. Grasped in the middle, these had flared convex ends and looked somewhat like a modern jogger's hand weights. Killing blows could be delivered upwards or with a chopping motion.

With their lines and nets, men fished far out to sea and in their double canoes bravely lassoed and captured sharks for food and skins and for their teeth, which the people used in tools and shark-tooth weapons, the latter inflicting horrible lacerations. The number of teeth in museum specimens vary from five to thirty. Users worked the teeth into a socket or longer groove in the handle, drilled holes through the handle and the base of the teeth, and secured the teeth by either lacing, sewing, or pegging.

Slings used cords of coconut fiber and human hair. Captain Cook described several sling missiles as "oval pieces of whetstone well polished, but somewhat pointed toward each end."

Another intriguing weapon was the *pikoi* or tripping cord, which consisted of a wooden or stone weight with or without a handle to which a long cord was attached. Similar in purpose to the *bola* or *bolus* of South America, warriors threw these through the air to entangle the legs of an enemy. They would then dispatch him with a club, dagger, or strangling cord or break his spine in a *lua*, the bare-handed art of breaking bones and backs in unarmed combat—regarded as the most prestigious of all skills.

Official executioners of the islands used strangling cords, so it is probable warriors also used these in close combat.

Such was the life of the Hawaiians until the arrival of Captain James Cook in 1778. These fertile islands supported the largest population in Polynesia—larger than the Society Islands and probably several times that of temperate New Zealand, which is almost twenty times their area. Believable estimates of Hawaii's people in that year vary from about 150,000 to 400,000. A reasonable guess is probably about 300,000.

3

Captain Cook Arrives

I solated in the North Pacific, Hawaii was the last group of islands to be reached by Europeans. Travel by sailing ship was snail-like, and European interest in the Pacific lay at first in finding a route to the Spice Islands (in Indonesia) and later in discovering the supposed great southern continent known as Terra Australis Incognita. No such continent was found except for Australia and New Zealand, much farther to the west.

Did the Spanish Land?

In 1520 the Portuguese explorer Ferdinand Magellan and his Spanish crews were the first Westerners to enter the Pacific. Magellan gave the ocean its name and made landfall in Guam and then the Philippines, named after his master King Phillip of Spain. During the following century, despite occasional incursions by individual ships such as the *Golden Hind* of Englishman Sir Francis Drake, Spain remained the main Pacific Ocean power. Spanish motives were not exploration but firstly, tapping into the spice trade, secondly, finding gold, and finally, converting the natives. For more than 200 years, their chief interest in the North Pacific became the annual Manilla galleons. One galleon sailed west from Acapulco in the new Spanish colony of Mexico to Manilla, capital of the Spanish Philippines. It brought Mexican silver and gold to purchase spices, silks, and other eastern goods. A second galleon sailed the reverse route east from Manila, carrying home the precious cargoes.

The prevailing winds and the counter-clockwise northern Pacific currents dictated the routes of such sailing ships. The western route passed far to the south of Hawaii and the eastern route far to the north, so Hawaii lay safely hidden somewhere in the middle. Still, given the unreliability of wind-borne travel and the possibility of straying off course, it remains fascinating that there is no hard evidence that the Spaniards ever saw or landed in Hawaii. There were after all more than 400 cross-Pacific voyages.

So why did they never sight the main islands or the 1,200 mi of low atolls to the northwest? Perhaps they did stumble upon some. Some have claimed that certain Spanish charts listed three islands, Las Monjas, La Mesa, and La Desgraciada about the right latitude but far to the east. (Determining longitude at that date was unreliable, and islands were often placed incorrectly on charts.) But if Spanish contact did occur, one would expect evidence— introduced diseases, elements in the Hawaiian language, or some detailed oral traditions, but these are all absent.

The Hawaiian islands lacked good harbors for the large galleons. (Honolulu and Pearl Harbors were difficult to find, and they only became useful after their entrances were cleared.) Even if they did land, there was nothing of value for them, no gold, no spices, no silk, so the Spaniards would show little interest in such islands.

Fascinatingly, there were small amounts of iron in Hawaii prior to Cook's visit. Hawaiians called it *meki* (*meti* on Kauai) and valued it highly. They said iron came from the sea. These facts can be accounted for by assuming that iron arrived on a beach as flotsam from some wrecked Spanish vessel. So the real proof of a Spanish landing still awaits: either a clue in some obscure Spanish monastic library or else the discovery of a Spanish shipwreck off Hawaiian coasts.

THE LAST ARCHIPELAGO

The North Pacific only became a center of more general European and North American interest after Englishman Captain James Cook had thoroughly examined the South Pacific from 1769 to 1774 in history's greatest sequence of ocean explorations. Cook then became the obvious choice to lead the British government's search for another long hoped-for piece of geography—the fabled Northwest Passage. Ever since Columbus stumbled upon the American continents, Europeans believed that during the northern hemisphere summer there might be a sea route from the far North Atlantic across the Arctic Ocean and into the North Pacific. Such a route would at the very least halve the travel time for Europeans to trade with China and the East. In fact, Cook's search for this northern passage had the unanticipated side effect of bringing to the world knowledge of the fourth, last, longest, and most populous Polynesian island group, the Hawaiian Archipelago.

Rather than try to find the passage directly from the North Atlantic (as Henry Hudson was attempting when he found New York's Hudson River), the British decided that Cook should try to enter the Arctic Ocean from the North Pacific. After the long journey down the Atlantic, around Cape Horn, and across the South Pacific, Cook's two ships, *HMS Resolution* (Cook was captain) and *HMS Discovery* (Charles Clerke as captain), anchored off the Society Islands. Here he and his crew renewed their stores and their friendly acquaintance with the Tahitians. From Tahiti, Cook proposed to sail to and then follow the northwest coast of North America to enter the Arctic Ocean through the Bering Strait.

To help the captains keep order, British marines sailed aboard both ships. One marine aboard the *Resolution* was John Ledyard, an American colonist who would later write his own account of the voyage. The expedition departed in July 1776.

About halfway along the proposed route at sunrise on January 18, 1778, Cook chanced upon the western Hawaiian islands of Kauai, Oahu, and Niihau. Cook and his men were astonished when several canoes paddled up to his ship and their robust brown crews hailed him in a language that sounded similar to the Polynesian of Tahiti. They were surprised because their Polynesian friends on Tahiti knew nothing about these islands in the north. The sides took part in a little trading, so for the first time in history (as far as we know) Hawaiians began trading with white men.

As the ships sailed along the south coast of Kauai, the sailors could see small villages of thatched huts, large cultivated gardens, and occasional tall, flimsy, whitish wooden towers—the last were a feature Cook had not seen anywhere else in his Pacific travels. Cook anchored off the village of Waimea, the seat of Kauai's *ali'i* rulers, but it seems they were on the other side of the island at that time. Cook reported that when the local Hawaiians tentatively climbed aboard, "Their eyes were continually flying from object to object. The wildness of their looks and actions fully expressed their surprise and astonishment... [and showed] that they never had been on board a ship before." John Ledyard made a similar observation.

During the two weeks the ships took on provisions, Cook commenced his study of the culture of the people. He found the Hawaiians similar in behavior to other Polynesians, and in approaching them he adopted the same methods that had succeeded on his earlier voyages. On Kauai, he began by giving gifts to show his peaceful intentions. In his ship's log he wrote that:

> Three things made them our fast friends, their own good Natured and benevolent disposition, gentle treatment on our part, and the dread of our fire arms; by our ceasing to observe the second the first would have worn off of course, and the too frequent use of the latter would have excited a spirit of revenge and perhaps have taught them that fire arms were not such terrible things as they had imagined.

Prophetically, given what would later happen to him on the Big Island, he added, "They are very sensible of the superiority they have over us in numbers and no one knows what an enraged multitude might do."

These "Indians," as Europeans of his time called all native peoples, seemed to him frank, warm, and welcoming, but also devious and deceitful—one might say rather like Europeans. Like other Polynesians, they were skilled at theft—though how they would have described these actions themselves might have been interesting to hear. Even before the ship's boat had found a suitable place for the Britons to land at Waimea, and despite a close watch by the crew, one man had grabbed a butcher's cleaver, disappeared over the side into a waiting canoe, and escaped inland.

Nevertheless when Cook landed, the natives showed astonishing deference. Several hundred carrying gifts stood on the beach and, as they would do with one of their own senior *ali'i*, they prostrated themselves when he stepped ashore, lying face down until he told them to rise. A local guide led the party through coconut, banana, paper mulberry, and other plantations to one of the whitish towers, itself standing upon a stone platform. Beside the platforms, which carried vegetable and fruit offerings to the gods, there were also several graves of *kanaka kapu*—men who had been slaughtered as human sacrifices.

There was much successful bartering. An average-sized iron nail bought enough pork to feed a ship's company for a day. Cook's crew exchanged small pieces of iron for bananas, chicken, taro root, and massive sweet potatoes of up to fourteen pounds in weight. To prevent the spread of venereal disease from his crew, Cook attempted to limit the relationships between them and

First Known Contact

In January 1778 in his meticulously kept ship's log, Captain James Cook wrote the following words about the first Hawaiians he met, the people of the most westerly of the main inhabited islands, Kauai:

> At this time we were in some doubt whether or no the land before us was inhabited; but this doubt was soon cleared up by seeing some canoes coming off from the shore toward the ships. I immediately brought to, to give them time to join us. They had from three to six men each; and on their approach we were agreeably surprised to find that they spoke in the language of Otaheite [Tahiti] and of the other islands we had lately visited. It required but little address to get them to come alongside, but no entreaties could prevail upon them to come on board. I tied some brass medals to a rope and gave them to those in the canoes, who in return tied some small mackerel to the rope as an equivalent. This was repeated; and some small nails or bits of iron, which they valued more than any other article, were given to them. For these they exchanged more fish, and a sweet potato....

Some courageous Hawaiians went aboard the following day.

the Hawaiian women, but he was unsuccessful. Some women did board the ship. The writings of Thomas Edgar, master of the *Discovery,* provide a sailor's account of relations with native women; according to him, the young women "used all their arts to entice [the sailors] into their houses and even went so far as to endeavour to draw them in by force."

Sandwich Islands

The two ships also visited the smaller island of Niihau, which proved to be less prosperous and less populated. Lieutenant Gore's sailors went ashore but, being ordered against fraternization, tried to stay away from the local women. Edgar wrote: "ye extreme reservedness of the party excited so great a curiosity in the women that they were determined to see whether our people were men or not, and used every means in their power to provoke them to do that, which ye dread of punishment would have kept them from."

A route was then set for the North American coast. The Hawaiians had told Cook of other islands farther east (Maui and the others) and of smaller islands to the west (the extended stretch of small islands and atolls). On departure, Cook named the archipelago the Sandwich Islands after his chief patron, John Montague, the fourth Earl of Sandwich, First Lord of the Admiralty, i.e., the person in charge of the British Royal Navy at that time.

Cook spent most of the remainder of 1778 sailing through the Bering Strait between Alaska and Russia and into the Arctic Ocean, searching unsuccessfully for a passage through the ice. We now know such a route is impossible for sailing ships, though modern ice breakers and nuclear submarines have done it.

COOK AS THE GOD LONO

Returning south to winter in the warmer climes of Hawaii, Cook's ships reached the eastern islands, Maui, on November 25–26, and the Island of Hawaii a week later. Tacking clockwise around the coast for several weeks, he finally found comparatively safe refuge in the prosperous district at Kealakekua Bay in January 1779. The islands had, he wrote, enriched "our voyage with a discovery which, though the last, seemed, in every respect, to be the most important that had hitherto been made by Europeans throughout the extent of the Pacific Ocean."

Meanwhile the sighting of his ships offshore had caused extreme excitement among Hawaii's native people, especially the priests. Unknown to the Britons, both this visit and their earlier landing on Kauai took place during the key Hawaiian religious festival of Makahiki. This months-long celebration was in honor of the great Lono, god of agricultural fertility, and hence was a festival crucial to Hawaiian life. Lono, it was believed, always symbolically returned to the islands at this time. Cook had sailed clockwise, and the chief procession celebrating Lono also always travelled clockwise around the Island of Hawaii. A chief associated with Lono had lived in Kealakekua Bay and there was a large *heiau* dedicated to the god there.

Moreover the masts and billowing sails of the British ships resembled the poles and *kapa* cloth banners the Hawaiians carried in their processions during Makahiki. With this string of coincidences it was but a short leap, especially for the priests, to believe that the stranger Cook was in some mysterious metaphysical manner an incarnation of Lono. Though native Hawaiians and modern historians have much disputed the precise nature of this belief, the deference the people showed him and the excessive hospitality they offered him and his men supports such an identification. We must remember that the Hawaiians had never seen pale-skinned Europeans, and everything was new and strange: their clothing, habits, equipment, seemingly large amounts of iron, and even the sibilant English language. And though tiny by twenty-first century standards, Cook's ships were huge and godlike in contrast to Hawaiian double canoes. Still, there may have been different interpretations of the nature of Cook by different Hawaiians, such as the *ali'i* and the *kahuna* for instance.

In his log, Cook estimated that some 10,000 islanders in 2,500 canoes welcomed him, with hundreds of others skipping to the ships on their surfboards. He writes, "I have nowhere in this Sea seen such a number of people assembled at one place, besides those in the Canoes all the shore of the bay was covered with people and hundreds were swimming about the ships like shoals of fish." (It is assumed that they arrived from many other parts of the island besides Kealakekua.)

John Ledyard also wrote of the vast number of Hawaiian canoes that greeted the ships, while "[t]he beach, the surrounding rocks, the tops of houses and branches of trees were covered with people." He described their initial awe of the visitors and the multitudes who shouted, sang, danced, and clapped hands, backed up by their many squealing hogs: "A tumultuous and curious prospect!"

Once Cook came ashore, the people suspended other activities for weeks, carried the image of Lono in procession in many parts of the island, and traded heavily. Cook wrote, "It was not possible to keep the [women] out of the ship and no women I ever met with"—we must remember he'd seen many other Polynesians—"were more ready to bestow their favours. Indeed it appeared to me that they came with no other view."

The Britons passed some weeks repairing their ships, sails, and rigging, broken and worn after the long Arctic voyage. Meanwhile, chiefs, priests, and commoners gathered huge amounts of tribute. The priests showed Cook their *heiau* and stoically Cook cooperated in their ceremonies. Lieutenant King wrote that "[t]he captain recollecting what offices [the priest] Koa had officiated when he handled the putrid hog, could not get a morsel down [his throat], not even when the old fellow very politely chewed it for him."

DEATH OF COOK

Cook departed Kealakekua Bay on February 4, 1779, but a storm soon damaged the foremast of the *Resolution*, and he had no option but to return to Kealakekua Bay, the only nearby safe port he knew. Unfortunately for him and deeply problematic for his mana, Makahiki was now virtually over! Why would the god Lono return at this late date?

Though the native reception was muted, Cook's men established a little shore base and they were given some help in repairing the mast. But relations deteriorated. The Hawaiians would have noticed that a mast had been dismantled and sails removed—just as they had done with the poles and banners of their Makahiki festival.

Ashore, groups began to jeer at the sailors and even Cook himself. More ship's tools were stolen. On the night of February 13, the *Discovery*'s large cutter, which had been tied to a buoy close to the ship, was stolen. This could not be tolerated, for ship's boats were life and death matters in storms and shipwrecks and in gathering water and provisions.

Early in the morning Cook led a shore party of ten men, Lieutenant Phillips, and nine marines—in fact an ill-judged and pitifully small group—to challenge thousands of male Hawaiians, most of whom were warriors. (Cook was beginning to have bouts of ill-temper, and many now believe that after so many years of privation at sea his physical and mental health were deteriorating.) Several ship's boats with marines stood offshore at strategic positions.

Cook approached the great local chief Kalaniopu'u, who explained he knew nothing about the cutter. Cook persuaded Kalaniopu'u to accompany him back to the *Resolution*. The plan was to keep the chief as a hostage until the boat was returned. (Hostage taking had worked for Cook in several earlier confrontations in other parts of the Pacific.) Before they reached Cook's boat, however, Kalaniopu'u's favorite wife ran after them wailing and persuaded the chief to remain. With two lesser chiefs holding him, he sat down on the sand. Meanwhile a huge crowd had gathered, perhaps two or three thousand according to the Lieutenant Phillips, and pressed the marines close to the water. When despite Cook's urgings Kalaniopu'u would not move, Cook told Phillips they would be unable to keep the chief hostage without killing some of the Hawaiians, which he did not want to do, so he abandoned the hostage plan.

At that moment a Hawaiian chief arrived and reported to the crowd that one of the boats Cook had posted in the bay had fired upon a canoe trying to leave and had killed a chief. Immediately the mood of the crowd turned nasty. A melee broke out. Stones were thrown. (Thousands of handy weapon-sized stones still surround the bay.) Cook was forced to fire on the crowd and killed a man. The Hawaiians of the Big Island, unlike Polynesians elsewhere, had never seen muskets used as killing weapons. More Hawaiians attacked. The marines fired too. In the moments during which they were reloading their muskets, Cook turned his back and was hit from behind. In self-defense he swung his empty musket but was stabbed. Tumbling forward into the

shallows, he was clubbed and hacked to death by a multitude.

It was the tradition at this stage in Makahiki when Lono's procession had been completed that armed warriors would challenge the local chief on the beach and his own men would symbolically defend him. So the fact that Kalaniopu'u had been taken by Cook's party and then protected by his chiefs may have been interpreted by the Hawaiians as a confused enactment of this ritual. Hawaiian religious mysticism and the practical politics of hostage taking had all become terribly mixed.

Four of the marines were now dead. Phillips was wounded, and he and the remaining marines clambered into the boat. Everything happened so rapidly that only the nearer of the other boats of marines was close enough to help.

This painting shows Cook giving instructions when about to go ashore on February 14, 1779, to recover the ship's cutter, stolen during the night. Within an hour or so he is killed by enraged Hawaiians.
Captain Cook's Third Voyage by Bernard Finegan Gribble (1873–1962), in the private collection of Joy and Reg Grundy

Phillips realized that if he tried to rescue Cook's body they would all be killed, so he and the survivors sharply pulled away under a hail of stones. Cook had died from a combination of theft, bad judgment, religion, metaphysics, mayhem, and rivalry between chiefs and priests.

Reinforcements from the ships later arrived and arranged a truce further up the bay. The Britons were able to secure the *Resolution*'s foremast, sails, and astronomical instruments, but left everything else. By 12 o'clock everyone was back on the two ships.

Meanwhile Captain Clerke had seen the natives carrying the dead bodies inland. In the heat of the moment, some of the officers wanted reprisals, but Clerke decided that any further action would be counterproductive—there was no way to bring Cook back to life.

However, the sailors were sorely tested when canoes full of Hawaiians paddled close to the ships, shouting and gesticulating. Lieutenant King arranged a parley, telling the natives that if Cook's body were not returned the next morning the fleet would destroy the village. (Meanwhile the chief, Kalaniopu'u, was hiding in a cave in a cliff.) Secretly that night, in a move that revealed the divisions in the native community, a priest and a commoner silently came to the ships with a parcel of parts of Cook's body. As recorded in the Admiralty records, Lieutenant King observed:

> Our horror will be barely conceived and cannot possibly be described when the bundle was opened to see in it a piece of human flesh from the hind parts; this the man said was all he could get of the body; that the rest was cut to pieces and all burnt, but that the head and bones excepting what belonged to the trunk of the body were in the possession of Kalaniopu'u and other chiefs, and that if the flesh had not already been sent to Kaoo [a priest] he would have brought it to us because we desired the body so ardently.

The two Hawaiians believed they would be killed if the *ali'i* discovered their actions. In darkness they returned to shore. The immense complexity and confusion of the religious significance of Cook's arrival is shown in the extraordinary parting words of the two Hawaiians. In deep distress, they asked when Lono would return and how he would treat them!

In contrast the next morning, many canoes sailed past the ships blowing conch shells and hurling defiance. One man stood up, slung stones at the ships, and twirled Cook's captain's hat. Finding this insult too great, Clerke ordered some cannon to fire on the crowd on shore. (Kalaniopu'u's nephew, who would later become Kamehameha I, the first king of the archipelago, may have been wounded.) Further

John Ledyard, First American to Visit Hawaii

John Ledyard (1751–1789) was an adventurous colonial American who sailed with Cook to what Cook called the Sandwich Islands.

Connecticut-born Ledyard, who briefly attended Dartmouth College in New Hampshire (where a canoeing and whitewater kayaking club is named for him), went to seek new experiences in England and joined the red-coated Royal Marines (established in 1664). Fame would be his when Cook's expedition stumbled upon these islands unknown to the outside world.

Because the expedition left Portsmouth, England, on July 11, 1776, and news took two months to cross the Atlantic, neither Ledyard, Cook, nor anyone else on the voyage knew about the American Declaration of Independence on July 4 until years afterwards. Upon his return to North America in 1783 Ledyard published his observations, *A Journal of Captain Cook's Last Voyage to the Pacific Ocean*, the first account of Hawaii to be published in America.

He admired the bravery of the Hawaiians who approached the strange ships in canoes and "[a]ppeared inexpressibly surprised, though not intimidated. They shook their spears at us, rolled their eyes."

Ledyard's tricornered military hat at first puzzled the Hawaiians. Some Hawaiians called Ledyard's long-barreled musket a "water squirter," apparently because its smoke reminded them of water squirting through a bamboo tube.

Ledyard was also a guard on shore, and with Cook's agreement, he left the encampment to attempt the first non-Hawaiian ascent of the 13,679 ft volcano Mauna Loa. But his ambition exceeded his abilities and equipment, because it is easy to underestimate the height of such shield volcanoes, and he was halted by impassable rocky barriers far from the summit. Another advantage of being ashore was that Ledyard was able to leave camp secretly at night to dally with the Hawaiian women.

Near the Dartmouth canoeing club, a bronze plaque set in granite honors Ledyard with these words: "An officer under Captain Cook.... He, too, heard a voice crying in the wilderness."

fighting took place ashore and huts were burned before a truce was again arranged and Kalaniopu'u agreed to return Cook's bones. That the fighting did not become much worse shows the amazing restraint exercised by both sides.

The chief handed a bundle of bones wrapped in the pounded bark cloth known as *kapa,* covered in a valuable cloak of black and white feathers, to Lieutenant King. On opening it he found:

> ... the Captns [sic] hands (which were well known, from a remarkable Cut) the Scalp the skull, wanting the lower jaw, thigh bones & Arm bone; the hands only had flesh on them, and were cut in holes, and salt crammed in; the leg bones, lower jaw, & feet, which were all that remained... were dispers'd among other chiefs.

Some of Cook's possessions were also returned, including his musket with the gunbarrels bent and battered. The cutter that had been the cause of the conflict had been burned for its iron.

As was the practice at the time (though not always with a captain), Cook's shipboard possessions such as clothing were sold among the crew, who, several years away from home, would have been in considerable need.

The chiefs placed the bay under a *kapu.* The naval burial service took place with a salute of ships' cannon and Cook's bones were lowered into the waters of Kealakekua Bay, where they may still lie. The chiefs removed the *kapu,* canoes peacefully surrounded the ships, and a group of *ali'i* went aboard. They said they were sorry for what had occurred but were now happy at this reconciliation. At the end of the day, the ships sailed away to the west. It would be 1785 before the next European ship arrived.

Today, at Kealakekua Bay, an underwater plaque marks the site of Cook's demise together with an obelisk nearby on the beach (see opposite page).

Captain James Cook Monument, Kealakekua Bay. In 1825, after returning the bodies of King Kamehameha II and Queen Kamamalu from England, Royal Navy captain Lord Byron erected the first simple monument of oak and copper to Cook's memory. In 1837 a small copper plate memorial was fixed to the base of a coconut tree. In 1874, during Hawaii-based British astronomical observations to measure the distance between the earth and sun, the present Cook obelisk was constructed. The bay is popular for snorkeling.
Hawaii Visitors and Convention Bureau and Kirk Lee Aeder

Kauai Must-See Sites

Oldest and most beautiful of the inhabited islands, Kauai, "the Garden Island," has yellow beaches and lush tropical jungles. Earthquakes and rain erosion have sculpted some of the most striking landscapes in the world. The people of Waimea were the first to greet Captain Cook in 1778. Kamehameha could not conquer Kauai, so he compromised instead. The first major sugar plantation, owned by Ladd & Co., was here in the 1830s near Kohala and became Hawaii's first great financial scandal. The interior is mountain, canyon, high altitude, or vast waterlogged swamp, and resorts are concentrated in a limited number of locations around the coast. Modern tourism creates jobs, but locals decidedly do not want Kauai to become just another over-developed Oahu or Maui. Visit www.kauaigov.org or the website for the main local newspaper, the *Garden Island*, published in administrative Lihu'e at www.kauaiworld.com.

Mount Wai'ale'ale

Millions of years of erosion have reduced the once Mauna Kea-like volcano Wai'ale'ale ("Overflowing Water") to some 5,148 ft/1,577 m (nearby Kawaikini is about a hundred feet higher). With its astonishing world-record rainfall of some 440 inches (11,176 mm) a year, this height is sufficient to send endless and superb cascades of water crashing down Wai'ale'ale's often cloud-covered, green-velvet flanks.

Hanalei Bay, Princeville, Lumaha'i, Ha'ena

In the middle of the north coast are magnificent Hanalei Valley and Hanalei Bay, the largest bay on the island. The lush valley of the Hanalei River and its taro fields spreads out below Hanalei Valley Lookout. Just north on a former sugar plantation and cattle ranch is Kauai's largest resort, Princeville (www.princeville.com), named for the son of Kamehameha IV. In 1816 a Russian fort was built just in front of where the hotel stands. Viewable to the south are the beautiful ribbed green mountains used in films such as *Raiders of the Lost Arc* and *Jurassic Park*. To the west is a superb series of beaches called Lumaha'i with brilliant white sand and fingers of black rock promontories. In 1816, Hanalei Valley was the preferred headquarters of Georg A. Scheffer, the German adventurer of the Russian American Co. (he called it Schefferthal). He failed in his attempt at empire.

Several miles further west is Limahuli Garden, the National Tropical Botanical Garden, with hundreds of acres of forest preserving native species in the last valley before the beginning of the extraordinary Na Pali Coast.

Na Pali Coast

Along the northwest corner of Kauai stand the spectacular, sheer 10 mi (16 km) long cliffs of Na Pali Coast, one of earth's most magnificent locations. Hidden and mystical, you can visit this "must-see" by plane, helicopter, boat or kayak, or the fabled zig-zag, hair-raising Kalalau walking trail. Here are remains of vanished villages, house platforms, irrigation ditches, walls of taro fields, and impassable former trails. Here, in the verdant heights of superb Kalalau Valley, Koolau the leper, immortalized in the Jack London story, hid from, fought, and eluded the provisional government's police and soldiers. The valley was settled by native Hawaiians for many hundreds of years, but is now inhabited.

Waimea Canyon and Koke'e State Park

Waimea Canyon, Mark Twain's so-called Grand Canyon of the Pacific, is

Hawaiian Visitors Bureau and Ron Dahlquist

a mighty, lush slash a few miles inland but not accessible from the Na Pali Coast. It is about 10 mi (16 km) long and about 3000 breathtaking ft (1,150 m) deep with spectacular streams and waterfalls and massively dense rainforest. Millions of years of rainfall and rushing waters have cut the canyon and produced the fantastic shapes and colors.

Most visitors view the canyon from points along Koke'e Road on the canyon rim. At the canyon's north end lies Koke'e State Park with its many hiking trails and a corner of the great, high Alaka'i Swamp. The road ends not far past Kalalau Lookout, giving a majestic 4,120 ft high view down Kalalau Valley to Kalalau Beach and cliffs on the Na Pali Coast.

4

Kamehameha Conquers

Childhood, Youth, and Rise to Power

By the mid-1700s, there was much skirmishing and raiding among the islands. The several chiefs of the Big Island and the one or two chiefs of the second largest island, Maui, were becoming ambitious for more territory. The military power of cannon and muskets revealed to them during Cook's visit were later included in their plans. The greatest of these conquerors would be Kamehameha.

Kamehameha (the "Lonely One") was born on the Island of Hawaii in the district of Kohala on the far north coast, though exactly where is not known. His year of birth is debated too, most likely 1758. Later it was said that a strange light appeared in the sky at his birth, and we know that late in 1758 Halley's Comet was indeed visible from Hawaii. (This claim about a light may of course be a rationalization made years later by the *kahuna* and Kamehameha's acolytes to bolster his mana.)

Kamehameha's parentage is also debated. Though his mother was Kekuiapoiwa, the daughter of a chief from Kona, we are not sure who his father was. Most historians believe it was the chief of Kohala, Keoua Kupuapaikalani. In any case, Kamehameha was hidden for the first five years after his birth in the magnificent, secluded Waipi'o Valley, lest he be murdered by chiefs who saw him as a rival. He was then returned to his mother and Keoua Kupuapaikalani.

Keoua Kupuapaikalani died when Kamehameha was fourteen. Kamehameha was then adopted by his uncle, the chief Kalaniopu'u, ruler of the western part of the Island of Hawaii and the chief connected with Cook's death. Kalaniopu'u treated Kamehameha as a son and ensured that he learned all the beliefs and mastered all the abilities needed for ruling in peace and war. This training involved memorizing his genealogy, prayers, *kapu*, and other religious beliefs; navigating at sea; slinging stones; throwing, avoiding, and catching spears; experiencing personal close combat with daggers, clubs, and the *lua*; and understanding general battle tactics. Kamehameha was physically strong and agile, and it was said, more skillful than anyone else at avoiding and catching spears. From an early age, Kamehameha was prepared to lead, and given his later huge success in war and government, these claims ring true.

A few years later, Kamehameha won Kalaniopu'u's gratitude by representing the now elderly chief in personal combat with the eastern chief of Hilo and winning.

Kamehameha was present when Kalaniopu'u visited Cook on the *Discovery* in 1779. Lieutenant James King wrote an interesting description: "his disposition... was good natur'd and humourous, although his manner shewd somewhat of an overbearing spirit, and he seemed to be the principal director in this interview."

Kamehameha continued to grow in skill and a personal mana of power and violence. In exchange for a splendid feather cloak, he acquired several iron daggers from Cook's officers. After Cook's assassination, it was said that he took and kept some of Cook's hair, thereby increasing his mana considerably. Some British officers believed he had been one of those who slew Cook.

Although authority on Oahu, Maui, and other islands to the west usually passed down through the senior chief's blood line, on the Island of Hawaii, charisma, warrior skills, and a little luck made it possible for men from lesser bloodlines to challenge and fight their way to the top.

A little more than a year after Cook's ships had departed, Kalaniopu'u was dying. Debilitated by decades of drinking *awa*, no longer stimulated by his wives and hula dancers, he gathered his retainers. He made Kiwala'o, his son, heir to the chiefdom. Kamehameha, his nephew, was given charge of the two-foot-high, rare, red-and-yellow-feathered image of savage Ku, the god of war and fiercest of the gods. The image had a snarling mouth lined with sharp rows of dogs' teeth. (Several splendid examples of Ku can be seen today in Bishop Museum in Honolulu.) Kalaniopu'u must have known that this division of authority would pit Kamehameha against his son in a challenge for the chieftainship. Perhaps he was testing his son's mettle.

Before European contact, as a small child King Kamehameha I was hidden in Waipi'o Valley, this magnificent (1 mi/1.6 km wide by 6 mi/9.7 km long) verdant red earth valley in the north of the Big Island, to escape rivals who wanted him dead. For hundreds of years the valley had been home to thousands who fished and farmed with water from Waipi'o Stream in irrigated terraces for growing taro. As a sacred place it held heiau *(temples) and a refuge. Waterfalls stream down its sides and there is a stunning lookout at its landward end. Nowadays its few farmers carefully conserve ancient Hawaiian values.*
Hawaii Visitors and Convention Bureau and Kirk Lee Aeder

Soon after Kalaniopu'u's death, various ritual confrontations occurred. Keawema'uhili, a powerful chief from the east side of the island and uncle of Kiwala'o, precipitated matters by presuming that he alone had the right to redistribute the lands of Kalaniopu'u. He allotted himself and his allies the largest and best sections and disadvantaged Kamehameha and other western chiefs. Several of Kamehameha's assumed allies then traitorously joined what appeared to be the more powerful alliance of Keawema'uhili together with Kiwala'o and his younger brother Keoua.

Olowalu Massacre, 1790

On January 30, 1790, the American brig *Eleanora*, captained by Simon Metcalfe, lay at anchor in the shallow indentation of Olowalu Bay, Maui. (The bay is about midway between the modern towns of Lahaina and Ma'alaea and is today a popular snorkeling and diving area.) Near midnight, the ship's cutter was stolen by Hawaiians who wanted its metal framework. The cutter's Filipino guard was stabbed and killed—probably the first Filipino to die in Hawaii.

The following day and night there were skirmishes between the local people and the crew, including an attack on the village. For a few days normal relations resumed. A chief came aboard and offered to return both the cutter and the Filipino, and Captain Metcalfe offered generous rewards.

The next day, only the Filipino's thighs were produced. In frustration Captain Metcalfe threw them into the sea. Soon after, the same chief came aboard asking for the reward. It was given and he was also told that if he returned the cutter the second reward would be paid. Soon the chief paddled up to the *Eleanora* in his canoe, in the bottom of which lay merely the keel of the cutter. He asked for his reward. Ignoring the chief and addressing his crew, the furious Metcalfe said something to the effect that the chief would indeed receive a reward, but one the Hawaiians would never expect.

Some of the crew tried to restrain Metcalfe, but he was out for blood. As one of the sailors wrote in a Boston newspaper a year later, Metcalfe decided to

> … station one man at each port cannon and others at the guns below
> decks, whilst others were on the quarter deck at the swivelling cannon
> and four brass guns. When all were ready, at his command they were
> to fire immediately into the canoes. The guns below decks had in each
> of them 100 musket balls and 50 landgradge nails. There were seven
> of the above guns, each containing the like quantity. The four guns on
> the quarter deck had in them 50 balls each, some of the swivels 20,
> others 10 balls.

The visiting canoes were full of foodstuffs to barter, and carried men, women, and children. They were directed to paddle around to the starboard side. When the native people were nicely in line to be slaughtered, Metcalfe gave the order to fire. The killing was terrible, with blood and bits of bodies littering the sea. Later it was learned that the chief responsible for stealing the cutter was not in the canoes of the slaughtered.

Simon Metcalfe would in turn be killed by the natives of the Tuamotu Islands in the South Pacific.

Meanwhile, the main obstacle to Kamehameha's control of the archipelago and the most formidable chief in the islands was the great Kahekili who ruled Maui and the smaller islands of Lanai and Molokai. Kahekili had taken the name of the thunder god and had one side of his body tattooed dark black like thunder clouds. He also captured the island of Oahu on which Honolulu now stands, killing its ruler, his own foster son. The latter was then sacrificed to the war god, and many of the other *ali'i* of Oahu were tortured (including being slowly grilled) and killed, their skeletons used in the walls of a special house of bones. Kahekili also had a convenient arrangement of non-aggression with a half-brother, Kaeokulani, ruler of the islands of Kauai and Niihau. Between them they ruled all the archipelago except the Big Island.

In his domains, Kahekili allowed no competition. He organized a special fighting force like modern commandos or rangers, the *pahupu*. Also tattooed black, they added a terrifying touch by having their eyelids turned and fixed inside out. Kahekili used the skulls of enemies for diverse purposes, among which was bathroom duty. Crafty as well as cruel, he, rather than Kamehameha, looked most likely to become ruler of the whole archipelago.

A SERIES OF BATTLES

Kamehameha strictly observed religious ritual, recognizing its importance in social control. In mid-1782 while Kamehameha was consulting his priests, a war party led by his leading *ali'i* Ke'eaumoku chanced upon Kiwala'o and brother Keoua at Mokuohai. At the height of the skirmish, a slung stone felled Kiwala'o, and Ke'eaumoku, though badly wounded, dragged himself to his enemy and used a shark-tooth dagger to slit Kiwala'o's throat. Though Keoua escaped, the battle made Kamehameha one of the three most powerful chiefs on Hawaii Island, the others now Keawema'uhili and Keoua. But despite four more years of skirmishing, none could overcome the others.

Maui and the Battle of Iao Valley
Because Cook had discovered sea otters and fur seals along the coast of what is now British Columbia and Oregon and Washington states, the ships of fur traders began to stop

over in the islands and Kamehameha and his rivals bought firearms.

Using some of those arms, Kamehameha decided to attack Maui in 1790 while Kahekili was away visiting Oahu. It was said that when Kamehameha landed, the red feathers of his war god Ku stood straight up—considered a very favorable omen. There must have been a good onshore wind that day! Kamehameha killed the leader of his first battle in personal combat, then sailed around to land in Kahului Bay, now the site of Maui's main port and airport for tourists.

Though the opposition under Kahekili's son Kalanikupule fought gamely, they were forced into the narrowing and steep Iao Valley a few miles inland. Observed by noncombatants on the hillsides, the Battle of Iao Valley then took place. Making deadly use of his cannon called *Lopeka*, operated by his two British helpers John Young and Isaac Davis, Kamehameha won a great victory. Though Kalanikupule himself managed to escape along a path over the cliff at the end of the valley (nowadays almost obliterated by landslides), the bodies of the dead Maui defenders dammed up the mountain stream. Today the area is called Kepaniwai (meaning "water dam") Heritage Gardens.

Kamehameha's British Helpers

The two Britons, Young (English) and Davis (Welsh), came into Kamehameha's service by accident. John Young was a skilled boatswain on the American trading ship *Eleanora* under notorious Captain Simon Metcalfe. It was planned that the *Eleanora* and the *Fair American*, captained by Metcalfe's son Thomas, would rendezvous off the Kona Coast of Hawaii Island. After a cutter was stolen, Captain Metcalfe carried out the Olowalu Massacre of perhaps a hundred Hawaiians. Innocent of and still unaware of the massacre, Thomas Metcalfe was attacked by Hawaiians in retaliation when the *Fair American* reached the Kona Coast. They boarded and killed by bashing and drowning Thomas and all the crew except Isaac Davis, who somehow survived despite serious wounds.

In 1790 Young went ashore on the Kona Coast of the Big Island, but the Hawaiians prevented him from returning to the *Eleanora* in case he told Metcalfe about the killing of his son Thomas. (Young actually knew nothing about it.) So

Hawaiian Flag

Newcomers to Hawaii are often astonished by the presence of the British ensign in the corner of the Hawaiian state flag. How did it get there?

Before Cook arrived in the archipelago, no flags were in use. Instead there were long feather cylinders on top of tall staffs (*kahili*); there was a triangular *puela* insignia for canoes and sail-like tapa standards carried on poles during the Makahiki festival season.

When Captain George Vancouver accepted Kamahameha's cession of the Island of Hawaii to Britain in 1794, he presented the king with the British ensign of the time. Apparently Kamehameha made use of that Vancouver ensign. During the War of 1812 between Britain and the fledgling United States, he seems to have decided he should have a flag of his own, and Otto von Kotzebue, the Russian navigator who visited the islands in 1816, makes reference to Kamehameha's Hawaiian flag.

Whether Kamehameha's flag had the same design as the present flag is not known, though experts say it seems likely. Following monarchs retained the flag. Today the eight horizontal stripes of red, white, and blue are considered to represent the eight main islands of the group.

After the coup d'etat of 1893 and the annexation to the United States in 1898, the same flag was retained despite the presence of the British "Jack." In 1959 it became the official ensign of the newly constituted state of Hawaii.

Modern sovereignty activists see it as a symbol of Hawaii's former independence from the United States, and some fly it upside down as a symbol of protest.

Young was stranded. Soon afterwards he met Kamehameha and also Davis, who was being nursed by local Hawaiians and making a rapid recovery. In April 1791 Young and Davis tried to escape, but they were brought back and became reconciled to living in Hawaii. In fact, they soon came to prefer Hawaiian life to that of their homeland.

Both were skilled seamen and fighters and could operate cannon, and Kamehameha immediately realized their potential for his own plans of conquest. Within a few years they had become his friends and key advisors and were made chiefs. They helped Kamehameha in all the important battles, leading to a united archipelago under his rule.

Davis was overseer of all the king's Honolulu interests by 1898. He acquired much wealth and had hundreds of commoners working for him. When in 1810 he warned Kaumualii, ruler of Kauai, that some of Kamehameha's chiefs intended to poison Kaumualii, the frustrated chiefs poisoned Davis in his place.

Young's home was made at Kawaihae on land given to him by Kamehameha. His was the first stone house in the islands. In 1795 he married Namokuelua, a young Hawaiian woman of noble descent, who died in 1804 but bore two sons, Robert and James Kanehoa. In 1803 Young imported the first horse into Hawaii, a mare with foal. The American sea-captain who brought the horse ashore noted the "incessant exclamations of astonishments" among the local Hawaiians. In 1806 Young married Kaoaneha, a niece of Kamehameha. She and Young had three daughters and one son. From 1802 to 1812, while the king was often living in Honolulu, Young was made governor of the Big Island and also governor of Oahu for a time in 1812. In 1819 the official artist aboard the French ship *Uranie* painted his portrait.

Sacrifice of Keoua on Pu'ukohola Heiau

Meanwhile, conveniently for Kamehameha, Keoua had killed his own ally Keawema'uhili, leaving only himself and Kamehameha sharing the Big Island. Inconveniently, Keoua began attacking Kamehameha's lands on the northeast coast to burn villages, break fish ponds, and destroy taro patches. Kamehameha returned and fought two evenly matched battles before Keoua withdrew from the Hilo area toward his home district of Ka'u in the south.

His route passed close to the active Kilauea Volcano, which suddenly erupted from Halema'uma'u Crater, trapping him. A monstrous plume of steam, smoke, ash, and volcanic particles shot four or five miles into the sky. The plume was seen from the northwest coast 60 mi away (and recorded by John Young) across the 13,667 ft Mauna

Loa Volcano, which indicates its great height. This volcanic material rained down upon Keoua's people and perhaps a third of them perished.

It is difficult to assess how much Keoua's loss affected the military balance of power, but it was obvious to all Hawaiians that the volcano goddess Pele, who many believed to inhabit Halema'uma'u Crater, was angry with Keoua. We may therefore assume that Keoua was in anguish and deeply disturbed and that Kamehameha's morale was equally boosted.

Still, as nine years of war had passed and neither Kamehameha nor Keoua was in the ascendant, the battle for power required some new tactics. It was told that a

From the edge of Kilauea Caldera these tourists have been peering at the oval Halema'uma'u Crater about a mile away in the distance. At one time the crater was full of boiling lava. It remains the mythological home of petulant Pele, the female volcano goddess. In 1790 a stupendous volcanic eruption from Halema'uma'u, perhaps the greatest since Hawaii was settled, destroyed many of the warriors of Kamehameha's rival Keoua. In the early 1900s, pioneer vulcanologist Thomas Jagger used to climb down into Halema'uma'u to take his measurements.
Hector L. Torres

The Russians Are Coming, 1816

After the Russians had seized Siberia from its native peoples and colonized it, they proceeded up the long chain of the Aleutian Islands, taking these from the Aleuts, and into North America to claim Alaska. To further their trade, they established the Russian American Company in the town of New Archangel (Sitka).

In 1816 an expedition under Georg A. Scheffer, a German-born doctor, was dispatched by the Russian American Co. to salvage the cargo of a Russian ship wrecked on Kauai. Were he unsuccessful, he was instructed to demand compensation from the ruler of the island, Kaumualii, who was at this time a subject-king under Kamehameha.

Scheffer first cleverly deceived King Kamehameha into helping him. This occurred despite warnings to the king by John Young and various US traders. Queen Ka'ahumanu even granted Scheffer estates on Oahu.

Scheffer proceeded to Kauai where he fed the anti-Kamehameha feelings of Kaumualii, who, happy to have what he believed to be an ally, concluded an agreement giving the Russian American Co. huge swathes of land and a monopoly on the island's sandalwood. Kaumualii apparently told Scheffer that most of the islands really belonged to him and that if Russia would help him to reconquer them he would, according to Scheffer, "give [Russia] half of Oahu and all the sandalwood forever, and also whatever provinces I might want to select on the other islands." In great hopes, Scheffer raised the tsarist Russian flag over Kauai.

But on returning to Honolulu, Scheffer met the determined mass opposition of John Young and the American traders, some of whom then pursued him back to Kauai. They tried to destroy his relationship with Kaumualii, who drove them off the island with his warriors.

Scheffer renamed many of the areas of Kauai that he claimed to control, calling the spectacular northern Hanalei Valley on Hanalei Bay, "Scheffertal." To Scheffer's chagrin, the Russian American Co. disowned his deals, and when Otto von Kotzebue's official Russian naval expedition visited Honolulu in late 1816, Kamehameha was told that Russia had nothing to do with Scheffer's claims or his opportunistic alliance with Kaumualii. Soon the American traders in Honolulu were threatening Kaumualii that if he did not rid himself of Scheffer and the Russians, they would sail eight ships to Kauai to toss the Russians into the sea and kill all Kaumualii's "Indians" (natives) as well.

By May 1817 Kaumualii realized he had grossly miscalculated Scheffer's power, and Scheffer was forced to depart hastily. By July he was ignominiously fleeing for his life to Guangzhou (Canton) in China.

kahuna advised Kamehameha to construct a massive *heiau* at Pu'ukohola, a hill just above Kawaihae Bay on the northern peninsula and dedicated to the war god Ku, so he could "gain the kingdom without a scratch to his skin." This Hawaiian dry-stone equivalent of a Mayan pyramid took more than a year to construct, and Kamehameha dragooned thousands of workers from all of his lands to build it. *Ali'i* and commoners alike sweated hefting the stone, passing it hand to hand in vast human chains over many miles—for we must remember that there were no draft animals on the islands. Special care was taken to have everything correct—the location, carved figures, an oracle-tower, and a hole for the unlucky tortured human sacrifices (John Young said he saw thirteen sacrifices)—with careful, appropriate prayers at every stage. Completed in 1791 and strikingly restored, it is one of the largest *heiau* in the islands and is today a national historic site.

Kamehameha invited Keoua to discuss peace at Kawaihae Bay. From Kamehameha's viewpoint, Keoua would make the perfect high status human sacrifice for his new *heiau*. Keoua well knew the purpose of Pu'ukohola Heiau. Perhaps he believed Pele had passed her judgment on him and was resigned to death, for amazingly he accepted. He even brought his close friends and high chiefs, 26 men sailing on his double canoe. On entering the bay, he was immediately surrounded by Kamehameha's canoes. On the beach was Ke'eaumoku, who had killed Kamehameha's enemy Kiwala'o. Keoua landed. In the blink of an eye Ke'eaumoku fatally speared him. Other warriors fired their muskets at Keoua's friends and companions and many died before Kamehameha intervened to save the remaining lives, including that of Keoua's younger brother Kaoleioku. The body of Keoua became the high-ranking sacrifice to Ku on Pu'ukohola Heiau. Though some have blamed a "trigger-happy" Ke'eaumoku, it is inconceivable to most historians that Kamehameha with his detailed *heiau* preparation had not planned this deviousness. An instant of brutal and treacherous action made him master of the whole island.

Keoua was a popular chief with his own subjects, and in despair they mourned him. Until the mid-1930s there

were old people in his Ka'u District who despised the
memory of Kamehameha.

But Kahekili of Maui still lived. He, together with his
bizarre *pahupu*, Kaeokulani, and his warriors from Kauai,
attacked Kamehameha's north coast in a great fleet of
canoes. Besides their traditional weapons, they had muskets
and a cannon controlled by a European gunner.

Battle of the Red-Mouthed Gun

Most likely in the spring of 1791, Kamehameha caught up
with his two enemies then at sea off the north coast. He, too,
had a cannon, the already proven *Lopaka*, and swivel guns
on the sloop *Fair American*, an ocean-going vessel he had
luckily acquired through the two massacres already
mentioned. Once again the gunnery of Young and Davis
proved crucial, this time on the water in which they were
expert. Though the victory was not clear-cut, historians
generally award it to Kamehameha and call the battle
Kekuwaha'ulaula, "Battle of the Red-Mouthed Gun."
Kahekili and Kaeokulani returned safely to Maui,
anticipating an attack from Kamehameha.

In 1792 or early 1793, the English fur trader and gun
seller Captain William Brown first recognized the
commercial possibilities of Honolulu Harbor. He made an
agreement with the fearsome Kahekili, which Brown
seems to have believed ceded the island to him and Britain,
his payment being to help Kahekili fight Kamehameha.

Kahekili died, succeeded by his son Kalanikupule on
Oahu and by Kaeokulani on Kauai, Maui, Lanai, and
Molokai. These two chiefs soon squabbled and fought, and
with the help of the crew and muskets of Captain Brown,
Kahekili's son Kalanikupule was victorious. These Hawaiian
chiefs were shrewd and never satisfied, and Kalanikupule's
thoughts soon turned to the conquest of Kamehameha and
the Big Island. When a group of Oahuans murdered Brown
and some of his men, Kalanikupule took advantage by trying
to seize Brown's ships to use in his intended invasion. His
hijack failed, the ships and their surviving crews escaped to
sea, and in revenge they sent a letter warning Young, Davis,
and Kamehameha.

Paniolos *(Hawaiian cowboys) at Independence Weekend Rodeo.*
Descendants of the cattle given to Kamehameha I had become a massive
nuisance by the early 1800s. In 1814 John Palmer Parker, with the
king's approval, began rounding them up. Thus began Hawaii's cattle
industry and the Parker Ranch, worked by Hawaiian cowboys, on the
uplands of the Big Island. Cattle ranching then spread to other islands.
Parker Ranch and Gladys Suzuki

VANCOUVER & THE CESSION OF HAWAII ISLAND

Captain George Vancouver, who had been a midshipman
under Cook, was sent to further explore and chart the
northwest coast of North America in the *HMS Discovery.*
On the same expedition he visited the Sandwich Islands
three times. The first was for three weeks in early 1792. In
February and March 1793, Vancouver returned and this
time landed on the Big Island.

Vancouver and Kamehameha had met on Cook's ship in
1778, and when they now saw each other again, their surprise
and pleasure was shared and they became friends. As
Vancouver reported, "I was agreeably surprised in finding
that his riper years had softened that stern ferocity which his
younger days had exhibited... [he now showed]... an open,
cheerful, and sensible mind, combined with great generosity
and goodness of disposition." During this visit, the two
discussed the idea of Hawaii's cession to Britain. Because of
the loyalty of Britons Young and Davis in both peace and war,
Kamehameha was very favorably disposed toward Britain.
Leading *ali'i* also seem to have agreed to cession.

During Vancouver's third and final visit in 1794, the two

leaders held long conversations. A deeper friendship developed and once again, as Vancouver puts it, "Cession to his Britainnic Majesty became now an object of his [Kamehameha's] serious concern." The perceptive Kamehameha may have concluded that ceding the Island of Hawaii to Britain would provide him with protection from the interference of other foreign powers. Some historians have suggested that while he was agreeing to a cession, it was not in the sense Vancouver believed, though clearly he wanted Vancouver's and Britain's military support.

Attended by Kamehameha and all leading *ali'i,* Vancouver's ship held a ceremony of cession, watched and apparently approved by thousands in surrounding canoes. A plate of copper was fixed to Kamehameha's house acknowledging the establishment of the protectorate. Presumably, Vancouver intended to inform the British government of these arrangements.

At this point the historical record becomes cloudy. The protectorate was never formalized by the British government. Several causes may have been responsible for this oversight. During these years, Britain was engaged in a life-and-death struggle against France and Napoleon Bonaparte in Europe. In such circumstances it is understandable that the British might just have forgotten about ratifying the agreement with the king of this island on the other side of the world. Also, on his return, Vancouver was hounded by his former crewman, the foul-tempered Thomas Pitt, who, as a nephew of the British prime minister William Pitt, made enemies for Vancouver in government circles—a situation that may have led to the rejection of his agreement with Kamehameha. Vancouver himself fell ill and died by May 1798. In any case, the lack of ratification had little effect on Kamehameha's position because other countries believed that a British protectorate had been established. As a secretary of the Hawaiian Historical Society wrote in 1913, "The sailing vessels in the Pacific felt the restraining influence of what might be called an imaginary force and did not make trouble for the people who might be under Britain's protection." Such a situation must have given great confidence to Kamehameha as he fought his later campaigns to unite all the islands under his control.

In return Vancouver gave Kamehameha sheep and

cattle. A *kapu* was placed on the cattle that were allowed to run loose and bred enormously in the island's uplands. Within a few years these strange beasts became the basis of Hawaii's cattle industry. Vancouver's crew and twenty local carpenters, supervised by his shipwright and helped by Young and Davis, also built the *Britannia* for Kamehameha. This vessel had a keel of 29 ft and a width of over 9 ft. From Kamehameha's point of view, *Britannia* was his first "battleship." The British influence in Kamehameha's campaigns was certainly significant.

FURTHER CONQUESTS

Kamehameha had never been stronger. In 1795 he captured Maui and Molokai. His ships the *Britannia* and the *Young American* and his great fleet of canoes were on the way to conquer Oahu when a long-time ally, the handsome *ali'i* Kaiana, went over to the enemy with his followers. (Kaiana had earlier committed adultery with Kamehameha's favorite wife Ka'ahumanu.)

Great Battle of Nu'uanu Pali, near Honolulu
With some 16,000 men (a larger force than that with which William the Norman seized England in the famous invasion of 1066), Kamchamcha landed in the south. His invasion fleet beached on a vast stretch of coast from Waialae Beach, just east of Diamond Head, through what are now the multibillion-dollar sands and high-rise hotels of famous Waikiki, and to Honolulu Harbor. Kamehameha's forces attacked from several directions, pursuing his enemies inland. The warriors of Kalanikupule and Kaiana decided to make their stand on the high ground at the head of Nu'uanu Valley behind Honolulu Harbor and the area of modern downtown Honolulu. The valley's sides quickly become steep and it ends in a heart-stopping drop down the thousand feet of rock known as Nu'uanu Pali (cliff) on the windward side of the Ko'olau Range.

The defenders were pushed to the end of the valley, and Kalanikupule and a few others fortuitously found their way out to the north. Many others tried to hold their ground but were pushed to the lip of the cliff and then forced over the edge. Others, rather than be captured, tortured, and sacrificed, chose to jump to their deaths.

Queen Lydia Namahana Gormandizes, 1816

Otto von Kotzebue, the Russian navigator, visited Honolulu in 1816. In his book *Voyage of Discovery, 1815–1818*, published in London in 1831, he reports on the gastronomic behavior of the Maui queen, Lydia Namahana (he calls her Nomahanna), mother of Kaʻahumanu:

A number of Chinese porcelain dishes containing food of various kinds were ranged in a semicircle before her, and the attendants were busily employed in handing first one and then another to her majesty. She helped herself with her fingers from each in turn, and ate most voraciously whilst two boys flapped away the flies.…

My appearance did not at all disturb her: she greeted me with her mouth full, and graciously nodded her desire that I should take my seat in a chair by her side, when I witnessed, I think, the most extraordinary meal upon record. How much had passed the royal mouth before my entrance, I will not undertake to affirm; but it took in enough in my presence to have satisfied six men! Great as was my admiration at the quantity of food thus consumed, the scene which followed was calculated to increase it. Her appetite appearing satisfied at length, the queen drew her breath with difficulty two or three times, then exclaimed, "I have eaten famously!" These were the first words her important business had allowed her time to utter. By the assistance of her attendants, she then turned upon her back and made a sign with her hand to a tall, strong fellow, who seemed well practiced in the office; he immediately sprang upon her body, and kneaded her unmercifully with his knees and fists as if she had been a trough of bread. This was done to favor the digestion; and her majesty after groaning a little at this ungentle treatment and taking a short time to recover herself, ordered her royal person to be again turned on the stomach, and recommenced her meal.…

Nomahanna is vain of her tremendous appetite. She considers most people too thin, and recommends inaction as an accelerator of her admired embonpoint.… On the Sandwich Islands, a female figure a fathom [6 ft] long and of immeasurable circumference is charming; whilst the European lady laces tightly and sometimes drinks vinegar in order to touch our hearts by her slender and delicate symmetry.

Today visitors can drive to the top of Nuʻuanu Pali and, buffeted by the continual and wayward winds that blast up the valley, look over the cliff and ponder Kamehameha's triumph and the fate of his enemies. In 1897 when the road was being cut across the mountains, workers discovered the skulls and skeletons of an estimated 800 warriors at the foot of the cliffs. (This total shows that large numbers of defenders were still fighting at Nu'uanu.) In cutting the road, massive blasts of dynamite dislodged thousands of tons of rock from the cliff face, which rained down to bury the skeletons. The battle captures the modern Hawaiian imagination, and artists have produced some striking paintings of it.

In 1907 the Daughters of Hawaii unveiled a plaque at the site commemorating the battle and the Kamehameha dynasty that united the islands. In 1997 hundreds of Hawaiians walked from Waikiki to the site for a sunrise re-consecration. (Hawaiians since the time of Kamehameha have increasingly honored his achievements in uniting the archipelago and ignored his opportunism and savagery.)

Oahu is striking, beautiful, green, and extremely fertile, and Kamehameha now possessed its great valleys planted in taro and its strings of well-maintained fish ponds along the coasts. This largesse seems to have meant little to him, for Kamehameha now ruled all the islands but for Kauai and tiny Niihau. Like his contemporary, Napoleon, Kamehameha could not stop himself. He had to possess these islands too, wanting the whole archipelago under his single rule.

Kauai Invasion Plans

He ordered his carpenters to build him another vessel, a 40-ton European-style ship, and again organized a campaign. In the middle of 1796, the great invasion fleet was ready and passed out into the 70 mi wide Kauai Channel, by far the widest waters between any of the islands—and the most unruly. Despite all the prayers to the gods, high winds rose, his canoes foundered and overturned, and he was frustratingly forced back.

His thoughts of a second attempt were squashed by a revolt on the Big Island, which he crushed. Now he began to settle and concentrate on his achievements, and for the time being he abandoned the ambition to capture Kauai. Perhaps for the first time since its early years of settlement, the entire Hawaiian Archipelago was at peace.

Kamehameha's mind then turned to government—how to create a state that, in contrast to too much of the political history of the archipelago, would not be at continual risk from revolts by ambitious *ali'i*. Only if there were such peace and good order could Kamehameha amass all the wealth produced by farming, fishing, and trading with visiting European and American ships.

Kamehameha was highly intelligent, shrewd, and endowed with practical common sense. He kept the stability of the old ways but mixed these with useful innovations. He liberally celebrated the annual Makahiki festival but also built large storehouses that he filled with produce to trade. The highest chiefs were removed from district authority but acquired the prestige of living at Kamehameha's court—where he could also keep an eye on them. He appointed lower-born *ali'i* as governors to control each island, men who owed their position to him rather than genealogy or family influence and had no ties of blood or kin to the former chiefs of their islands. The most famous of these was Boki, governor of Oahu, site of Honolulu, which, as the years passed, began to outpace other towns in wealth, population, and importance.

Like most political leaders and wealthy men outside Christian European or lands colonized by it, many Hawaiian chiefs had multiple wives. Kamehameha as autocratic ruler was able to indulge his fleshly passions in a manner denied to ordinary men and married twenty-one women. Two were most significant. One was his seventeenth and favorite wife, Ka'ahumanu, daughter of the chief Ke'eaumoku, who killed Keoua. It seems Kamehemeha took her into his household as a child of eight, and by age sixteen their regard for each other was remarked upon by the visiting Vancouver. (Years later Ka'ahumanu confessed to the missionary Bingham that Kamehemeha regularly thrashed her.) The other favorite was the sacred Keopuolani, the mother of his two eldest sons, so sacred that she did not go outside in daylight. Nine of Kamehemeha's wives bore him a total of fourteen children. After his favorite son Alexander Stewart disappeared on a voyage to China, he made his son Liholiho heir to the kingdom.

He encouraged and rewarded commensurately a number of faithful white men, of whom Young and Davis held pride of place. At and near his court, there eventually gathered skilled men of every kind—carpenters, canoe makers, boat and ship builders, blacksmiths, ropemakers, feather workers, carvers, surfers, genealogists, and not least, religious orators and diviners. The more exotic of his European helpers were several escaped convicts from the British penal settlements in the colony of New South Wales in Australia. In 1808 Kamehameha gave them jobs as royal distillers.

Control of Kauai at Last

Kamehameha had never abandoned his life's ambition to be supreme ruler of the archipelago, and in 1804 and 1805 began the build-up in the Big Island for a second attack on Kauai. His white shipwrights constructed more schooners and his native carpenters cut specially designed broad twin-hulled war canoes, or *peleleu*, which carried a covered platform supporting a main sail and a jib. An enormous fleet of about 800 vessels was assembled. The armada left the Island of Hawaii in 1802 but remained over a year in Lahaina on Maui, from where Kamehameha dispatched never-answered letters to the ruler of Kauai, Kaumualii, demanding he surrender.

In early 1804 Kamehameha set up camp farther west in Oahu and in spring, when he was almost ready to sail into Kauai Channel, Oahu was struck by an horrendous epidemic—cholera, or typhoid, or even perhaps bubonic plague—the latter a possibility because of the rapidity with which the disease progressed. Most likely the crew of a visiting ship brought the disease, but to the priests the only explanation was that the Hawaiian gods were extremely angry and had to be placated.

The people made offerings and sacrifices with mountains of fruit and pigs and coconuts—and humans too. Three men who had infringed an eating *kapu* were seized, for perhaps it was they who had annoyed the gods. Their arms and legs were broken, then their eyeballs were removed. Their tortured screams and unending pain ignored, they were not killed until the appointed time as determined by the *kahuna* and then placed on the *heiau* at Waikiki. The plague continued.

Thousands of Oahuans died. No group or class was immune. Kamehameha abandoned his intention to invade Kauai once again, and as historian Gavan Daws puts it, "along the shore at Waikiki the war canoes were left to rot in the sun."

As the years passed, Kamehameha mellowed or grew tired or just realized how much could be lost in another invasion. He decided to compromise. Kaumualii of Kauai was now prepared to acknowledge Kamehameha's overlordship and to pay tribute, but, understandably remembering the fate of Keoua, he did not want to come to Oahu.

Finally, through the mediation of an American trader, Nathan Winship, the two rulers met peacefully. In 1810 Winship carried Kaumualii and his court to Honolulu. Delicate negotiations resulted in Kaumualii's being allowed to continue governing Kauai and Niihau as a tributary king who acknowledged Kamehameha's rule over the whole archipelago. At last, in his early fifties, Kamehameha had achieved his life's ambition. Nevertheless, Kaumualii seems to have accepted this subordinate status reluctantly.

No other Pacific chief so imposed his will on his people—or on the self-seeking Europeans who lived in his territory—as Kamehameha. For 25 years his Hawaii was easily the largest and most stable kingdom, not just in Polynesia but in all the Pacific islands, despite this being a period of enormous social change brought about by foreign contact and commerce.

FINAL YEARS AND DEATH

Because the foreign trade of Honolulu continued to grow, Kamehameha left the Big Island in 1804 and moved his capital there, where he remained until 1812, by which date he could fully rely upon Boki, his governor of Oahu. (By that time Kamehameha had a tax on all forms of commerce, including sex.) He also wanted to pass his declining years in the valleys and hills of his native island of Hawaii. Here he constructed the royal compound Kamakahonu (Turtle Eye) at Kailua. But in 1816, at John Young's insistence, he also agreed that a strong fort should be constructed in Honolulu near the harbor entrance.

In 1818 Vasily Golovin, the Russian navigator on a voyage around the world, described the mature Kamehameha:

> Still strong, active, temperate and sober. He does not use liquor or eat to excess. We can see in him a combination of childishness and ripe judgment.... His honesty and

love of justice have been shown in numerous cases. One fact which shows his good sense is this. None of the foreigners visiting his country enjoys any exclusive privileges, but all can trade with equal freedom. Europeans are not allowed to own land.

In early 1819 Kamehameha fell ill and died on May 8. Young, "his favorite foreigner," was at the king's deathbed. (In 1833 Young would go to live in Honolulu with his daughter and his son-in-law, Dr. Thomas C. B. Rooke, where he died two years later at age ninety-one. So important had Young become and his integrity so universally acknowledged that he was interred in the royal mausoleum and later transferred to the new Royal Mausoleum in the Nu'uanu Valley where his body still lies.)

Old friends prepared the king's body, many *kahuna* offered prayers, and several of his closest *ali'i* gathered his stripped bones and buried them somewhere in North Kohala, taking this secret to their own graves. The site has never been discovered and may even be underwater because the west coast has been sinking about an inch a decade for centuries. At least, that is the most accepted version. But there is a mysterious passage by Queen Lili'uokalani written in code in one of her diaries in 1901 and only translated in 1971 by a Bishop Museum researcher. It says that she and a relative interred Kamahameha's bones in the Royal Mausoleum early on May 14. If she did so, again, no one knows where these bones are now.

In accordance with the late king's will, Liholiho became king with the title of Kamehameha II. The questions then became: Without Kamehameha I, would the social-political cement of the *kapu* system retain its force? Would the Hawaiians be able to resist the pressures and encroachments of foreigners and retain their independence?

Must-See Sites: The Island of Hawaii

Youngest and largest of the islands, the "Big Island" was the location of the earliest settlements and the last *heiau* to be built. It was also the birthplace of Kamehameha the unifier, the site of Captain Cook's demise, the locality where Protestant missionaries first landed, and home of Kilauea, the world's most active volcano. The Island of Hawaii is key to Hawaiian culture (see www.hawaii-county.com or www.bigisland.org). This discussion follows a roughly counter-clockwise direction around the island, beginning at Hilo on the central east coast.

Hilo and Hamakua Districts
Hilo
Hilo (hee-low), the second largest and the wettest town (120 in/ 3,050 mm of rain per year) of the state, lies on the east coast of the Island of Hawaii, 200 mi southeast by air from Honolulu. Hilo sits between the flanks of the volcanoes Mauna Kea and Mauna Loa.

The town was hit by devastating tsunamis in 1837, 1946, and 1960. A clock on a tall green pedestal on Kamehameha Avenue is still frozen at the moment (1:04 AM) when in 1960 the 35 ft tsunami hit, killing 61 people. That tsunami was generated by an 8.6 magnitude earthquake in Chile that sent the tsunami about 6,200 mi before it reached Hawaii. To prevent a repetition, Hilo bayfront is now long stretches of undeveloped grass and park land, and the administrative and business section of town has been raised 26 ft (8 m). The Pacific Tsunami Museum explains tsunamis.

The rain and the soil make Hilo lush, with luxuriant trees and flowers and many commercial gardens. The trees of Banyan Drive were planted by 1930s celebrities such as King George V, Cecil B. DeMille, and Amelia Earhart. One of the best remaining examples of a mission home, Lyman Museum & Mission House built in 1839 of koa hardwood, has what was perhaps Hawaii's first corrugated "tin" (zinc-iron) roof, imported in 1856. Built in 1925, the refurbished Palace Theatre (hilopalace.com) is once again a center of activity. High above the town, the turreted Shipman House, where Queen Lili'uokalani stayed when visiting Hilo, has superb views. Each year about 20,000 visitors are attracted to the colorful Merrie Monarch Hula Festival. The local newspaper is the *Hawaii Tribune-Herald* (www.hilohawaii tribune.com).

Mauna Kea Volcano and Astronomical Observatories
At 13,796 ft this great dormant volcano has visitors' centers and, because the clear ocean air gives the best astronomical viewing in the world, upon it rests the world's greatest cluster of astronomical observatories (those of the United States, Britain, Australia, Japan, Chile, France, Brazil, Netherlands, Taiwan, and Argentina). The first was that of the University of Hawaii in 1968. Britain built the first infrared telescope, which can be operated by remote control from Greenwich Observatory near London.

The NASA telescope has measured the temperature of volcanoes on Io, one of the moons of Jupiter; Io's largest volcano is even called "Pele," after the Hawaiian volcano goddess.

The 8-story-high, 300-ton (270-tonne) twin Keck Telescopes built in 1992 and 1996 are the world's largest optical and infrared instruments; they operate with nanometer precision. Keck has a visitors' gallery and is open during the day. In 1996 Keck discovered the most distant galaxy ever observed to that date (see www2.keck.hawaii.edu/).

About halfway to the summit stands the Onizuka Center for International Astronomy (www.ifa.hawaii.edu/info/vis), named after Ellison Onizuka, Hawaii's first astronaut, who was killed in the *Challenger* space shuttle explosion. This center is about 28 mi (45 km) from Hilo along Saddle Road. There is a lookout and a star-gazing program. A stop here is necessary for adjustment when driving to higher altitudes. At the very summit is a cairn of rocks from which, when weather permits, there is a 360-degree view of the Pacific. Skiing and snowboarding are popular in winter.

Upon the great dormant volcano sit the astronomical observatories of ten nations, making use of the clean, high-altitude ocean air that provides the earth's best viewing.
Hawaii Visitors and Convention Bureau and Kirk Lee Aeder

Saddle Road
Built by the US Army during World War II and cutting across the northern third of the Big Island, Saddle Road climbs from Hilo to more than 6,500 ft (getting cold!) with splendid views of Mauna Kea and Mauna Loa. It passes through a thickly wooded section and then harsh areas of lava, broken here and there by isolated clusters of trees and parched grasslands, then winds farther west again through the rolling cattle pastures around Waimea. Be prepared: The road has no service stations.

North Kohala District
This northern peninsula has some of the most spectacular scenery on the island: towering sea cliffs that open into the deep, meandering valleys of the Kohala Mountains, the remains of an ancient volcano. Here waterfalls cascade thousands of feet into tropical rainforests, and the remnants of ancient Hawaiian settlements hide in the greenery. This is helicopter country.

Mo'okini Heiau and Kamehameha Statue
Near the little artisan town of Hawi stands Mo'okini Heiau, lichen-covered, in ruin, and perhaps dating from the 800s—another immense basalt temple, on the windswept northern tip of the island. Its stone seems to have been brought (by hand) from Pololu Valley 14 mi (22 km) distant. The current resident *kahuna* claims descent from the very earliest *kahuna*. About 2 mi (3 km) east of Hawi in the tiny town of Kapa'au stands the original statue of King Kamehameha I (the copy is in Honolulu).

Waipi'o Valley
The spiritual heartland of the ancient Big Island, the "Valley of the Kings" is the largest of seven ampitheater-shaped verdant valleys along this far north coast. Majestic Waipi'o is about a mile wide and six deep, its near vertical walls laced with waterfalls, some about 2,000 ft high. The Waipi'o Stream splashes the rich taro fields of the valley floor, crossing a black sand beach to the angry ocean. Access requires four-wheel drive.

Some thousands of people lived here in pre-contact times, the stream stocked with fish, the valley speckled with *heiau*, and its own place of refuge like Pu'uhonua O Honaunau. But tsunamis have devastated this valley, and now it supports merely a handful of farmers. Kamehameha I passed the first few years of his life hidden here, protected from those who wished him dead.

South Kohala District
Pu'ukohola Hieau National Historic Site
On the northwest coast of the Big Island, Pu'ukohola Heiau, a triple-tiered, lava dry-stone temple about 225 by 100 ft, was constructed above Kawaihae Bay to achieve the favor of the war god Ku in Kamehameha I's plan to conquer the island. Today it is fully restored. Kamehameha's rival,

Keoua of the Ka'u district, was killed and sacrificed to Ku on the *heiau*, and Kamehameha became chief of all the Big Island (www.nps.gov/puhe).

Puako Petroglyph Preserve

About five miles south of Pu'ukohola Heiau, west of the Highway 19 and near the ocean, are approximately 3,000 distinct images carved in rock—the Puako Petroglyph Archeological Preserve, perhaps the Pacific's most extensive collection of petroglyphs. The earliest images date from around 1200 CE, the most recent from the 1800s after Westerners arrived. Many petroglyphs seem to trace genealogies, though most are difficult to see when the sun is overhead.

Waimea

Sometimes called Kamuela, this up-country, up-to-date northern ranching town standing at 2,500 ft is often cool and misty. It grew in concert with the Parker Ranch founded by John P. Parker. Mid-town is Parker Ranch Visitor Center telling the history of ranching. W. M. Keck Observatory headquarters on the town's outskirts provides information on the world's most powerful telescopes.

Originally cattle were herded through the surf to waiting ships in Kawaihae Bay, which took them to the Parker slaughterhouse in Honolulu. There are graceful homesteads, including a rebuilt version of *Mana Hale*, originally erected by Parker, in which the interiors are done in striking koa wood and the house filled with shining handmade furniture. *Puopelu*, a lavish home built in 1862, has a Regency interior, antiques, and a European art collection.

North Kona District

"Kona Coast" (meaning leeward) refers to most of the dry, sunny west coast.

Kailua-Kona

Often just called "Kona" and lying in the shadow of the impressive 8,271 ft (2,551 m) volcano Hualalai (last eruption in 1801), this town is the center of the Big Island's burgeoning west coast and the island's busiest vacation destination. Here the missionaries first landed. In town on the shore of Ali'i Drive on Kailua Bay sits neat little Hulihe'e Palace, built in 1838 by Queen Ka'ahumanu's brother, Big Island Governor John Adams Kuakini, and preserved and beautified by King Kalakaua in 1885. Until 1916 it was a summer "getaway" for royalty. Opposite is missionary-built Moku'aikaua Church, probably the first church in the islands (just ahead of Kawaiahao in Honolulu). The original structure of 1820 was of pandanus thatch. The present church, also built by Kuakini in 1837, was constructed from coral and lava rock, the latter drawn from a 1400s *heiau* on the site. The simple interior is of koa hardwood. A few hundred yards away is King Kamahameha's Kona Beach Hotel, built where King Kamehameha I had his final royal compound, *Kamakahonu* (Turtle Eye), on small but striking Kamakahonu Bay from 1812 to 1819. Here is the Ahu'ena Heiau dedicated to the god Lono that he restored, and in the hotel are many historical artifacts. The local newspaper is *West Hawaii Today* (www.westhawaiitoday.com).

South Kona District
Kealakekua Bay Area
Kealakekua Bay is where Captain Cook was killed. Although the monument erected on the site in 1874 at the north end of the bay is easy to approach by sea, it is a difficult hike from land. The cliffs behind the monument are honeycombed with burial caves. The bay is excellent for snorkeling. There is also a plaque dedicated to Cook at the place he was killed.

The Amy B. H. Greenwell Ethnobotanical Garden of Bishop Museum, on twelve acres southeast of Captain Cook town, encourages native Hawaiian land use, researches ancient botany, and maintains a repository for Hawaiian and Polynesian plants. Its interesting remnant of the ancient local Kona Field system has four vegetation zones varying from coastal to mountainous, preserving about 250 native species.

Pu'uhonua O Honaunau National Historical Park
Built on a rocky lava point five miles south on Route 160 and marked by lines of tall royal palms is Pu'uhonua O Honaunau ("the City of Refuge"), surrounded inland by the 182 ac Pu'uhonua O Honaunau National Historical Park, founded in 1961. This is the site of one of Hawaii's greatest construction feats, the mighty dry stone "Great Wall" built in the mid-1500s, 17 ft thick, 10 ft high, and about 1,000 ft long. It encloses the sacred area where traditionally no blood could be shed. It was a place where the very lucky, the very skillful, and the very few might escape the fearsome retribution for breaking a *kapu*. Offered sanctuary, the offender would be absolved by the *kahuna*. Defeated warriors and non-combatants could also take refuge. Kamehameha's willful favorite, Queen Ka'ahumanu, once fled from him here. Two ruined *heiau* in the lava rock area apparently predated the wall. The reconstructed Hale O Keawe Heiau near the ocean at the north end of the Great Wall, first built around 1550, held the bones of the great chief Keawe and many later chiefs and thus their mana for some 250 years.

On the landward side of the Wall in the "palace grounds," a number of thatched A-frame structures have been recreated. Near the Hale O Keawe Heiau, Keone'ele Cove was the canoe landing place for local chiefs, *kapu* to commoners. Nowadays it provides prime snorkeling. Nearby are other archaeological sites such as royal fishponds, *heiau* platforms, sled tracks, and coastal village sites. Native Hawaiians still believe Pu'uhonua O Honaunau is a sacred place (see www.nps.gov/puho).

Mauna Loa Kona Coffee Lands

Inland and south of Kealakekua Bay and Captain Cook town on the rising slopes of Mauna Loa Volcano, the cooler climate and fertile volcanic soil combine to produce one of Earth's best coffees. In the little hamlets, many "boutique" mills welcome visitors with tasting rooms and shops, exhibiting varieties of gourmet Kona coffee.

Puna District

Hawaii Volcanoes National Park

Set in the southeast of the Big Island, the park is best approached from Hilo. More than half of the Hawaii Volcanoes National Park is designated wilderness and provides novel hiking and camping. Within the park is the Hawaiian Volcano Observatory (hvo.wr.usgs.gov), established by Thomas Jaggar in 1912. Nearby at the Jaggar Museum visitors can view the tools of the vulcanologist's trade. Some of the best views of Kilauea Caldera and Halema'uma'u Crater are from the overlook just outside. Amazing Kilauea is the youngest volcano. From the air it looks like a bulge on the southeastern flank of Mauna Loa, and it was at first considered to be a kind of satellite rather than a separate volcano. Intensive research has shown clearly that Kilauea has its own magma-producing system, which plunges more than 36 mi (58 km) into the earth.

Kilauea has been erupting since between 600,000 and 300,000 years ago. It is slowly transforming itself layer by layer into a shield volcano like Mauna Kea. The caldera was the site of regular activity during the 19th century and the early part of the 20th century. From 1952 to 1982 there were 34 eruptions. The present eruption of Kilauea has continued regularly since 1983. The lava that erupts from the cinder-and-spatter cone of Pu'u 'O'o in great red-yellow rivers (black when it cools) that flow along the surface or through a lava-tube system down Pulama Pali about 6 mi (9.6 km) to the ocean to the south. In 1960, near the Cape Kumukahi Lighthouse, the lava flow parted, passed around the rocky mound below the structure, then closed to continue entering the ocean—and added a new 500 yards of land to the point.

Since 1983, Kilauea has covered over 16,000 ac, threatening wildlife, destroying power lines and water supplies, crushing about 200 houses, and leaving some areas covered in lava 80 ft (24 m) deep. It destroyed the black sand of Kaimu Beach and covered a twelfth century *heiau* and the hundred-year-old Kalapana Mauna Kea Church. Chain of Craters Road runs down the escarpment to take viewers close. Park rangers mark trails that end half a mile or so from moving lava thrusting into the ocean. Strict caution is needed. Helicopter flights over Kilauea Caldera and the lava flow are available. The park is as an International Biosphere Reserve and a World Heritage Site (see www.nps.gov/havo).

5

Missionaries versus Whalers

Sandalwood and Seals

By 1810 some excited European sea captains had found that, as in many other Pacific islands, the Hawaiian Archipelago had stands of sandalwood that grew profusely in upland areas. They knew the Chinese loved to burn *jos* sticks of this silky smooth sandalwood for incense and that Chinese traders would pay them handsomely for it. Suddenly Hawaii was developing a new industry.

Canny European and American sea traders could win vast profits by buying cheaply from these Hawaiian chiefs and selling dear in the port of Guangzhou (Canton) in Guangdong in southern China. Encouraged by Kamehameha's example, most Hawaiian chiefs had acquired an indiscriminate taste for Western manufactured goods. It was sandalwood which allowed these *ali'i* to pay for their expensive new and wasteful taste. But as they were poor businessmen and often taken advantage of, it was sandalwood that ran them into debt.

Americans soon dominated the trade. In 1812 three Bostonians, the leader of whom was Nathan Winship, the man who had reconciled Kamehameha and Kauai's king, persuaded Kamehemeha to give them a ten-year monopoly. Within a few years John Jacob Astor of New York had illegally broken this monopoly. Other traders also operated illegally, encouraging local chiefs to ignore Kamehemeha's authority. When Liholiho ascended the throne, he had to share the sandalwood trade officially with them to secure their loyalty.

The chiefs dragooned the commoners into cutting the wood and hauling it down the mountainsides. The work was tough and physically harmful. Years of frenetic cutting and no program for replenishment destroyed much of the sandalwood forests and the Hawaiian industry itself within twenty years. Greed contributed too, because during the early years supply finally far exceeded demand and the law of diminishing returns began to apply.

As a result of the trade, the Hawaiian Islands became a center for provisioning ships and providing recreation for crews (in a sense the first tourism). Over the next decade or so, these functions became the basis for the islands' economy. Prostitution, unfortunately, became ordinary, assisting in the spread of European diseases that would decimate the native population.

Soon to be supplemented by US missionaries and whalers, the sandalwood traders began an American presence that in less than a century would become overwhelming.

Cook's discovery of vast schools of seals and sea otters sporting on the North American west coast began an American and European trade with the northwestern Native Americans, taking the pelts from them to Guangzhou. (A good pelt was worth about $100 in China—an enormous sum at that time.) Once again the Hawaiian Islands became a rendezvous for replenishment, rest, and recreation for ships on this long route. The islands were also ideal for trade ships to spend the winter. Reversely, hundreds of Hawaiians also migrated into what is now British Columbia and Washington state, the source of the pelts and furs.

THE CATTLE INDUSTRY

It may be recalled that Captain Vancouver gave Kamehameha some cattle. Placed under a *kapu*, they had multiplied into a problem within twenty years, roaming at will on the Big Island, knocking down fences, destroying gardens, and terrifying the people.

A young ship's clerk from Massachusetts, John Palmer Parker, had jumped ship in Hawaii in 1809. In 1814 he approached Kamehameha with a proposal as a result of which he gained the right to solve the cattle problem. Parker had the intelligence and ambition to realize that if domesticated, cattle could become the basis of an industry for meat and hides. He began by salting beef to sell to passing ships. His dedication and decades-long persistence (and marriage to Kipikane, a Kamehameha grand-daughter) brought prosperity. Parker moved to the village of Waimea in 1835, establishing his koa wood homestead at Mana. Though he cleared vast areas of land, it still belonged to the king. In 1847 he became one of the first whites to receive a royal land grant—two acres from Kamehameha III.

Parker sponsored the arrival of Mexican cowboys who in turn trained native Hawaiians in cowboy skills, men who became known as *paniolos*. The word comes from the Hawaiian pronunciation of "Espanoles" (Spaniards). It was dangerous work. The American writer Herman Melville wrote, "Many of these dissipated fellows, quaffing too freely of the stirrup-cup, and riding headlong after the herds, when they reeled in the saddle, were unhorsed and killed."

For decades the little town of Waimea might have come out of the Wild West, except that it was in the foothills of the Kohala Mountains. Parker and his descendants eventually developed the ranch into one of the most successful in the world. Parker built *Mana Hale*, a house to match his ambitions. The French diplomat Charles de Varigny describes it:

> When we arrived ten natives ran out to take the bridles of our mounts. A group of young girls hearing the hubbub also appeared. Some of them then departed for their duties in the dairy and the kitchen. The cattle bellowed, the sheep bleated, and a sweet aroma of dinner wafted on the evening air. We were given lodging in this huge box… this house of compartments all constructed from varnished koa wood—a timber of this land that resembles mahogany. Everything, roof, doors, partitions, floors and ceilings, all of the interior as well as the exterior, was made from koa. The whole building gave one the feeling, one might fancy, of an enormous toy.

At various times in the second half of the 1800s, cattle rearing developed on the other main islands. On Molokai, cattle grazing destroyed the native vegetation, and the soil eroded and washed into coastal aquaculture fishponds. Soon these were useless for fish, and a centuries old, natural, inexpensive source of food was no more.

Questioning the *Kapu*

The isolation of the islands had protected the native religion. But the *cordon sanitaire* of the North Pacific Ocean had been broached by Cook. Kamehameha was a traditionalist who helped to keep the old religion, its mana, and its *kapu* system strong for so long. As with everything else, Kamehameha judged religious beliefs by their results. When the Christian captains of visiting ships suggested that their god was superior, he would make such response as: "Please climb to yonder cliff, jump off, and I shall carefully observe if he saves you." No captain obliged. Kamehameha's successors would be less strict in their empirical tests of Christianity.

Challenges to Hawaiian religious beliefs, both implicit and explicit, arrived with Cook and continued. If Cook were really the god Lono, why was he killed so easily? If visiting sandalwood ships and sailors so consistently broke the *kapu* and ignored the holy ceremonies at the *heiau*, why were they not punished by the gods?

Women Test the Kapu

Skepticism about the religion spread. Women were the most discriminated against, and thus had most to gain. It was aristocratic women who first began to question the *kapu* system that prevented them from eating certain foods and forbade them from ever sharing a meal with men.

So, little by little, they began to test and challenge by flouting some *kapu*, then seeing what happened. Even in the late 1700s, visiting captains reported how aristocratic women would sometimes eat with their men when both came aboard ship or report that while the body of a common woman might be floating in the harbor, slaughtered by the priests or chiefs for infringing upon a *kapu*, at the same time royal women might infringe upon that *kapu* with impunity. By 1810 Archibald Campbell, who lived in Honolulu for a year, noted that "[t]he women very seldom scruple to break them [*kapu*] when it can be done in secret; they often swim off to ships at night during the taboo [*kapu*] against fraternization."

Ka'ahumanu, Kamehameha's favorite wife, had resistsed these restrictions from the beginning. Soon after her marriage, she began to ignore *kapu*. At one point, though Kamehameha put a *kapu* on her body, she continued to sleep with other chiefs. By the date of Kamehameha's death, she was easily the most powerful of his wives, and she and the sacred Keopuolani ever more openly began to flout the *kapu*. Wanting to control politics,

King Liholiho's Beautiful Yacht

Cleopatra's Barge was originally owned by a rich Salem, Massachusetts, merchant. America's first ocean-going yacht, she measured 83 ft on the waterline. Her hull was picked out with golf leaf and decorated with bright horizontal and herringbone stripes. Guests were served on pink luster ware and used ivory-handled cutlery. The inside was opulent with Grecian motifs carved into the bulkheads, and decorative cabinets held porcelain and silver. The yacht and her owner crossed the Atlantic, visiting such places as Gibraltar, Barcelona, Marseilles, and Genoa, but the owner died soon after.

Some American traders bought the ship, and it was sailed to Hawaii where the new king Liholiho, Kamehameha II, purchased it for $80,000 in sandalwood (the equivalent to many millions now), renaming it *Ha'aheo O Hawai'i* (Pride of Hawaii). Liholiho was enchanted and used it as his official vessel to travel around his tropical kingdom while indulging his passions for good food and drink.

When Liholiho departed for Britain in 1823, he left the ship in the care of his ministers, who seem to have been criminally cavalier and carefree with their enormously expensive responsibility. On April 5, 1824, (about five weeks before Liholiho had even landed in Britain) *Ha'aheo O Hawai'i* entered beautiful, cup-shaped Hanalei Bay on the north shore of Kauai and in good weather was allowed to founder on a reef in only five feet of water. It is believed that captain and crew were drunk.

Local Hawaiians tried to haul the yacht off the reef, but she turned on her side and sank in the enormous surf. Some of the wreck still rests at the mouth of Waioli Stream in Hanalei Bay, but hurricanes and tsunamis have taken their toll. She was located in July 1995 using electronic remote-sensing equipment. Excavations have produced a conch shell, poi pounders, glass, copper sheathing, weapons, gilded beads, oil lamps, and ivory pieces. Liholiho never learned of his loss, however, because he died of measles contracted soon after landing in Britain.

they pressured young King Liholiho to dispense with the *kapu* system. Among other things, women were banned from taking part in the *luakini heiau*, during which political as well as religious decisions were made. The 22-year-old Liholiho, unsure of his own power, gave way.

In November 1819, he agreed to hold a huge feast at which *ali'i* males and females could eat in the same place.

But he was so appalled by the implications of his decision that for two days prior to the feast he went on a mighty drinking binge out in the bay.

Overthrowing the Kapu

Two long tables were set up in the Western way, one for the male chiefs, a second for the women. At the women's table even the *kapu* foods of pork, coconuts, and bananas were served. The nervous Liholiho wandered around the tables for a while and suddenly took a seat with the women. He then set to voraciously eating and drinking.

No one choked on the food. The great god Kane did not seem to care. Lono, universal provider of sustenance, did not destroy any fields. Sea god Kanaloa did not mount a hurricane or send a tsunami across Waikiki. Lesser gods also did nothing—the goddess Pele did not cause Mauna Loa or Kilauea to erupt.

Ka'ahumanu possessed a powerful personality not to be denied (and by this date a monstrous size as well; the visiting Jacques Arago wrote, "she is prodigiously fat, but her face is interesting"). She forced Liholiho to agree to her being *kuhina nui*, virtually a new office, with powers as great as those of any modern prime minister. It was she who really ruled the kingdom for the next thirteen years, first as *kuhina nui* and later as regent during the minority of Kamehameha III.

Encouraged by Ka'ahumanu, Liholiho sent his heralds to every part of the islands of Hawaii with orders to desecrate the *heiau*, overthrow the idols, and end the sacrifices.

Supported by *kahuna*, a number of traditionalists among the chiefs rebelled at this appalling affront to their gods and to the power structure on which they themselves relied, and when attempts by both sides to reach agreement failed, the rebels used firearms to challenge the king. In December 1819, they and Liholiho's army led by the formidable Kalanimoku fought a battle at Kuamoo just south of Kailua in the Big Island. Liholiho's forces won with much superior weapons inherited from Kamehameha I and also crushed all subsequent small revolts.

Liholiho, Kamehameha II, remained king, but no longer was he supported in office by the Hawaiian gods and the fear instilled by the *kapu* system and the punishments for infringement—a fact potentially devastating to monarchial authority that Ka'ahumanu appears to have overlooked. Still, tradition has its own inertia, royalty has its own high charisma, and the danger to the monarchy passed. Hawaiians retained a deep and abiding respect for the king, and the ruling system survived. But for hundreds of years, the *kapu* system had maintained "law and order," so naturally misbehavior increased.

Hikers seen on the spectacular Pele's Paint Pot section of the Halemau'u Trail, deep inside the caldera of Haleakala Volcano. Depending upon the chemical composition of the lava and its degree of oxidation, colors vary from red ochre to lavender. Itself near 1,000 ft high, Pu'u O Maui Cone stands in the distance. Eight miles behind the hikers, on the rim of the caldera, is a telescope where astronomers have searched for planets orbiting other suns. Hawaii Visitors and Convention Bureau and Ron Dahlquist

Early Cowboys Catching Bulls in Hawaii

The cattle industry dates to 1793 when British naval captain George Vancouver gave King Kamehameha I some Santa Barbara longhorns. Francis Allyn Olmsted (1819–44), a student at Yale and in the Pacific to improve his health, describes the bull hunters of the Big Island in 1840 in his book, *Incidents of a Whaling Voyage*, published in New York in 1841:

> The lasso, the principal instrument in their capture, is made of braided thongs, upon one end of which is a ring forming a slip noose, which is thrown with astonishing precision around any part of the animal. Even while at full gallop in pursuit, the hunter grasps his lasso, and giving it two or three twirls around his head with the right hand, throws it unerringly and entangles his victim by the horns or limbs. And now, be wary for thy life, bold hunter; for the savage animal is maddened with terror. See, he turns upon his pursuer, with eyeballs glaring with fire and his frame quivering with rage. But the well-trained horse springs to one side, and braces himself, while the unwieldy animal plunges forward, but is suddenly caught up by the lasso, and falls with a heavy momentum upon the ground. Again he rises, and tears the ground with his hoofs, and loudly roars; then doubly furious comes down upon his pursuer, but is again avoided and again dashed upon the ground. Exhausted by repeated shocks like these, his fury is subdued and he allows himself to be secured to a tame bullock, which soon removes all his ferocity.

Until the end of 1820, Liholiho lived mainly at Kailua, but Honolulu was becoming ever more important in the culture and trade of the islands, and the king was persuaded to move his main home there. Using sandalwood deals, Liholiho had recently bought himself a beautiful yacht in which he sailed to Honolulu. But the congenital difficulty Liholiho found in remaining in the same place for a day or more meant that he was often in transit between islands.

As always in Hawaiian history, the nobles had led the way in killing the *kapu* and the commoners followed, and this would soon happen with Christianity too—for the second unintentional result was to make the Hawaiians vulnerable to spiritual reconquest by any new, self-assured religion that might arrive on their shores. Had the newcomers been Muslims or Buddhists or Hindus, perhaps the Hawaiians would have adopted one of those religions first, but in fact the first arrivals would be Calvinist New Englanders.

For decades many people still worshipped the old gods in secret. Indeed, some *ali'i* joined the priests and commoners in continuing to make offerings at the *heiau*. There has been a resurgence of native religion in recent decades and offerings by native Hawaiians are common.

Fundamentalist American Missionaries

It had been planned that the first Christian missionary to Hawaii would be Opukahaia, a young Hawaiian who had been taken to the United States. He studied English and trained in the foreign mission school in Connecticut. Opukahaia learned the Book of Genesis by heart in Hawaiian and, though now prepared for his great work, contracted typhoid and died.

Every age sees its own time as one of challenge, change, concerns, conflict, and war. For more than a thousand years, this viewpoint has led many Christians to believe that the problems of their own day were a true sign of the soon-to-occur second coming of Christ. In the early 1800s, some members of the American Board of Commissioners for Foreign Missions had such a premonition and convinced themselves that Christ was indeed about to reveal himself. There was thus no time to be lost in saving the souls of benighted savages (as they regarded them), such as the natives of the Sandwich Islands. Though the board believed that a religious training in Boston by New Englanders of Congregationalist faith was superior to all others, they decided to accept any good man of general Calvinist persuasion who was prepared to sail to far Hawaii to preach the fundamental truths "upon which every good Christian would agree."

Unrighteousness, Fornication, Wickedness...

The first ministers accepted for this task were the strict and straight Hiram Bingham of Vermont and Asa Thurston from Massachusetts. Their task was formidable, because in order to turn the Hawaiians into Christians they believed they had to "civilize" them at the same time—which for them seems to have meant turning Hawaiians into Calvinist New Englanders. So they had to wean them away from the sensual live-for-the-day Hawaiian lifestyle.

Decades later Bingham wrote a book of his experiences in which he described the Hawaiians' way of life as: "unrighteous, fornication, wickedness, murder, debate, deceit, malignity... whisperers, backbiters, haters of God, despiteful, proud, boasters, inventors of evil things,

The 28-year-old Reverend Hiram Bingham was the leader of the first missionaries to arrive in the islands in 1820. Sybil, his wife, proved to be an able helpmeet in home and mission.
Hawaii State Archives

disobedient to parents, without natural affection, implacable, unmerciful." Implacable himself, he believed he was ready for the task of changing the lives of such people. In the same volume he wrote that the Hawaiians were: "… too stupid and ignorant to farm lands and become self-providing." Bingham just ignored the fact that prior to the disorienting arrival of North Americans and Europeans like himself, the people of the Hawaiian Islands provided for some hundreds of thousands of themselves in great abundance for a thousand years in complete isolation from the rest of the world.

A farmer with five children, a printer, two teachers, and a physician joined the mission party, along with four young Hawaiians who had been trained at the mission school. Except for the farmer, the party were bachelors. Several engagements formed prior to the decision to sail to Hawaii were dissolved by women unprepared for such sacrifice. The organizers of the mission feared that single men would be a liability, too likely to "succumb to temptation," and so hastily found six young New England women who were prepared to marry men they hardly knew and share a mission life a third of the way around the world. The wedding bans were announced and the marriages performed—all within two months.

Then came the awful and tedious five month voyage on the brigantine *Thaddeus*, cramped two couples to a cabin, all the way down the Atlantic, around Cape Horn, and northwards across the Pacific—about 18,000 mi (29,000 km). There was no Panama Canal then and no well-worn western routes or railways across North America to the Spanish-controlled Pacific coast. At sunrise and sunset the New Englanders, led by Bingham, prayed.

On March 30, 1820, the voyagers at last spied the shining snow-capped volcanoes on the Big Island, and on April 4 they lowered the anchor in Kailua Bay. Other than the original settlement and Cook's arrival, this was the most significant turning point in Hawaiian history, a time portentous.

Then Bingham, Thurston, and the others saw the Hawaiians. They did not see them with even the tolerance of James Cook, nor as the "noble savages" described and admired (if patronizingly) by the European Enlightenment philosophers. Nor did they see sharing, fulfilled people. They saw merely savages. Expecting the worst, they certainly saw it, and, wrote Bingham, "Some of our number, with gushing tears, turned away from the spectacle."

Bingham sent a message to Liholiho for permission to land. But why would a king who had just rid himself of the constraining Hawaiian religion want to greet a group of Americans who hoped to introduce another? So he kept the New Englanders waiting on their ship for a while, but after consulting with old Englander John Young and checking with the powerful Ka'ahumanu, he allowed them to land— on a year's probation. When the newcomers first heard that the Hawaiian religion had been rejected mere months before their arrival, they were elated, assuming this change was God clearing the way. In fact the destruction of the native religion made their task much easier than that of Christians in many other Pacific islands such as Tahiti and Tonga. Thurston stayed in charge of the mission on the Big Island, and Bingham sailed to the larger, growing town of Honolulu to take control, arriving on April 19. During three decades, eleven more mission groups would land before it was considered that the Hawaiian enterprise had become self-perpetuating.

But success was hard to achieve. Two of the Hawaiian trainees set a good example, but another was excommunicated for drunkenness. Dozens of native people listened to outdoor sermons or were fascinated by singing in harmony, but just as many were more interested in giggling at the Calvinists' style of dress—dark, heavy, heat-holding woolen suits of the men or the bonnets and corsets covered by multiple petticoats of the women. Having to wear clothing to become Christian was hugely unappealing, though in time the missionaries achieved that goal.

Though time and human nature would eventually subvert their rigidity, these missionaries were racial segregationists at heart. John Young had favored their landing, but they were disgusted that he had married a Hawaiian. When some years later the Hawaiian chiefs suggested that the daughters of the missionaries would make suitable brides for the young princes Alexander Liholiho and Lot, Bingham and his fellows strongly refused. When Samuel G. Dwight, a bachelor who arrived in a later mission group, married a Hawaiian woman, he was dismissed.

Canadian Hawaiians

Seal and sea otter pelts bought from northwestern Native Americans to be sold in China brought European trading ships to Hawaii. The first to arrive was the *Imperial Eagle*, actually a British ship under an Austrian flag, in May 1787. When the ship was to leave, a young Hawaiian woman, Winee, pleaded to remain on board. As the servant of the captain's wife, she became the first Hawaiian known to have sailed to the American northwest.

Kaiana, who traitorously fought to the death against Kamehameha, was another early Hawaiian visitor to America. His ship's captain said that when Kaiana and a Nootka tribal chief met, there was immediate enmity. Kaiana thought himself superior to the local Native Americans, as did many of the Hawaiians who arrived later.

Hawaiians, usually called "Kanakas," served in the British North-West Company (NWC) and even more in the Hudson's Bay Company (HBC), and part of their job was to defend the trading company's outposts against Native American attacks. One NWC clerk wrote that they were "not wanting in courage," especially "against the Indians for whom they entertain a very cordial contempt." During one up-river expedition, the leader of the NWC party asked the Hawaiians if they would fight those who were trying to rob the company. Their answer was, "Mr. Keith, we kill every man you bid us."

In 1820 three Hawaiians were murdered while hunting beaver among the Snake tribe, and the river there became known as the Owyhee (Hawaii). By the mid-1840s, there were several dozen Hawaiians serving at inland HBC posts. They married local British Colombian settlers or Native American women. Even more worked at Fort Vancouver (now the city of Vancouver).

In 1849 came the California gold rush. As one scholar reports, "Suddenly the HBC lost its Kanakas.... They had some success on the fields but little social standing and frequently were involved in conflicts with other miners because they preferred to dive for gold in the rivers rather than use conventional methods!"

By the 1880s, there were Hawaiians resident in Vancouver, Victoria, the capital of British Columbia, the Gulf Islands, and in northern Washington state.

The Gulf Islands were the only place where sufficient numbers settled to form a true Hawaiian community and where they even built their own churches. Here Hawaiians could marry others of their race and keep their ethnic identity through several generations. Here remain people who proudly acknowledge their ancestry.

Nevertheless, to convert, the converters had to make contact. Their strategy was always to cultivate the Hawaiian leaders. They had great success on Kauai with King Kaumualii, but Boki, Liholiho's governor on Oahu, was intransigent. Bingham strode down dusty Fort Street to Honolulu Fort (the landmark Aloha Tower now stands approximately on the site). In a tall stovepipe hat and claw-hammer tailed coat, he asked Governor Boki to help them with accommodation, but Boki seemed not to hear him at all. Fortunately for Bingham's self-image, he did not have to settle in a little grass hut, because Winship, the sandalwood trader, had agreed that if necessary the mission could use his own Honolulu house.

At first the powerful dowager-queen Ka'ahumanu haughtily ignored the newcomers, but fortunately for the mission she fell gravely ill. Bingham's wife Sybil devotedly nursed her and she recovered. She said she repented her sins and she certainly began to attend church regularly each Sunday—in a carriage pulled by several strong Hawaiians, usually with her back to the direction of advance, her huge legs dangling over the edge. Her husband King Kaumualii, whom she had married soon after he had been brought from Kauai, also rode in the carriage. At its side was Kaumualii's handsome son, whom Ka'ahumanu had also married. It was not clear what of her conversion was genuine, what pretense. King Liholiho himself would have nothing to do with church attendance.

The Hawaiian Alphabet
The missionaries wanted to teach the natives to read and write in Hawaiian in order for them to be able to study the Bible for themselves; for the Bible, rather than an all-wise church, was the foundation of their Protestantism. But establishing an orthography into which to translate a Hawaiian Bible was itself an enormous task. There was little difficulty with Hawaiian vowels as long as they were allocated a single sound, but the consonants seemed many, and in some cases unclear to both missionary and native speaker: Hawaiian "k" and "t" could sound inter-changeable and "t" was sometimes like "d." The sounds "l" or "r" and "w" or "v" were also problematic.

The first spelling primer listing written Hawaiian words was printed in 1822 on a press the mission brought out. By coincidence it used the five vowels and seven consonants that, after much debate, were finally agreed upon in 1826 as standard. In the meantime up to a dozen additional consonants had been tried. Various missionaries then worked long years on translating the New Testament, which was printed in 1832; the Old Testament was completed in 1839. A complete Hawaiian Bible of 2,335 pages was available by mid-1839.

But for the first few years, the missionaries' attempts at spreading literacy were mostly unsuccessful, with a few exceptions, such as John Ii and David Malo, who gained literacy early on. The missionaries were generally unable to see any virtue in native culture and unwilling to try to build cultural bridges. Nevertheless, in teaching the Hawaiians to read and write and in creating a written form of the language, the mission made it possible to preserve much of Hawaii's cultural heritage for posterity, an invaluable service. By the early 1830s, reading had become immensely popular, with thousands of well-drilled Hawaiians diligently learning to read and write on slates and taking the literacy examinations. (In Kauai the first school desks were surfboards.)

On July 19, 1831, Reuben Tinker, a new missionary, recorded in his journal one of the teaching techniques:

The shell horn has been blowing for examination of the schools in the meeting house. About 2,000 scholars present, some wrapped in large quantities of native cloth.... It was a pleasant occasion in which they seemed interested and happy.... The king and chiefs were present, and examined among the rest. They read in various books, and 450 in 4 rows wrote the same sentence at the same time on slates. They perform with some ceremony. In this exercise, one of the teachers cried out with as much importance as an orderly sergeant... and immediately the whole company began to sit up straight. At the next order they stood on their feet; at the next they presented their slates, i.e., they held them resting on the left arm as a musician would place his fiddle—at the next order they brought their pencils to bear upon the broad sides of their slates ready for action. Mr. Bingham then put into the crier's ear the sentence to be written, which he proclaimed with all his

Astonishing Procession Commemorates Kamehameha I, 1823

Just prior to the 1823 commemorations of the death of King Kamehameha I, a second party of missionaries arrived in Honolulu. One, Charles Stewart, astonished, overwhelmed, attracted, and repelled, wrote the following account of the climax:

> [Kamamalu, Liholiho's favorite wife was] a conspicuous object. The car of state in which she joined the processions... consisted of an elegantly modelled whale boat, fastened firmly to a platform thirty feet by twelve, and borne on the heads or shoulders of seventy men... formed into a solid body, so that the outer rows only, at the sides and ends were seen; and all men forming these wore the splendid scarlet and yellow feather cloaks and helmets....
>
> The only dress of the queen was a scarlet silk pau, or native petticoat, and a coronet of feathers. She was seated in the middle of the boat screened from the sun by an immense Chinese umbrella of scarlet damask... supported by a chief.... On one quarter of the boat stood Kalanimoku the prime minister; and on the other Naihe the national orator; both also in malos [girdles] of scarlet silk and helmets of feathers, and each bearing a kahili or feathered staff of state, near thirty feet in height....
>
> Pauahi, another of the wives of Liholiho, after passing in procession with her retinue, alighted from her couch... [and to recall her narrow escape as a child from fire] set fire to it and all its expensive trappings, and then threw into the flames the whole of her dress except a single handkerchief to cast around her. In this she was immediately imitated by her attendants; and many valuable articles, a large quantity of kapa, and entire pieces of broadcloth were thus consumed.... The dresses of some of the queens-dowager were expensive, and immense.... One wore seventy-two yards of kerseymere of double fold, one half being scarlet and the other orange. It was wrapped around her figure till her arms were supported horizontally....
>
> The young prince [Kauikeaouli, the future Kamehameha III] and princess wore the native dress, malo and pau, of scarlet silk. Their vehicle consisted of four field-bedsteads of Chinese wood and workmanship, lashed together side by side....
>
> The king and his suite made but a sorry exhibition. They were nearly naked, mounted on horses without saddles and

> so intoxicated as scarce to be able to retain their seats as they scampered from place to place in all the disorder of a troop of bacchanalians. A body-guard of fifty or sixty men... attempted by a running march to keep near the person of their sovereign....
>
> Companies of singing and dancing girls and men, consisting of many hundreds met the processions in different places, encircling the highest chiefs, and shouting their praise in enthusiastic adulation... sounds of the native drum and calabash, the wild notes of their songs in the loud choruses and responses... the pulsations on the ground of the tread of thousands in the dance, reached us even at the missionary enclosure.

might, and a movement of the 450 pencils commenced which from their creaking was like the music of machinery lacking oil.

King Liholiho was an enigma to the newcomers. Paid for with sandalwood, his "grass palace" contained a heterogeneous collection of furniture: sets of crystal and china, solid writing desks, Empire-style European chairs, brass bedsteads—but the king and his retainers usually preferred to relax naked on the matting on the floor of the palace, drinking from a calabash. Nonetheless, when occasion demanded, Liholiho and his court donned the expensive and beautiful clothes cut for them by the European tailors of the town or specially prepared in far Guangzhou.

A Disastrous Voyage to Britain

Liholiho decided to take himself and his Queen Kamamalu to Britain "to see his friend" the king. He also wanted to discuss the reaffirmation of a British protectorate over the islands. Under the guidance of faithful Governor Boki, the royal party departed in November 1823. Typically, the disorganized king did not inform the British of his plan, and Liholiho's unexpected arrival was inauspicious.

The British government decided the Hawaiians would need some coaching in social graces before they could be presented to the king of the British Empire without embarrassment to either side. The Hawaiians proved able learners, were introduced to society, and were almost ready for the great occasion. Then disaster struck. Liholiho and his queen contracted measles, and, having no immunity to this common European disease, Queen Kamamalu died on July 8, 1824. Liholiho, apparently as much from despair as disease, died six days later. In his hastily scribed will, he appointed his young brother Kauikeaouli king to be guided by Ka'ahumanu and the *kuhina nui* Kalanimoku.

Boki took control, discussed diplomacy, and Britain agreed to send a consul to Hawaii. This appointment of a consul meant that despite the quasi-protectorate established by George Vancouver over the Big Island, Britain now recognized the independence of the island kingdom. Britain also agreed to pay for the transport of Boki, his party, and the royal cadavers to the other side of the world in the 46-gun frigate *HMS Blonde* captained by Lord George Byron. The Hawaiians were grateful for the return of their king and, among other gifts, Byron and his officers were presented with feather cloaks. The magnificent red, black, and yellow Kintore Cloak in Bishop Museum is one of these. It was returned to Hawaii in 1969 at the wish of its owner.

By this time it was already clear to the non-mission community in the islands that Bingham was ignoring the instructions of his superiors to refrain from politics. His idea of political influence was not the US Constitution, the Bill of Rights, or the US separation of church and state, but the imposition of the Ten Commandments.

Bingham succeeded in making it a crime for natives to wear leis made of flowers, for as he explained in a letter home, "The way they are worn may have a vicious meaning." As early as 1821, the mission managed to have surfing banned. And the open, unrepressed sexual experimentation indulged in by the young was condemned as beastly, degrading, and sinful. Coming so soon after the ending of the *kapu*, such wholesale rejection of practices, which for many centuries had been considered healthy, proper, and normal, was bewildering for the Hawaiians and psychologically deeply destructive.

Despite this cultural crucifixion, it was not the Hawaiians who most strenuously resisted the proselytizing of the mission but the foreign commercial community and the ships' crews who saw the missionaries as interfering busybodies and ridiculed their leader as "King Bingham." Even his fellow Richard Armstrong, who admired

Bingham's dedication, called him, "a compound of vanity, self-importance, forwardness, obstinacy, self-complacency." The Honolulu merchant Stephen Reynolds described Bingham as "a lazy, lying wretch." In contrast, John Young admired what the mission was achieving: "Good morals are superseding the reign of crime... a code of these things is what I have longed for but have never seen until now."

WHALING AND WHALERS

In the long-term it was whaling that became far more important than either sandalwood or sealskins. In 1819 the first whale was caught by an American ship off Hawaii. It presaged a fifty year industry dominated by whaling companies from New England, especially from the tiny islands of Nantucket and Martha's Vineyard off Cape Cod, Massachusetts.

Weeks of mind-dulling routine aboard ship would be followed by a few days of adrenaline-rushing danger harpooning from tiny six-man boats; for long months this pattern would repeat itself. Most desirable was the fine oil in the head of the sperm whale. Whalebone (baleen) was used in chair seats and ladies' corsets and horse whips. Occasionally someone would find the fantastically valuable waxy ambergris (mostly cholesterol!) that is secreted by the sperm whale's intestine and was used to fix perfumes in Europe and as a rare spice in east Asia.

Finally, after months at sea, the celibacy, salt pork, and ship's temperance came to an end and there followed several weeks or sometimes months of fresh food, excess grog, and satiation with girls in Hawaii while the ship was provisioned or remained in port during the off-season. There were about 200 US whale ships in the Pacific in the later 1820s, and almost 600 at the height of the industry ten years later. Honolulu in Oahu and Lahaina in Maui became the busiest ports in the whole ocean. Self-seeking newcomers and old-hand locals in the whaling ports seized their opportunities, became merchants, and formed companies to supply the ships so far from their home ports. Relatively quickly, chandlering ship repair and food provisioning merged, and powerful foreign-controlled Hawaiian trading companies developed. Entertainers travelled from the United States to grab the whalers' dollars.

Many Hawaiian men became crew members on whaling ships to earn money and see the world. They were efficient and well accepted for they came from a history of hundreds of years of working on the ocean. In fact, at the height of the industry there were some nineteen whalers owned by Hawaiians themselves. As a contemporary seaman wrote during the 1840s:

> These Kanakas are large and well built men, as active as monkeys and make the best seamen. It is almost impossible to drown them. In time of a storm they will sport in the surf where a white man could not live for a minute. They will even attack and kill sharks in the water. The mate pointed one out... who was cast overboard one dark, stormy night. When they found him an hour afterward he was swimming straight for the nearest land, twenty miles away, and did not seem to be afraid.

In time the whales were depleted, but this merely meant that ships pushed farther into the North Pacific. However, it was not the shortage of whales that finally brought an end to the great days, but the discovery of petroleum in Pennsylvania in 1859 and the production of inexpensive kerosene. Reading and doing night chores became novel after-dark activities for most Americans and Western Europeans. In consequence, the whaling ships that had made Honolulu and Lahaina two of the Pacific's wildest towns rotted by the hundreds.

Ten Commandments or Seven Deadly Sins?
Religion and whaling, missionaries and whalers, were anathema to one another. The discord began when the newly righteous dowager queen and regent Ka'ahumanu (immensely fat and fifty years old, she had had her own fun for decades) and the *kuhina* Kalanimoku banned "vice, drunkenness, debauchery, theft and other violations" and ordered the sabbath to be strictly kept. Ka'ahumanu also persuaded as many Hawaiians as possible to her point of view, crushed native culture, and actively preached to large numbers.

When the crew of the British whaler *Daniel* landed in Lahaina ready to play, they found the local women banned to them. Blaming (with justification) the local missionary

Converted by Tsunami, 1837

Rev. Titus Coan had been preaching in the Hilo area since 1835. In autumn 1837 he was convinced a change was beginning in his parishioners and he looked for a sign from God. Later, in his book *Life in Hawaii*, he wrote about the tsunami of November 7, which occured during evening prayer:

> We were startled by a heavy thud, and a sudden jar of the earth. The sound was like the fall of some vast body on the beach, and in a few seconds a noise of mingled voices rising for a mile along the shore thrilled us like the wail of doom.... The sea, moved by an unseen hand, had all of a sudden risen in a gigantic wave, and this wave, rushing in with the speed of a racehorse had fallen upon the shore, sweeping everything not more than fifteen or twenty feet above high-water mark into indiscriminate ruin. Houses, furniture, calabashes, fuel, timber, canoes, food, clothing, everything floated wild upon the flood.... The harbor was full of strugglers calling for help, while frantic parents and children, wives and husbands ran to and fro along the beach, calling for their lost ones.
>
> As wave after wave came in and retired, the strugglers were brought near the shore... and the weaker and exhausted were carried back upon the retreating wave, some to sink and rise no more till the noise of judgment wakes them.... Had this catas-trophe occurred at midnight when all were asleep, hundreds of lives would undoubtedly have been lost. Through the great mercy of God only 13 were drowned.
>
> This event... greatly impressed the people. It was as the voice of God speaking to them out of heaven, "Be ye also ready."

William Richards, they surrounded his house, demanding vengeance. An equal number of even bigger Christian Hawaiians drove them off. The *Daniel* then sailed to Honolulu and its seamen, more angry than ever, challenged the missionaries in their homes at Kawaiahao.

At a riotous public meeting, Ka'ahumanu and Kalanimoku and their upper class supporters pushed the idea that the laws of the Christian god should become the laws of Hawaii to bind the whole population, Hawaiian, British, European, and American. But the opposition lobby was strong too. The established traders of Honolulu and Lahaina realized the policy would kill their business. Moreover, the senior foreigners in Honolulu, Richard Charlton, the British consul, and the sepulchrally named John Coffin Jones, the US commercial agent, were united in opposing a theocracy, though they loathed each other.

The King Kamehameha III, not yet a teenager, was much too young to control the powerful passions of this conflict. Finally, in fear he told Boki that these new religious laws should be deferred. There then developed the disconcerting situation in which for a time Kaʻahumanu and the missionary party would be in control, then the secular businessmen and seamen and whalers would win, then the rules would revert to the mission, and so on.

The missionaries failed in 1826 when, commanded by Lieutenant John "Mad Jack" Percival, the US warship *Dolphin* arrived with orders to investigate the sandalwood debts of the Hawaiian chiefs to American traders and to "render all possible aid to American commerce." Percival was less than thorough in his investigations, seemingly more occupied with the supposed rights of his men to recreation. A mob of angry sailors in search of prostitutes surrounded Kalanimoku's house and smashed all his windows. Rev. Bingham, who was there preparing for a service, fled toward his church and home in Kawaiahao. He was about to be bashed by the sailors when Percival arrived just in time. Percival then persuaded the chiefs to lift the ban on contact between sailors and native women. Soon boatloads of young Hawaiian women were sailing round-trip from shore to ship. And at a dinner for the chiefs, Percival pointedly read the biblical passage about the wise King Solomon—who had 700 wives and 300 concubines.

In 1827 two shots from the cannon of frustrated whalers almost hit the house of Richards. And for some decades, as the whaling trade grew ever larger, the abuse, squabbles, and skirmishes between the sailors and the missionaries and the strict Christian Hawaiians went on unabated.

Complicating the religious tension in July 1827, six French Roman Catholic missionaries landed in Honolulu from the ship *Comete*, including three ordained priests. They arrived without permission, and Ka'ahumanu sent a message to Boki to force them to depart. Boki was inland at the time, and the *Comete* sailed without the priests. Soon Catholic converts were being arrested and imprisoned. The opposition of Boki and others to Catholicism would cause the government continuing trouble with France.

The sailors, both captains and men, thought that the problem was the missionaries' regulations, and not their conduct. The following protest, signed by twenty-four captains of American whaling vessels at Lahaina in March 1844 and submitted to the governor of Maui, complained:

> It is hard that peaceable men cannot walk through the street without having their lives endangered by stones thrown or clubs wielded by the authority of the police, to quell a disturbance originating with a few drunken men, made drunken at your LICENSED GROG-SHOPS. And we think it would redound to the credit of your government to punish the unprincipled men who sell rum to drunken sailors, than to drag from those miserable men a large part of their hard earnings as fines for breaking one law, when, by another, you compel the grog-shop keeper to sell as much as possible so he may be able to pay for his licence.

The fines themselves were harsh. Port regulations and fines in Honolulu in that same year of 1844 were listed as:

> All boats and seamen are required to return to their ships at 9 o'clock PM when the first gun is fired from the fort.
> $1 for desecrating the Sabbath for the first time.
> $2 for desecrating the second time, and then the fine is doubled for every repetition.
> $2 for every seaman on shore after the firing of the second gun at half past nine.
> $1 to $5 for hallooing or making a noise in the streets at night.
> $5 for fornication.
> $5 for racing or swift riding in the streets or frequented roads.
> $6 for drunkenness
> $10 for lewd, seductive, and lascivious conduct.
> $10 on every person who aids or secretes a seaman on shore after that hour or, opposes the police in their search.

$30 for adultery.
$50 for rape.
[Murder was a hanging offense.]

Sometimes punishments of whalers were counter-productive, as occurred in 1852 after a whaler jailed in Honolulu Fort for swift riding was killed by the police. When nothing was done to arrest the murderer, hundreds of whalers rioted (there were then about 150 whale ships in the harbor, a record). As one of them, Alonzo Samson, describes in his 1867 book:

> ... although [we were] mostly unarmed, there were probably no 5,000 men on the islands who could have withstood our charge. In a few minutes the streets were cleared and in about an hour the entire population was flying pell mell... for the mountains. The custom house was fired and the assailants pushed on to the fort, which was given up without a struggle by the horror stricken native soldiers who retired and took up a position on Punch Bowl Hill [nowadays the site of the military's National Memorial Cemetery]....
>
> We now returned to plunder the city. Stores, grog-shops, dwellings, all were thrown open and ransacked. The king dispatched a messenger to Lahaina for assistance where there were ships of war, but in the meantime, having held the town for three days without molestation and having gratified our vengeance and enjoyed our spree we retired quietly... on board our several vessels....

In the 1840s and '50s, more US ships called at Honolulu and Lahaina than any other port in the world. As a result, United States consulates were busy places. Malfeasance was so common that the Hawaiian ports became the most eagerly sought in the whole US Consular Service. By the later 1850s, approximately $150,000 a year was being spent on the "relief" of American sailors in Hawaii (hospitalization, treatment, clothing, repatriation), more than half the sum appropriated for Americans in the entire world.

What Counts as Conversion?

The missionaries were dedicated and never gave up. By 1838 there were about 90 Calvinist mission workers, 37

Waikiki to Diamond Head 1865, *by Enoch Wood Perry. From a site near the grounds of present-day Halekulani Hotel, Perry (1831– 1915), an American artist, painted this peaceful pastoral scene of what is today frenetic Waikiki. At the tip of Diamond Head Perry places a cluster of grass structures that were reserved for Hawaiian Royalty, now a group of hotels. Painted long before the Ala Wai canal channeled the water that flows from the Manoa and other valleys, the stream shown (probably the Kanewai) was one of several that ran into the ocean across Waikiki. The lone paddler in his outrigger canoe mirrors the shape of Diamond Head and seems to connect to the strolling female holding a gourd. The crossed palms in the foreground are a feature of many of Perry's Hawaiian paintings.* Bishop Museum

ordained, preaching at 17 missions around the islands. But though about half the population attended church regularly, conversion was slow and only some 1,200 had been accepted into full church membership—less than 1 percent of the population after 17 years of missionary toil.

This was because men like Bingham and Thurston believed that genuine conversion was rare and relapse common, and they preferred to be slow and certain rather than superficially successful. To some of the mission newcomers fired with the impatient optimism of youth, this rate of conversion was unacceptable. This was also the time of the great revival in the United States, led by Charles Grandison Finney, whose fire and brimstone preaching

Must-See Sites: Maui

Maui possesses old towns like Lahaina and Wailuku, tremendous waves like "Jaws," the verdant Hana Coast, the huge shield volcano Haleakala, and splendid beaches like Wailea on the leeward west coast (see www.co.maui.hi.us or www.visitmaui.com).

Haleakala National Park and Volcano

The National Park encompasses the caldera of Haleakala ("House of the Sun"), the world's largest dormant volcano, now about 10,000 ft (3,084 m) high, once perhaps 12,000 ft, that last erupted 200 years ago. The huge caldera is dotted with about a dozen cinder cones from later eruptions, several themselves pressing 1,000 ft (308 m) in height.

Magnificent views of the multitudinous sandy colors of the floor present themselves from the caldera rim. Equally spectacular are the sights along the miles-long Sliding Sands and Halemau'u Trails which cross the caldera a thousand feet down (www.nps.gov/hale).

From the coast Haleakala seems to rise up almost forever, but its great bulk makes its height deceptive. Sunrises and sunsets are awesome. The endlessly zig-zagging drive to the top from Kahului takes about two hours. Cycling down the volcano in daylight is matched by organized star-gazing on top at night.

Hana Highway, Hana, Piilanihale Heiau

With some 600 turns, more than 50 one-lane bridges, and numerous waterfalls cramped into an awesome 52-mile spectacular emerald stretch of road, the Hana Highway is exciting. Hana itself is one of the last native Hawaiian rural towns where the general lifestyle has changed little. Ka'uiki Head on the right side of the Hana Bay is a natural fort, the scene of battles between Maui's fierce Kahekili and the Big Island's Kalaniopu'u. Here too is the birthplace (a cave) of Queen Ka'ahumanu, favorite of Kamehameha I. The back country is beautiful. About a mile down a remnant of the King's Highway, the footpath that once circled the island, stands Piilanihale Heiau, the size of a football field, covered with moss and algae, and Hawaii's largest and perhaps most poignant *heiau*. Built in the 1400s, its walls rise a spectacular 42 ft (13 m). It stands in Kahanu Garden (guided tours only), a 465 ac (188 ha) site that focuses on indigenous trees and species Hawaiians used for food, clothing, medicine, and religious ceremonies.

Lahaina

A significant village for centuries, then the country's capital (1820–45), for much of the 1800s Lahaina was a wild whaling port with mighty confrontations between whalers and missionaries over local women. From the late 1800s to the 1960s, Lahaina remained a backwater, a sugar

Hana Coast Road. Hawaii Visitors and Convention Bureau/Ron Dahlquist

plantation town. Then Amfac developed Kaanapali to the north and Lahaina began to boom—not unlike the whaling days. Chiefs and missionaries are buried in a small cemetery at Waiola Church. A famous Banyan tree planted in 1873 is now the largest in Hawaii. The 1834 missionary house, Baldwin Home, with its several-feet-thick coral and stone walls, distributes maps. Completed in 1859 with stone from an earlier building belonging to a chief, Lahaina Courthouse on Wharf Street originally performed many functions. About two million people visit Lahaina yearly and go whale watching, fishing, and snorkeling, or take a ferry to Lanai and Molokai.

Kahului, Wailuku, and Iao Valley

Maui's main port and airport is at Kahului. Close to the airport is the Alexander and Baldwin Sugar Museum, which has good displays of sugar history and processing and of the cultures of the workers. A few miles east is the old sugar town of Pa'ia, now a center for the spectacular world-class windsurfing at nearby Ho'okipa Beach. A little farther on is the reef that extends from shore and generates the fearsome waves called "Jaws."

Wailuku, the administrative center of Maui county and built in the foothills of the striking green West Maui Mountains (actually a single eroded volcano), features interesting wooden structures in the old town. Stone and plaster Ka'ahumanu Congregational Church, built in 1876, was originally a grass hut attended by Queen Ka'ahumanu. Nearby on a former native Hawaiian sacred site is the one-time missionary turned sugarcane plantation manager's residence, Bailey House.

North and west of Wailuku are Iao Valley and Iao Stream where in 1790 Kamehameha I won a great victory. The bodies of the defenders clogged the stream. Today the area called Kepaniwai Heritage Gardens (Kepaniwai means "water dam") is a section of Iao Valley State Park. Nearby is the striking 1,200 ft high (364 m) volcanic spur Iao Needle.

could reduce whole congregations to terror. One of Finney's graduates was Titus Coan, who believed he could repeat Finney's success in the Sandwich Islands.

Coan arrived in 1835 at Hilo on the east coast of the Big Island. By late 1837 he was looking for a sign from God to guide him. To his mind the great tsunami of November 1837, which hit and destroyed much of the town of Hilo and drowned 13, was that sign, and it deeply impressed the local Hawaiians who tramped in droves to hear him. Coan was at war with the Devil and saw conversion as a mighty battle. God was a great general "whose arm is omnipotent... whose eyes are as a flame of fire and whose spear gleams lightning" and sinners were defeated by "the battle-axe of the Lord" and "the arrows of the Almighty."

His preaching had hundreds groveling on the ground. Fear of the old *kahuna* and *kapu* had been replaced by hellfire and the Devil. A revival spread out from Hilo. Kahului-Wailuku on Maui had also been struck by the tsunami and many people converted there. Hundreds and thousands responded to Coan's call and, unlike Bingham and Thurston, with no lengthy evidence of their sincerity he accepted most of them into the church. At Waimea, Coan's colleague Lorenzo Lyons was persuaded by a calculation of the American Millerites that Christ would come again in 1843, so he believed there existed a special urgency in converting as many as possible.

In six months from November 1837, Coan and Lyons admitted 3,200 Hawaiians to the church. On a single charismatic assembly line day in 1838, Coan baptized about 1,700 converts. During 1839 the two baptized 7,500 more. Church attendance increased everywhere, including at Bingham's services in Kawaiahao Church. But he and Thurston and many others who had been working endlessly and making themselves old in body and spirit for 17 years were unhappy at this tsunami of "conversion." It is too simple to say that Bingham and the others were envious. Rather they believed that conversion was not a matter of groveling for forgiveness or throwing convulsions, but that genuine repentance took place in people's minds, and the kind of change suitable for baptism was shown over a long period in consistent and reformed behavior. Just as thousands had converted, so thousands were soon deserting Coan and Lyons's churches.

6

Who Shall Govern the Nation?

The child king Kauikeaouli came to the throne as Kamehameha III in 1825. His reign, the longest of all, would last until 1854. Dowager Queen Ka'ahumanu acted as his regent until her death in 1832.

When Ka'ahumanu died, Kauikeaouli was seventeen. He felt freed from her moralistic control and began (for a time) to act like a king. Soon he abolished all the edicts promoted by the missionaries and Ka'ahumanu, keeping only those relating to theft and murder. Still, despite endless personal and political disputes between foreigners of the United States, Britain, and France resident in the Hawaiian Islands, they all wanted their own way, and all three could call on gunboats to support their views. So despite his good intentions to act like a Hawaiian king, Kauikeaouli and the chiefs would have to accommodate many of the wishes of the foreigners and suffer changes over which they had little control.

Kamehameha III and Dr. Judd

King Kamehameha III seems to have been a natural hedonist. Within weeks he was overindulging his previously suppressed passions in card playing, horse racing, rum carousing, and with the passing years in womanizing involving his sister (quite acceptable, indeed imperative for mana under traditional Hawaiian royal morality), relatives, commoners, and, rumor had it, at least one missionary wife. In his 1831 book, Charles Stewart, a naval chaplain, reports that while at the dinner table of an American merchant he was told that

> King Kamehameha III and his sister Princess Nahienaena were mutually and strongly attached, and that they themselves and all the chiefs wished a marriage

> to take place between them according to former usages in
> the royal family, but were prevented by the missionaries:
> adding that the ceremony however might as well be
> performed, for, it was well known, that they were already
> living in a state of licentiousness and incest! [This
> information] caused me to drop my knife and fork....
> [T]wo other Americans at the table corroborated the
> charge with the strongest asseverations.

Kamehameha III revived the dying culture, allowed
surfing again, supported canoe racing and spear throwing,
and encouraged the hula. For a time the missionary
conquest of Hawaii faltered.

But Kamehameha III was also the first of the Hawaiian
monarchs to have received his entire schooling at the hands
of missionaries, and Christian "shall nots" lay deep within
his psyche. For the rest of his life, disastrously for the native
Hawaiians, he was morally ambivalent, politically inconsistent, and usually controlled by others.

In the 1830s and '40s, the whaling industry continued
to flourish and relations with the West became ever more
complicated. Kamehmeha III needed help in dealing with
such matters and sought out the only people he believed
could provide it—the resident Westerners. Unfortunately
for him, they often had their own agendas.

The Rise of Dr. Judd

The man who became the real ruler during much of the
reign of Kamehameha III was not the king himself but an
American with medical qualifications from upstate New
York, Dr. Gerrit Parmele Judd. He arrived in 1828 ready, as
he wrote decades later, "to devote myself to the works of a
missionary among the heathen." Within a decade he had
withdrawn from the mission and become the most
powerful political figure on the islands, and within two
decades he would help draft legislation that allowed settlers
to buy land. This legislation would bring about the rapid
dispossession of the Hawaiian people, especially the
commoners for whom such ownership had no precedents
in their culture.

In 1843 Judd became minister of foreign affairs, in 1845
minister of the interior, and in 1846 minister of finance. In
fact, he always simultaneously performed many government

This 1850 studio portrait shows Dr. Gerrit P. Judd, the most powerful mid-century figure in Hawaii, with Prince Lot Kamehameha (aged 18, later King Kamehameha V) and Prince Alexander Liholiho (aged 16, later King Kamehameha IV). It was taken in Paris during their diplomatic and sight-seeing tour of the US, Britain, and Europe. Hawaii State Archives

functions and for most of the time was in effect the prime minister. In 1845 Judd would write to a friend in Boston, "You must know that I am at present the King Bingham of the Sandwich Islands."

But things were different in 1832. With Ka'ahumanu now lost to their cause, Judd and his colleagues were ignored by the king. They realized that unless they could find a patron to replace Ka'ahumanu, their mission was

John Papa Ii, Hawaiian Statesman and Historian

John Papa Ii (pronounced "ee-ee") (1800–1870) almost did not "live to tell the tale." As a youth and aristocrat at the court of King Kamehameha I, his job was similar to that of a page at a medieval European court. But death camped much closer to Hawaiian "pages" than to their Continental counterparts.

Ii's job was to carry the spittoon of the young Prince Liholiho. One day the spittoon's cover slipped off, and in falling, struck Ii's knee; amazingly, it bounced back up, where he caught it and neatly replaced it. His quick reaction had saved his life, for the political-cum-religious rules of ancient Hawaii were often appalling: The spitoon was *kapu* (taboo), and, as with many other trivial breaches of protocol, to drop any part of it on the ground meant immediate death for the carrier, even for an aristocrat. No extenuating circumstances were allowed; no trial was held. In fact, a stepbrother of Ii had been killed for a similar "misdeed."

Ii was born into the *ali'i* (chiefs) of old Hawaii and grew up with many privileges. When the missionaries landed, the highly intelligent young man immediately learned to read. Within a year he was helping Rev. Bingham to translate parts of the Bible into Hawaiian and acting as interpreter for sermons.

Later Ii had a long and distinguished career in the government of Hawaii under Kings Kamehameha III, IV, and V. Natives and foreigners alike agreed upon his unassailable moral rectitude. But John Papa Ii is best remembered for his crucial historical writings, which appeared as a set of articles in the Hawaiian-language newspaper *Ku'oko'a* (Independent) between 1866 and 1870. These articles provide a fascinating firsthand account of life under the ancient *kapu* system, an insider's view of court life with details available nowhere else. In 1959 they were translated and published by Bishop Museum as *Fragments of Hawaiian History*. Though he admired the American values of hard work and persistence, Ii remained rigorously and permanently opposed to annexation by the United States and absolutely loyal to the monarchy.

nullified. As a doctor, Judd had helped and befriended the *ali'i* Kina'u. She had been a wife (and half-sister) of Liholiho but held no formal position. In a masterly maneuver, Judd persuaded Kina'u to approach the king: "By our advice she presented herself… and she was… proclaimed as Kuhina." Kamehameha III lived to regret this action because the mission manipulated Kina'u to impose their political, religious, and cultural designs, whereas he wanted the monarchy to retain its full powers and the country to keep its culture.

Within a few years, through ingratiating himself to Kina'u, Judd had become principal advisor of the king. He worked tirelessly at learning the Hawaiian language, became fluent, and was made royal physician and the official interpreter. Perpetually opposed by the kuhina and the many Christian chiefs, by the early 1840s Kamehamaha III gave up trying to impose his will and his Hawaiian values, increasingly retreated into alcoholic hedonism, and so opened the way for foreign control.

Still, political and social changes brought by foreigners were complex and thus often positive too. In 1834 for instance, as a direct result of the reading campaign, the first printed newssheet in the Hawaiian language, *Ka Lama Hawaii* (The Hawaiian Luminary), was produced in Maui at the press of Lahainaluna Seminary (established 1831) by the students. Also as a result of the growth of reading, that year saw the start of the first real newspaper in Hawaiian, *Ke Kumu Hawaii* (The Hawaiian Source). In 1836 the first proper streets in Honolulu were surveyed and laid out. The same year saw the first newspaper in English, the *Sandwich Islands Gazette*. Due to the arbitrariness of political authority, the paper had much trouble beginning, yet Honolulu resident Melchior Bondu was able to note in his diary for June 30, "The printers who live at our house have printed today their first newspaper. They are to issue one paper a week at six dollars a year." In 1839, through mission efforts, the Chiefs' Children's School was opened and for decades provided high quality schooling for the children of *ali'i*, and, helping the growth of democracy, the first declaration of the rights of citizens was promulgated.

Though they were pleased with the spread of Christian principles in the governance of the country, many of Judd's missionary colleagues had long disapproved of his being a government minister, for he was contravening the board rules banning political interference—yet within a few years other missionaries were joining Judd in government. So Judd formally resigned from the mission. In what in hindsight can scarcely be accepted at face value, he explained to the US consul in Honolulu: "It is impossible for me to express to you the deep anxiety I feel for the young government of these Islands. I have unaware been drawn into the deepest assimilation of all my interests with theirs, and ready to sacrifice everything for the welfare of the nation [Hawaii]." Judd acquired his own Parisian-designed coat of arms. At official functions, he wore a bright blue jacket with gold insignia over a white vest and white trousers, together with a plumed hat. He travelled in a gilded coach, plushly upholstered, and enjoyed seventeen-gun salutes.

Judd and most other Protestants produced large Victorian families. He had nine children, of whom two died young. The views and values of such offspring were those held by their parents. The Protestant work ethic, as it has been called, was important in their thinking—work hard and accumulate, *in Hawaii*.

CONSTITUTIONS, FRENCH AND BRITISH TROUBLES

Roman Catholics

Meanwhile, the Calvinist ministers had always shown antipathy to the Catholics. Bingham, Judd, and others openly and behind the scenes had long been pressuring and politicking for their exclusion. In 1837 Bingham and Judd finally persuaded King Kamehameha III to ban Roman Catholicism:

> Therefore, I with my chiefs, forbid... that anyone should teach the peculiarities of the Pope's religion, nor shall it be allowed to anyone who teaches those doctrines or those peculiarities to reside in this kingdom; nor shall the ceremonies be exhibited in our kingdom, nor shall anyone teaching its peculiarities or its faith be permitted to land on these shores; for it is not proper that two religions be found in this small kingdom.

Herman Melville in Hawaii, 1843

The American writer Herman Melville (1819–1891) is most famous for his classic *Moby Dick*, the story of compulsive Captain Ahab and the great white whale of the title. But only because Melville went to sea were *Moby Dick* and his great Polynesian books *Typee* and *Omoo* ever composed, and his experience in Hawaii made it possible.

In January 1841, Melville shipped out on the 104 ft long (32 m) whaler *Acushnet* from New Bedford, Massachusetts, bound for the Pacific. Like his hero in *Moby Dick*, he could with truth suggest, "a whale ship was my Yale College and my Harvard."

Melville's adventures in various Polynesian islands provided the basis for *Typee* and *Omoo,* the first modern novels of the Pacific. Each makes allusions to his experiences in Hawaii. In them and with astonishing confidence and candor, which brought him much ill feeling at a time, he criticizes both missionaries and ships' captains. On his final whaling voyage on the *Charles & Henry*, Melville took on the dangerous job of harpooner and left the ship in Honolulu. After four months there, he returned to Boston as crewman on the naval vessel *United States*.

Melville had an explanation for the Hawaiian and Polynesian habit of taking items from Western ships:

> The strict honesty which the inhabitants of nearly all Polynesian islands manifest toward one another is in striking contrast with the thieving propensities some of them evince in their intercourse with foreigners. It would seem that, according to their peculiar code of morals, the pilfering of a hatchet or a wrought nail from a European is looked upon as a praiseworthy action. Or rather—bearing in mind the wholesale forays made upon them by their nautical visitors—they consider the property of the latter as a fair object of reprisal.

Melville's ironic eye also appears in this passage from *Typee:*

> Not until I visited Honolulu was I aware that natives had been civilized into draught horses. I saw a robust, red faced missionary's spouse who took her regular airings in a little go-cart drawn by two of the islanders, both being, with the exception of the fig-leaf, as naked as when they were born. Rattling along the streets the lady looks about her as magnificently as any queen…. A sudden elevation disturbs her serenity… to be sure, she used to think nothing of driving cows to pasture on the old farm in New England…. She bawls out 'Hookee! Hookee!' (Pull! Pull!) and rap goes the heavy handle of her huge fan over the naked skull of the old savage: while the young one shies on one side and keeps beyond its range.

The chiefs agreed, because the worship of idols had been banned when the *kapu* system was abolished, and the rites and images used in Catholic churches and services looked like idol-worship to them.

But knowledge of the ban and ill treatment of Catholics soon reached Paris. In mid-1839 the French frigate *L'Artemise*, captained by C. P. T. Laplace, portentously appeared off Honolulu to force the Hawaiian kingdom to honor Frenchmen and France and to allow Catholic worship. Laplace had orders from his Parisian superiors:

> ... to destroy the malevolent impression which you find established to the detriment of the French name; to rectify the erroneous opinion which has been created as to the power of France; and to make it well understood that it will be altogether to the advantage of the chiefs... to conduct themselves in such a manner as not to incur the wrath of France.

Laplace demanded that the government make available a site to build a Catholic church, free all imprisoned Catholics, provide a bond of $20,000, and sign a treaty agreeing to all of the above while 21 cannon of Honolulu Fort saluted the French flag. Worried Honolulu merchants quickly helped the government to raise the money. Now Kamehameha III's frightened white government ministers and influential missionaries advised him speedily to comply. As a result, the king agreed to religious toleration.

But the Hawaiians held one political plus in the affair: the French priests were all celibates, produced no children, and did not intend to make their homes in Hawaiian lands.

First Constitution, 1840

In 1840 the government took responsibility for the country's elementary schools. By this date the king, encouraged by his advisors, had decided that because economic and political relationships within Hawaii and with other nations were changing so much, a formal constitution was necessary.

A number of intelligent, educated (mostly in Lahainaluna Seminary) native Hawaiians, in particular Timothy Ha'alilio, John and David Ii, and David Malo, drafted a 64-page Constitution. The king signed it on

October 8, 1840. Part of the preamble stated that it had been promulgated, "... for the purpose of protecting alike, both the people and the chiefs of all these islands... that no chief may be able to oppress any subject, but that chiefs and people may enjoy the same protection, under one and the same law."

An elected legislature was set up. So although final authority remained with the king, there were now three centers of power: the king (and *kuhina nui*), the senior chiefs, and the legislature representing the people. Freedom of religion was guaranteed. The constitution explained that though land ownership derived directly from the king and was his to disburse, no longer did he lay claim to own all the land, and neither chiefs nor commoners nor foreigners could be removed without good cause.

Indeed, traditional Hawaiian practice treated the property of foreigners much as it did that of natives, namely, to be held at the pleasure of the chief or king. But foreigners with their churches, schools, stores, and plantations believed they should be able to own their property in the way they did in their home countries. So during the 1840s land rights became the great issue that foreigners pressed to have changed. Such trends deeply worried thoughtful Hawaiians like Malo.

The Peculiar Paulet Interlude
A dispute over land in Honolulu became the indirect cause of one of the most bizarre episodes in Hawaiian history: the unauthorized takeover of Hawaii by a British naval officer.

Differences with the Hawaiian government over land claims by himself and other British residents of Honolulu led the British consul Richard Charlton to believe that British subjects were being discriminated against. In September 1842, Charlton sailed for London to explain his position to the British government and to get help in changing the situation. His deputy, the youthful Alexander Simpson, was left in charge of the British Consulate. Anti-British sentiment was common among the New England mission community, including Judd, and presumably affected government attitudes. (The American author Herman Melville says Judd was "animated by an inveterate dislike to England.") It was generally known that, in turn, Simpson believed Judd to be of poor character. Then the

Mark Twain and Hawaii, 1866

After staying in Hawaii for 124 days in the spring of 1866, the diverting American author Samuel Clemens, with the pseudonym "Mark Twain," spent the rest of his life thinking of it, talking about it, giving lectures about it, and longing to return.

His sojourn became the dividing line between his earlier, less sophisticated work and his mature writings. A mere two years later, he produced the celebrated *Innocents Abroad*. Near the end of his life, Mark Twain claimed that it was the "circumstance" that had sent him to the Sandwich Islands that took him from journalism to a life in literature.

The Hawaiian experience was also seminal in producing a parallel, well-paid, and permanent career: that of popular public lecturer, for something had to fill the people's need for entertainment in those nineteenth century days before radio, film, television, and the Internet. Twain's first ever lecture, which became his star lecture, concerned Hawaii; it remained central to his repertoire for seven years, while variations appeared throughout his later life.

During his stay in the islands, he sent twenty-five reports, or "letters," to his employer, California's top newspaper of the day, the *Sacramento Union*. The letters described sugar, whaling, natural beauty, political and religious matters, legends and history, reciprocity, and annexation. All were written in a marvelous mix of jaunty journalism (he spoke of "smoke-dried children… clothed in nothing but sunshine"), shrewd poetic observation, accurate economic prophecy, tall tales, and what would become a characteristic of his writing, a sort of sardonic comic character assassination. (His later Hawaiian lectures were titled, "Our Fellow Savages of the Sandwich Islands.")

Twain always wanted to write a great novel about Hawaii—a century before Michener. For decades he worked out ideas for it. In 1870 he wrote to A. F. Judd mentioning that after his current contracts he would, "do the Islands." There is also an 1884 letter in which Twain alludes to engaging in a "most painstaking revision" of a manuscript on Hawaii, but no one has ever found that manuscript. Some think Twain never wrote it. Its absence is a monumental loss for literature of and about the islands.

In an 1889 lecture he said: "No alien land in all the world has any deep, strong charm for me but that one, no other land could so longingly and so beseechingly haunt me sleeping and waking, through half a lifetime, as that one has done. Other things leave me, but it abides."

Mark Twain passionately wished to return, and in 1895, after twenty-nine years of waiting, he almost had his wish—he sailed to within a mile of Honolulu. As fate fashioned it, Honolulu had been struck by a cholera epidemic, was quarantined, and no ships were allowed into port. Amid what must have been aching disappointment, he wrote, "If I might I would go ashore and never leave."

government refused to recognize Simpson's new status.

Following further complex difficulties and messy court cases connected with Charlton's land debts, Simpson sent for a British warship to come to Honolulu to protect British interests.

Coincidentally and ironically given subsequent events, just before Charlton's departure the British Foreign Office issued a statement instructing British diplomats to support Pacific island native governments. It said that though genuine grievances should be investigated, island rulers should be allowed "great forbearance and courtesy," that local laws and customs be respected, that the islanders' sense of independence should be strengthened, and that visiting naval captains ought not to compel decisions in favor of resident foreigners by "peremptory menace" or "physical force."

But given the slow pace of communications in the first half of the 1800s, none of this official British moderation was known to anyone in Hawaii. And on February 10, 1843, the British man-of-war *Carysfort,* captained by Lord George Paulet, arrived in Honolulu Harbor in response to Simpson's request.

Because he wanted to resolve the disagreements as efficiently as possible, Paulet thought it reasonable to request direct access to the king. Hawaii was after all a small nation; the king was the ultimate source of authority, and there was no huge bureaucracy continually demanding the king's time. It made little sense to work through intermediaries such as Judd. Moreover, Paulet did not trust Judd. But the king thrice refused to see him (Judd had control of and was the translator of the correspondence between the king and Paulet). Two diplomatic letters, from the king to Paulet and Paulet's reply, show the stubbornness of the both parties.

HONOLULU, February 17, 1843.

Salutations to you, Lord George Paulet, Captain of Her Britannic Majesty's Ship Carysfort.

SIR: We have received your communication of yesterday's date, and must decline having any private interview, particularly under the circumstances which you propose. We shall be ready to receive any written communication from you to-morrow, and will give it due consideration. In case you have business of a private nature, we will appoint Dr. Judd our confidential agent to confer with you, who, being a person of integrity and fidelity to our Government, and perfectly acquainted with all our affairs, will receive your communications, give you all the information you require (in confidence), and report the same to us.

With respect,
KAMEHAMEHA III.
KEKAULOUHI.

I hereby certify the above to be a faithful translation,
G. P. JUDD,
Translator and Interpreter for the Government.

HER BRITANNIC MAJESTY'S SHIP CARYSFORT,
Woahoo, February 17, 1843.

SIR: In answer to your letter of this day's date (which I have too good an opinion of your majesty to allow me to believe ever emanated from yourself, but from your ill-advisors) I have to state that I shall hold no communication whatever with Dr. G. P. Judd, who, it has been satisfactorily proved to me, has been the punic mover in the unlawful proceedings of your Government against British subjects.

  As you have refused me a personal interview, I inclose [sic] you the demands which I consider it my duty to make upon your Government, with which I demand a compliance at or before 4 o'clock p.m. to-morrow (Saturday); otherwise I shall be obliged to take immediate coercive steps [meaning he would fire upon the town] to obtain these measures for my countrymen.

I have the honor to be your majesty's most obedient, humble servant,
GEO. PAULET,
Captain.
His Majesty KAMEHAMEHA III.

Intimidated, Kamehameha III and his white advisors considered what to do, including thwarting Paulet by ceding the kingdom to the United States and France jointly, an idea the king thought extreme. Eventually the king decided that Paulet was being so unreasonable there was no way to compromise with him. So he thought he might as well cede control of the kingdom to Paulet until some higher British authority could constrain him.

Unauthorized by the British government to accept any such arrangement, Paulet agreed, the transfer of control took place within Honolulu Fort, and the British flag flew above Honolulu. The king and his advisors would continue to decide native affairs, but a commission including Paulet would deal with business affecting foreigners (Paulet's main concern). Paulet later also interfered with native affairs by repealing the mission-inspired laws against fornication and the selling of alcohol—both moves popular with the section of the community not controlled by the mission faction. (Paulet had learned that Kekuanoa, governor of Oahu, was pretending to abide by the Christian fornication laws while actually secretly promoting the transport of women to ships at night and pocketing most of their earnings himself.)

When knowledge of Paulet's acceptance of the "cession" and awareness of the British Foreign Office instructions reached Paulet's superior, Admiral Sir Richard Thomas, then in Chile, he hastened to Honolulu to reverse what had happened. Conferring with both Paulet and the

Rear Admiral Sir Richard Thomas arrived in Hawaii to reverse the unauthorized 1843 annexation of the islands by British naval captain Lord George Paulet. Hawaii State Archives

king (this time the king did not use Judd as go-between) and asking only for equal treatment for British subjects and other foreigners, on July 31, 1843, Thomas announced the restoration of full Hawaiian control.

The restoration ceremonies were held on the plains east of Honolulu, just outside the present day downtown at what is now Thomas Square (named after Admiral Thomas). The king and his chiefs then walked in procession back to Kawaiahao Church to give thanks. King Kamehameha III there uttered the famous words, "Ua mau ke ea o ka aina ka pono." ("The life of the land is preserved in righteousness"—still the motto of the state of Hawaii.) Paulet sailed away and Thomas remained for some months to smooth any ruffled Hawaiian feelings. In November 1843, Britain and France issued a joint statement:

> Her Majesty the Queen of the United Kingdom of Great Britain and Ireland, and His Majesty the King of the French, taking into consideration the existence in the Sandwich Islands of a government capable of providing for the regularity of its relations with foreign nations, have thought it right to engage, reciprocally, to consider the Sandwich Islands as an Independent State, and never to take possession, either directly or under the title of Protectorate, or under any other form, of any part of the territory of which they are composed.

The United States had been asked to join them, but wishing to refrain from all foreign alliances, declined, though it had recognized Hawaii's independence in 1842. President Tyler, however, stated that the United States "would regard with dissatisfaction any attempt by another power to take possession of the islands."

Historians have generally been critical of Paulet. But Herman Melville, who worked in Honolulu during Paulet's period, wrote in *Typee*, "… to this hour the great body of the Hawaiian people invoke blessings on his head, and look back with gratitude to the time when his liberal and paternal sway diffused peace and happiness among them." (Some modern native Hawaiians who seek sovereignty might regard Paulet positively. For given the subsequent history of the British Empire and Commonwealth, it is clear that had the British government supported Paulet's control and annexed Hawaii in 1843, it, like Tonga, Samoa, Fiji, and many other places in the Pacific, would long ago have been independent. Moreover, given British colonial land laws in such islands, the land would still be in native Hawaiian hands.)

Meanwhile, Honolulu and environs continued to develop. In 1845 King Kamehameha III and two members of his court were the first horse-riders to cross the *pali* (cliff) of the Ko‘olau Range to the north of the city on the newly improved, though still hair-raising, pathway linking the capital to the windward side of Oahu.

The French Invade

The Unites States and Britain remained conciliatory, and treaties of mutual respect had been signed with several minor European powers such as Denmark, Norway and Sweden, and some of the German principalities. But despite the revising of the Laplace Treaty in 1846 and the French return of the $20,000 bond, the French were often uncompromising. The new consul, Guillaume Patrice Dillon, made himself obnoxious by abusing the king and demanding special concessions, such as for the tiny amount of French wine that trickled into the kingdom. As historical accidents happen, in 1849 French Rear Admiral Legoarant de Tromelin arrived in Honolulu for an unrelated friendly visit in the ship *La Poursuivante*. Deceived by Dillon's exaggerated complaints, he informed the government that unless all of Dillon's demands were immediately met, he would make use of "all the means at his disposal."

De Tromelin plastered circulars around Honolulu warning the citizens he would attack the town the next day. The US and British consuls fiercely protested. In a panic, foreigners placed the equivalent of about $45,000 (millions now) in silver and gold in the keeping of the missionaries in Kawaiahao Church. The following afternoon, the French marines stormed ashore. Their major punitive objective for both real and symbolic purposes was Kamehameha I's Honolulu Fort. The small native guard did not resist. The French demolished some of the fort, ransacked Governor Kekuanoa's fort home, spiked the cannon, smashed the muskets and swords, threw all the hundreds of barrels of gunpowder into the sea, opened the town prison inside the fort, and freed all the inmates. (The broken fort was leveled in 1857 and the rubble used as fill to extend the sides of the harbor.

The French posted guards at key buildings and seized the king's striking personal yacht, *Kamehameha III*. In addition to the value of the yacht, they had caused more than $100,000 in damage, which in the mid-1800s was an entire year's revenue for the country. The yacht was sailed to the French colony of Tahiti. In the 1850s and '60s the French threat died away, but the king's yacht was never returned.

THE GREAT *MAHELE* OF 1848 AND LATER LAND LAWS

By the mid-1840s there was immense discontent among native Hawaiians at the control exerted by foreigners. In 1845 the native Hawaiian statesman David Malo and others collected thousands of names on Maui and the Big Island to petition the king. They warned that the whites would use their economic power to take Hawaiian land. The reply they received from the king was that foreigners were in government only temporarily until educated Hawaiians could take their place. Given that at this time natives outnumbered foreigners almost a hundred to one, perhaps the small number of non-natives seemed to the king to pose no threat. If so, he was deceived.

In the 1846 cabinet, three naturalized Americans were appointed: Judd to finance, William Richards to public instruction, John Ricord to attorney general, and Robert C. Wyllie, a naturalized Briton (Scottish), to foreign affairs, with no native Hawaiians given positions of significance. From that date, Malo and most native Hawaiians lost all respect for their often drunken, vacillating "Little King" (he was small), as they now called him. By this time the American commissioner Anthony Ten Ecyk was writing to the state department in Washington DC: "The king and his native chiefs are mere automatons in the hands of his ministers.... I think of Dr. Judd as a man of ordinary talents... [who] allows his personal feelings to control his public acts."

Foreign affairs being relatively quiet, foreigners in the government now pressed to have the control of land reorganized. The rules for division and ownership of land and the actions taken thereunder would become known as "The Great *Mahele*" or "The Great Division."

Father Damien of Molokai Island

Joseph de Veuster was born in Belgium in 1840 and died in Molokai, Hawaii, in 1889. His farmer father wanted him to go into business, but as the result of hearing some dedicated priests, he decided to become a priest himself in the novitiate of the Fathers of the Sacred Heart of Jesus and Mary at Louvain. He took the name of Damien. In 1864 Damien was sent to the Hawaiian Catholic mission, where he was ordained two months later in Honolulu's Catholic Cathedral of Our Lady of Peace. Sent to the Big Island, zealous and fit, he even built a number of chapels himself.

Aware of the distressing conditions of the 600 lepers at the settlement in Molokai, Damien pleaded with his bishop to be allowed to become resident priest there. "As long as the lepers can care for themselves," wrote the superintendent of the board of health to the bishop, "they are comparatively comfortable, but as soon as the dreadful disease renders them helpless, it would seem that even demons themselves would pity their condition and hasten their death." In May 1873 Damien arrived and built churches.

Though there were others who helped, including various Protestant clergy, Father Damien showed the greatest dedication, compassion, and perseverance. He acted as a priest but also helped with their illness. He dressed their wounds, made their coffins, and dug their graves. Twelve years on in 1885, he began to show signs of having contracted the disease himself. Within four years he died, following fifteen years of selfless service.

The Great Mahele

Legislation was now instituted to give the chiefs the land that they controlled under the traditional system and to meet the foreigners' demands for full ownership. One meaning of the Hawaiian word *mahele* is "division"; though the king had always opposed the idea of a formal *mahele* or division of land, he was finally persuaded that this was the time to make land ownership available to commoners too. He believed ownership would create a prosperous farming community, which would help native Hawaiians who had become destitute in Honolulu and Lahaina and might reverse the serious native population decline that had continued throughout the 1800s.

Strictly speaking, the "Great *Mahele*" refers to the many meetings of Kamehameha III and more than 240 of his chiefs in early 1848 at which they agreed to share out and formalize their previously traditionally held lands. But "Great *Mahele*" and *mahele* are often used more loosely to refer to all the activities of land redistribution over a decade or so, and *mahele* is used in this way below. The agreements made by the chiefs did not give title. Claims made by chiefs, commoners, and settlers still had to be heard and awarded through the specially established Land Commission set up in 1846. The legislature could have stipulated that only native Hawaiians could claim land, but, under the pressure of powerful foreigners in the cabinet, it did not.

Judd was deeply involved in the Land Commission. As he later wrote, "There was no one but myself who had the knowledge and... resolution to act efficiently. I therefore volunteered my services to the King... and on condition of his appointing as my fellow-laborers those whom I named, pledged myself to make the division [of land]." And on many occasions, as the Commission Chairman Chief Justice Lee later pointed out, "Dr. Judd acted as sole judge in land disputes."

Soon Judd and his close colleagues were preparing a bill that would make it possible for non-natives to own Hawaiian land, but only citizens of the Hawaiian kingdom could do so. When news of this bill became an open secret just before it was to pass through the legislature, there occurred, as one historian puts it, "a stampede of missionaries" suddenly wanting to renounce their

American citizenship and become naturalized. Then an Act of July 1850 also allowed the sale of lands in fee simple, giving the owner outright and unconditional disposal rights, to resident foreigners who remained aliens. Foreigners would make full use of these new opportunities.

The Land Commission visited all islands and received testimony for about 12,000 claims. After almost 10 years of difficult work, the commission closed in March 1855.

The 6,423 sq mi of land (16,636 sq km or 4,110,720 ac) on the eight main islands were distributed in the following categories. First, the king renounced his right to own all the land of the kingdom, but retained certain estates, about a million acres, called the King's Lands. He and his successors, Kamehameha IV and V, could mortgage, lease, or sell this land. Much was in fact sold over the years. In 1865 the remainder of these lands was made inalienable, after which time they became known as Crown Lands.

Second were Government Lands, about 1,500,000 acres set aside to generate government revenue from lease or sale. Buyers did not have to approach the Land Commission but acquired Royal Patent Grants from the government. Sales of Government Lands were rapid, mostly to naturalized citizens or to aliens. In 1849–50 some 27,292 ac were alienated, in 1850–51 some 31,518 ac, and by 1886 about two-thirds of all Government Lands was gone.

Third were Chiefs' Lands, also about 1,500,000 ac. Chiefs most closely related to the ruling family received larger tracts. Chiefs too had to have their claims approved by the commission. To receive title, they were required to pay a commutation fee, which, because they lacked cash to pay, in most cases became a third of their land. This land then became Government Lands. Short of cash and in debt to foreigners, chiefs began to sell much of their land.

Fourth were Kuleana Lands. In keeping with the idea of encouraging Hawaiian commoners to own their own land to farm, they were now allowed to claim land on which they were living or cultivating. To acquire this land in fee simple, they had to go before the Land Commission to request it. There was no commutation fee because this land was taken out of Government or Chiefs' Lands. Special arrangements were made to give fee simple ownership to people who lived on lots in the towns.

The legal knowledge of the Hawaiian commoners was inadequate for such a process, and nothing in their previous cultural history was concerned with owning land, so they failed to seize their rights. The majority of them did not approach the Land Commission. Though Malo and men like him had wisely suggested that if there were to be a *mahele*, then there should be a ten-year period in which to prepare the Hawaiian people for it, there was no government effort to properly inform and educate them.

In time some 8,750 Hawaiian commoners received about 28,600 ac of land—mostly fertile land, as it happens. This averages only about 3.27 ac each for those commoners who gained any land at all. But even these lands often did not include the water and fishing rights that were a central part of the traditional system. So when they could not make a living, many commoners left their land and moved to the port towns, and title reverted. Other commoners lost their land because they did not sell their produce but exchanged it and so had no cash to pay land tax.

For more than 2,000 years in their *ahupua'a*, the Hawaiians and their Polynesian ancestors had always farmed common land and produced what was sufficient for their own family needs, but knew nothing about owning land or growing a surplus for sale—giving, sharing, exchange, yes; selling, no. In the Hawaiian economic system, surplus was given away, not hoarded. The Western economic system was just the opposite.

But it seems that the Westerners who argued for the *mahele* (and there were many who genuinely cared for the natives and truly believed the *mahele* would help) were incapable of understanding that most Hawaiians did not think in Western ways. In one form or another, chiefs and commoners continued to lose their land to resident foreigners and foreign businessmen who came to the islands.

Because of the immense confusions and complexities of surveying and registration, frustration mounted and land redistribution continued for decades. No district had only one surveyor, and there were, for instance, about a dozen different surveyors operating in Waikiki alone. The final relevant legislative act did not pass until 1892.

In contrast to the plight of the Hawaiian commoners, within four years of the passing of the first land laws, sixteen leading members of the Congregational Mission gained title in fee simple to 7,888 ac of first-class land on Oahu, i.e., nearly 500 ac each. In his privileged position of minister and judge in land disputes, Judd managed to acquire 22 choice ac in Waikiki, 3,081 ranchland ac at Kualoa on Oahu's windward coast (the ranch is still in the family), 2,184 on the green Hana coast on Maui and elsewhere, for a total 5,295 ac.

In 1851 the missionary Amos Cooke summarized the situation thus:

> While the natives stand confounded... and doubting the truth of the change on their behalf, the foreigners are creeping in among them, getting their largest and best lands, water privileges, building lots, etc. The Lord seems to be allowing such things to take place that the Islands may gradually pass into other hands. This is trying but we cannot help it. It is what we have been contending against for years, but the Lord is showing us that His thoughts are not our thoughts, neither are his ways our ways. The will of the Lord be done.

By the end of the 1800s, white men would own four acres for every single acre owned by a native. The dispossession suggested by this fact has fed much of the contemporary revival of the immensely complex movement toward Hawaiian sovereignty.

JUDD'S JOURNEY WITH THE PRINCES & HIS FALL

The year after the *mahele* began, the French troubles described earlier occurred. Judd outmaneuvered the foreign minister, Robert Wyllie, and, bearing the title of "Plenipotentiary Extraordinary," was given the task of trying to settle the French problem in France itself. He was to discuss French reparations and other international matters by visiting Europe, Britain, and the United States in 1849 and 1850. Accompanying him for general education and diplomatic experience were Prince Alexander Liholiho (fifteen years old), later to be Kamehameha IV, and his brother Prince Lot (eighteen years), the future Kamehameha V.

Society and Sights

The social side of the mission was a splendid affair. They saw the Californian goldfields, crossed the Isthmus of

This pretty 1862 portrait of Prince Albert, only child of King Kamehameha IV (Alexander Liholiho) and Queen Emma and hope of the Kamehameha dynasty, was painted shortly before his death. Godchild of Britain's Queen Victoria, Prince Albert was named after her German consort, Albert of Saxe-Coburg. Bishop Museum

Panama in a coach, strolled in Manhattan, and visited the Houses of Parliament and other sights of London, during which time Alexander became enchanted by Anglican Church ritual and met Queen Victoria. They crossed the Channel to Paris, browsed in the National Library, and attended the opera and the Bois de Boulogne. In front of a multitude, they met the president of France, Louis Napoleon, the nephew of the first Napoleon.

The young princes' trip was a great success because, as they favorably impressed royalty and diplomats, their eyes were opened to the vast Western world, furthering their diplomatic and general education. However, not so in Baltimore. There, Judd was occupied with the luggage at the end of the train when young Prince Alexander Liholiho sat down in his reserved seat in the parlor car. He was rudely ordered to depart by the conductor, who had no tolerance for black people. Alexander, soon to be Hawaii's king, was profoundly insulted and carried the affront to the grave, his attitude to Americans being permanently soured. As he wrote in his journal, the conductor probably had "taken me for somebody's servant just because I had a darker skin than he had." This was the most serious of several incidents in which the princes were mistaken for African-Americans.

Judd was successful in the United States, and a treaty of reciprocal respect with Hawaii was agreed to. But there was no success in Paris, the main source of problems, for which he was strongly criticized when he reached home. In fact there is ample criticism of him by contemporaries. Soon after his return, William Lee, Judd's protégé and friend, wrote: "Judd... is bold and cunning.... His arbitrary temper, his wounded pride, his hate of all rivals, his solicitude to promote his relatives, and his ambition... all conspire to render his position grievous to himself and his friends."

Disastrous Epidemic
The native population continued its decline. In 1848 a vicious epidemic of measles, influenza, and whooping cough, to which native Hawaiians had little immunity, killed thousands of them, further reducing the population. Late that year George Kenway, living on the Big Island, wrote to Robert Wyllie that

It can scarcely be said that there is any Native population at all. The hillsides and the banks of watercourses show for miles the ruins of the "olden time"—Stone walls half sunk in the ground, broken down and covered with grass—large broken squares of trees and imperfect embankments—remains of old taro patches and water runs now dried up and useless and many other such tokens… impress one with a melancholy curiosity about a people that cannot now be found.

A few years later a smallpox epidemic accelerated this disastrous trend. Early in 1853, the ship *Charles Mallory* entered Honolulu from San Francisco with a passenger suffering from smallpox. He was promptly quarantined; the community thought the disease was contained, but it broke out after three months. Soon smallpox was spreading almost uncontrollably, resulting in a huge death toll.

At this point, the historical record becomes muddy and disputed. Explanations of the disaster have mentioned the unreliable mid-1800s vaccine, the refusal of many native Hawaiians to be vaccinated, and unhygienic native burial practices. Some accounts say that the deaths occurred despite isolation of areas, burning of contaminated houses, and a large-scale vaccination campaign. Others add that there was a dispute between Wylie, who also had medical training and preferred to develop a smallpox vaccine from the infected passenger, and Judd, who wanted a cowpox vaccine. The difficulties continued when Judd appointed himself commissioner of health and for weeks refused to release funds for any form of immunization program unless his preferred vaccination was agreed to. Certainly two Honolulu doctors, Wesley Newcomb and George A. Lathrop (though the latter disliked Hawaiians), openly criticized Judd for "most wickedly" stalling the immunization program.

Honolulu and Oahu suffered terribly, with yellow flags of warning hanging from almost every second door. William Farrer, a Mormon elder who arrived in Honolulu in late June, wrote:

I shall not soon forget the scenes of misery and wretchedness…. [In the hospital] the stench was almost unendurable although the natives in attendance… kept burning tar to purify the room. [One woman had lost so much of her face] to be almost unrecognizable and was near breathing her last… at the door lay two corpses ready to be carried off, to inter the one in a coffin and the other wrapped up in native mats. At Kaneohe [a village on the windward side of Oahu] the occupants had all died or had fled to some other place leaving everything behind, hogs, dogs, and pets to take care of themselves.

In 2003 when foundations were being dug for mega-stores just north of Honolulu's Ala Moana shopping center, dozens of skeletons were uncovered, probably from the 1853 epidemic. In May of '53, a visitor to Ewa (just west of Pearl Harbor) reported there were "1,200 deaths out of a population of 2,800…. The whole state of society became disorganized. Almost every family was broken up…"

Niihau, Molokai, and Lanai escaped, and Kauai seems to have had only one death, thanks to a rigorous quarantine and immunization by a local doctor. Maui and the Big Island suffered badly, though not as seriously as Oahu. Within months, about 11,000 smallpox cases were reported and some thousands died (sources vary from about 2,500 to 6,000), mostly native Hawaiians.

Judd's Fall

For the duration of his time in power, Judd also controlled the selection and collection of the significant government records, including those relating to his own career. These in time became the basis of the Hawaiian State Archives.

Encouraged by the two princes, the king finally demanded Judd's resignation. For a week Judd refused. He then went into private practice and business. Among the king's reasons was the fact that Judd had also recently been conspiring to sell the islands to an American millionaire. For good or ill, Dr. Gerritt P. Judd was one of the most influential figures in the history of the Hawaiian Islands.

EARLY MOVES FOR ANNEXATION

Judd's scheme to sell the islands was unknown to his fellow citizens. During his overseas tour, he had met Alfred G. Benson, a shipping millionaire from New York. Judd soon became the agent in Benson's attempt to buy the archipelago for $5,000,000. Once home, he presented the idea to the shocked king and incurred the wrath of the chiefs. Judd was not alone in wanting the islands to be American. As Gavan Dawes, the author of the most successful of all histories of Hawaii, points out: "A good many Americans in the kingdom were Manifest Destiny men... their minds inflamed by the election to the American presidency of the expansionist Democrat Franklin Pierce, who took office in 1853." Others, less determined, believed US annexation would end all possibility of control by France or Great Britain (neither of which were actually very likely). And all the Americans in the islands realized that their own part in the Hawaiian economy would benefit if Hawaiian goods could receive preference in the US market.

Businessman Charles Reed Bishop led another 1853 annexation scheme. Bishop had arrived in Honolulu only in 1846 by chance. Through his friendship with Judd and Lee (who had arrived with him), Bishop developed a massively successful banking and political career within a few years. He and other leading citizens who under the rules of the *mahele* had purchased substantial acreages took an unsuccessful petition to the king recommending rapid annexation to the United States. Their stated reason was "to preserve prosperity and political quiet in the Islands."

For most of 1853 and 1854, various groups continually varying in formulation devised plans for a republic or annexation to the United States, including the "Committee of Thirteen," most of whom despised the monarchy. Sometimes agitators were for straight-out US annexation. Sometimes they were more in favor of an armed coup d'etat to establish a revolutionary republic, then perhaps turn a neat profit by selling their republic to the United States. They encouraged men to come from California to support them in any insurrection. But they disliked the idea of statehood, because Hawaiians would then become citizens and they wanted settler control. There were false alarms of invasion, newspaper campaigns to persuade native Hawaiians to agree to annexation, and noisy public meetings, but no uprising. The king was too often intoxicated to act consistently, but the two princes, still smarting from the Baltimore incident, were resolutely set against annexation. At one point, the US Consul David Gregg and the captain of an American warship in harbor told Wylie, the foreign minister, that unless Hawaiian sovereignty passed immediately to the United States, insurrection was inevitable. Wylie, who wanted Hawaii to remain independent, turned the tables by formally requesting Gregg to give protection against any revolt—and requested the British and French consuls as well. When the latter two agreed, Gregg had to do so too. For some decades annexation went into eclipse.

ALEXANDER LIHOLIHO, KAMEHAMEHA IV

Over several years, the national legislature established by the 1840 constitution passed various acts that consolidated the existence of a cabinet, a permanent civil service, and a system of courts. In 1852, four years after the Great *Mahele* began, the legislature framed and adopted a new constitution, this time mostly the brainchild of Judd and Lee, and Kamehameha III was somehow persuaded to accept it. It gave every male subject, both native and naturalized, the right to vote for representatives in the lower house. This was the constitution that Alexander Liholiho, Kamehameha IV, inherited on his accession to the throne at the age of twenty on the death of his uncle in December 1854. Alexander immediately created a new style of ruling and a new kind of behavior at court and achieved a less abrasive relationship with the diplomats.

Protecting the Population and Keeping Hawaii Independent
Grandson of Kamehameha I, Alexander was tall, good-looking, intelligent, an English speaker, and perhaps as much European as Hawaiian in his values. Kamehameha III had encouraged Alexander's administrative education by giving the teenager a position in his cabinet. Alexander admired the British and had been well treated on his visit there. One of his first royal acts was to subscribe to the London *Times*. He received a number of British periodicals and planned to send his son to a British boarding school. His wife was the perfect partner: Emma Rooke Naea, whom he wed during the second year of his reign, was herself a chief as a great-grandniece of Kamehameha I and a granddaughter of John Young. Emma had been reared by her mother's sister and her uncle, Dr. T. C. Rooke. She was as British in her attitudes as Alexander. Indeed, after his death she sailed to England and stayed as a guest of Queen Victoria.

Low birth rates and epidemics since the arrival of foreigners had rapidly reduced the native Hawaiian population, and Emma and Alexander were deeply distressed by this trend. In 1855 Alexander proposed the legislative bill, "An Act to Institute Hospitals for the Sick Poor," to establish hospitals in Honolulu and Lahaina.

During his short reign, Alexander was constrained by the constitution of 1852, and the legislature refused his act to establish the hospital. The two monarchs then took matters into their own hands and, going from business house to business house in Honolulu, personally pleaded for money. They were also aware of the special problems of victims of *mai pake* or leprosy (Hansen's Disease), most likely an unintended import in a ship from China, and a separate facility was provided for such cases. Alexander and Queen Emma also pledged their own money, and in 1860 the first hospital building was constructed from coral stone. When Queen Emma died decades later, she left the bulk of her estate to the hospital. This was the birth of the present-day Queen's Medical Center, Hawaii's largest private hospital, on Honolulu's broadest downtown block.

Together Alexander and his queen developed a Hawaiian Royal Court that elegantly blended the best of Hawaiian simplicity and British formality and court ritual and protocol, for they respected both cultures—Alexander enjoyed playing cricket and adored the hula, which he encouraged. Because he was unhappy with the political influence exercised by the American residents, he sought a counterweight in Britain and things British. British trade was much smaller than that with the United States, so he made other connections. He personally corresponded with Queen Victoria, whom he had met on his tour and who became godmother to his son, encouraged and made friends of British residents, and attempted to introduce into Hawaiian life elements of British culture.

As a religious counterweight to the overwhelming presence of the Presbyterian missionaries—and in Alexander's view a religion more suited to a monarchy than fundamentalist Protestantism—an Anglican mission was invited from Britain, and in the long-term the presence of the English-sandstone Cathedral of St. Andrew's (which became Episcopal after US annexation) in downtown

Honolulu was one result. Like its medieval predecessors, it took many years to finish—from 1867 to 1958. Alexander himself translated into Hawaiian the Anglican Book of Common Prayer. The new Anglican bishop, the Right Rev. Thomas N. Staley, actually encouraged the hula as well as ancient Hawaiian chants at chiefs' funerals. Annexation and Americanization now "on hold," the displeased missionary-business community criticized the royal couple at every opportunity.

But Alexander had a quick temper and sometimes drank to excess. In a fury based on false rumors about familiarity between his secretary, Henry Neilson, and Queen Emma, he shot Neilson, who eventually died from tuberculosis perhaps exacerbated by his chest wound. In another fit of passion, annoyed by his four-year-old son's tantrum, he punished the boy by dousing him with cold water. Soon after, the prince, the hope of the dynasty, sickened and died. These incidents destroyed the king's self-respect. He slid into continual depression, suffered increasingly from asthma, lived in virtual seclusion, and what promised to be an outstanding Hawaiian reign that might have ensured Hawaii's independence ended when he died from an asthma attack within fifteen months of his son's death.

Lot (Kamehameha V) and Lunalilo

King Lot, Kamehaheha V, who was king from 1863 to 1872, was the last direct blood relation of the unifier of the kingdom. Unlike the civil Alexander, he was more abrasive and refused to acknowledge Judd and Lee's constitution of 1852. Asserting that he knew the nature of his subjects better than such white men did and believing universal male suffrage unsuitable for them, he called a convention to revise the constitution along his own preferred lines.

When after much debate no agreement could be reached, Lot made an extraordinary speech to his advisors, both native and naturalized, showing emphatically where Hawaii's political power resided, stating: "as at the time His Majesty Kamehameha III gave the constitution of the year 1852, he reserved to himself the power of taking it away.... I make it known today that the constitution of 1852 is abrogated. I will give you a constitution."

King Lot's Flamboyant Parliament, 1872

The opening of parliament under the Hawaiian monarchy was usually a spectacular occasion. W. Bliss in his book *Paradise in the Pacific* (1873) describes the opening of parliament under the reign of King Lot (Kamehameha V).

> The parliament of paradise meets in Honolulu on the last day of April each alternate year. Its meeting is an event which astonishes the natives, and gives the white people an opportunity to air their well-preserved fashions in the splendor of a royal court.... Sauntering along the street I meet white women in black silks, and yellow women in white muslins, wending their way to the courthouse.... Its second storey is the legislative hall....
>
> Spectators occupy seats in the center of the hall, the whites in front, the natives in the rear. In this throng I recognize the oldest missionary, and the latest invalid from the states.... In front are seated the nobles and representatives comprising the legislature—a curious mixture of Hawaiian and Anglo-Saxon men, of which the Hawaiians are decidedly the best looking. On the right of the rostrum are seated the "ladies of the court" most of them Yankee girls once. On the left sits the black clothed minister of the United States, the British and French Commissioners, the officers of the British frigate *Scout*, now in port, and the consular corps all in gold lace, gilt buttons, swords, and whatever else adds pomp and circumstance.... There is an apothecary, Consul for Austria, a whaleman's agent, Consul for Italy, an auctioneer, Consul for Chile....
>
> The marshall of the kingdom enters, and throws over the Chair of State the royal mantle. It was the war cloak of Kamehameha I, made of bright yellow feathers... four feet long and spreads eleven feet and a half at the bottom.... [E]nter four native men in... capes and black silk hats of stovepipe style... with long staffs called kahilis [which] look like a gay chimney sweep's brush. These four stand at the four corners of the rostrum... then the King, Kamehameha V [enters]; then at a respectful interval, the ministers and staff officers—all white men in brilliant uniforms.
>
> I cannot repress a smile at the appearance of these civilized men, caparisoned with barbaric glory! There is our American-born banker, a scarlet ribbon around his neck, from which hangs the sparkling insignia of Hawaiian Knighthood. There is the little minister of finance, an excellent American-born dentist. There is the tall, scheming minister of

> foreign affairs, also minister of the navy that is yet to be, and of war not yet declared, once an American lawyer. There is the dignified minister of the interior, general manager and police supervisor of the kingdom, once a crusty Scotch physician. There is the attorney general of the crown, who recently went to New England and married a wife. All these are in cocked hats and blue broadcloth, brilliant with gilt bands, laces, and decorations; their rapiers buckled at their sides, and they themselves appearing to be very uncomfortable. When the king enters the audience rises, and every eye is turned upon him.

Proclaimed in 1864, Lot's own constitution rejected much of that of 1852 and stated that the kingdom was the king's. This constitution remained for 23 years until King Kalakaua was forced in 1887 to agree to the "Bayonet Constitution." Lot's constitution limited the franchise and members of the legislature to literate males owning a certain amount of property or an equivalent in earned income. In effect it disenfranchised many Hawaiians but, having deep respect for the king and nobles and the whole institution of monarchy, the majority acquiesced. Both appointed nobles and elected members sat in the legislature, so there was no longer legislative independence. Lot's constitution annoyed and frustrated the economically powerful foreign residents of Hawaii. Nevertheless, Lot was financially careful and tried to cultivate the business lobby—thus plantation owners were allowed to import Chinese laborers during his reign.

In Lot's time, the legislature was a bizarre sight: the white members mostly refused to learn Hawaiian and the Hawaiians refused to speak English. The impasse was solved by a brilliant young half-native Hawaiian, William Ragsdale, who interpreted. Mark Twain observed him and was astonished:

> [Ragsdale] fastens his eye... upon any member who rises, lets him say half a dozen sentences and then interrupts... and repeats his speech in a loud, rapid voice turning every Kanaka speech into English and every English speech into Kanaka.... His tongue is in constant motion from eleven in the forenoon till four in the afternoon, and why it does not wear out is the affair of Providence....

When he is translating the speeches [of pompous
members who do not understand the other language] he
will... drop in a little voluntary contribution occasionally
in the way of a word or two that will make the gravest
speech utterly ridiculous.

With the arrival of diplomats and sophisticated visitors
from overseas, people such as Mark Twain and the British
Duke of Edinburgh, Lot recognized the need for a proper
large-scale hotel. A lack of private capital meant the
government undertook construction. The Hawaiian Hotel
(later the Royal Hawaiian Hotel) on the corner of Hotel
and Richards Streets was formally opened in February
1872. (During World War I it became the Armed Forces
YMCA and, beautifully restored, is now the home of
various government agencies.) Elegant Aliʻiolani Hale was
another major project of Lot's reign. Intended as a palace, it
became the seat for the legislature and supreme court and
remains one of the great Hawaiian-style buildings.

But race relations deteriorated. Native Hawaiian fears of
American control were increased when Captain William
Reynolds sailed for Middlebrook Island, an atoll at the far
northern end of the Hawaiian chain, and claimed it as
American territory. The island was later renamed "Midway."

The new constitution also attended to the royal
succession, allowing for the legislature's election of the king
in a situation in which there was no legal heir. So when Lot
Kamehameha died, childless, aged 40 years, the legislature
elected his successor. The new king, William Charles
Lunalilo, defeated rival David Kalakaua and was the first
monarch to be elected. But within six months he became very
ill with little chance of recovery.

Meanwhile during the 1860s, the incidence of the
appalling disease of leprosy had been increasing, especially
among native Hawaiians, and from 1865 the Board of
Health had wanted to segregate its victims. Legislation to
quarantine all leprosy sufferers and strictly enforce the
segregation was passed in 1873. When King Lunalilo
signed the bill to legalize this campaign, he became very
unpopular with native Hawaiians, who held strong family
values. Popularity mattered little when he died soon after,
aged 39, having reigned less than thirteen months.

7

The Three Kings:
Sugar, Kalakaua, Immigration

Whaling had been welcomed as Hawaii's savior by the small but growing, mostly foreign, mostly American, merchant class. Whaling was unreliable, however, with good years followed by disaster. Agriculture would provide a permanent commercial base and solve the cyclical nature of the economy. Their best chance lay in developing a sugar industry. In fact, long before whaling died, sugar had become king of the kingdom. A crop native across Polynesia, sugarcane had always grown wild in Hawaii. The earliest attempts to produce crystal sugar were in 1802 by a Chinese on Lanai.

Sugar Boom

As we have seen with the Great *Mahele*, canny Westerners took advantage of unsophisticated Hawaiians to occupy land in increasing amounts, and land—leased, bought, grabbed—was crucial for the expansion of sugar. Plantation owners purchased large amounts of land from the chiefs and manipulated the rules of the *Mahele* so that they could always lease sufficient acreage from the "Government Lands."

California Gold Rush

The California gold rush of 1848 forged a new economic connection with the west coast of North America. Sugar became a significant part of the export trade. This relationship was much more convenient than that of whaling with the east coast of the United States around the far away horn of South America.

For a year or two it was not only sugar that went from Hawaii to California, but tents, pickaxes, lamps, and all the

paraphernalia miners needed. Unemployed whites and native Hawaiians also left the islands for the goldfields. For a time, native Hawaiians grew potatoes in the fertile soils of Maui and exported them to hungry miners.

But the end of the surface gold by late 1851 saw this sudden Californian source contract. The Australia gold rushes of the 1850s were just beginning, and sugar exported there helped to compensate and prevented recession for a year or so. Nevertheless many business people had over-invested and bankruptcies were widespread.

But California was not the only market. Waves of American settlers also crossed the continent from the midwest to Oregon and Washington during the 1830s and '40s, and by 1860 the west coast population had steadily increased. There were now twelve substantial Hawaiian sugar plantations aiming at that American market and the price of sugar was rising. More Americans began to see business opportunities in the islands.

Chinese peasants were first brought to Hawaii in 1852 on five-year contracts to work on the sugar plantations. They were the earliest of the many large immigrant groups that have contributed to the multiethnic nature of the islands. Hawaii State Archives

American Civil War

Sugar from the plantations of the seceded Confederate states of America was cut off by northern embargoes and blockades and the scorched-earth policies of its generals. Hawaiian sugar was thus able to replace southern sugar for the duration of the war. By 1866 there existed 32 prosperous plantations, and export had increased tenfold. And this occurred despite the high tariff that Hawaiian sugar, originating in a foreign country, had to pay.

Hawaii was officially neutral, but with the exception of a handful who prudently held their tongues, the Americans in Hawaii supported the Union. Women made bandages for Union wounded, fundraising was strongly supported, and northern victories publicly and noisily celebrated. A Hilo merchant, Thomas Spencer, even raised a body of native Hawaiians, "Spencer's Invincibles," to fight for the Union, but when it was pointed out that Hawaii was officially neutral, burst into tears.

By 1867 when the Civil War and the boom were over, eight plantations went bankrupt and Hawaii needed a new approach. It arrived when, after much dispute, many of the planters agreed to cooperate with one another and signed contracts and quotas with the Californian sugar importers and mills. The Hawaiian growers were now less free to sell wherever they liked. They still had to pay US duties, but to compensate they had a guaranteed market for eight years. By 1869, for the first time since the early days of sandalwood, exports exceeded imports. And Hawaii retained a favorable balance of trade until the later 1880s. This state of affairs was due almost entirely to the development and integration of the sugar industry.

A Treaty of Reciprocity?

To achieve a permanent market in the United States then became, for the next few decades, the key aim of the islands' planters, most of whom were Americans by birth or pro-American descendants of Americans who lived in Hawaii. If economic could also become political ties, so much the better.

But Washington DC regarded Hawaii as insignificant, and Hawaiian planters recognized that only a very large incentive could persuade the US government to agree to a treaty that gave the islands reciprocity in trade. Americans in Hawaii recognized the strategic naval significance of the superb anchorage of Pearl Harbor—if the coral that partly blocked the entrance were removed. So they pressed the Hawaiian government to offer Pearl Harbor's exclusive long-term use as the incentive for a US treaty. Not surprisingly, this offer to alienate Hawaiian territories to a foreign power brought about massive opposition. Dowager Queen Emma said, "There is a feeling of bitterness against these rude people who dwell on our land and have high-handed ideas of giving away somebody else's property as if it were theirs." In fact, though King Lunalilo had agreed to US use of Pearl Harbor, such was the native opposition that

'Iolani Palace

Built to replace its dilapidated predecessor, the foundation stone was laid by King Kalakaua in 1880 and completed in 1882 at a cost of around $350,000 (equivalent to many tens of millions today)—which the king's opponents considered a waste.

Its architects called it *American Composite* or *American Florentine*. It had electric lights before the White House did. After an elaborate opening ceremony, dismissed as barbaric by the king's enemies, it became the residence of Kalakaua and then of Hawaii's last monarch, his sister, Queen Lili'uokalani.

The palace has soaring Corinthian columns, gilded glass door panels, huge chandeliers, a mirrored and golden throne room, and not least a striking three-story-high koa hardwood staircase—and these are massive 20 ft (8 m) Victorian stories. There were four large bathrooms on the second floor, including the country's first flush toilets—a lustrous luxury in the 1880s, when, for instance, the Kaiser's palace in Berlin had no bathrooms. Local craftsmen were used when possible. The upper story balustrades were fabricated in the Honolulu Iron Works. Casts for the coat of arms and other pieces were crafted by a local Chinese worker. A Honolulu newspaper described the palace as "by far the most imposing building on the Islands." To many minds it still is.

Following the coup d'etat and royalist revolt, Queen Lili'uokalani was incarcerated in the palace as a prisoner of the republic for most of a year. Later it became the home, successively, of the provisional government, the government of the republic, the territory's legislature in 1898, and after 1959, the state legislature, until that moved into its grand new capitol just a block *mauka* (mountainwards) of the palace. Six million dollars were then spent upgrading the palace. In 2002 another multimillion restoration began.

just before he died he withdrew his support. But under the next monarch, such a treaty became possible.

KING KALAKAUA

It must be remembered that tradition required that the highest chief or the person with the most direct ancestral claim to lead should be chosen as ruler. So the legislature could not choose just anyone but was limited to those with ancestral right. In 1874 the two claimants were David Kalakaua and Dowager Queen Emma, Kanehameha IV's widow. Kalakaua's bloodline descended from the fierce chiefs of Kona on the west coast of the Big Island, who had supported Kamehameha I in his push for power. The elegant Queen Emma also possessed Kamehameha I's blood. Campaigns to persuade the legislators had begun before King Lunalilo's death. Emma's support was concentrated in Honolulu, Kalakaua's in the countryside and other islands.

King Kalakaua and the famous author Robert Louis Stevenson sit together on the lanai *(veranda) of the king's private retreat, the* Snuggery, *on Waikiki. Kalakaua ostentatiously supported Hawaiian culture, took key historic decisions, and was the first reigning monarch of any nation to travel around the world. He was aptly called the Merrie Monarch. In a letter of February 1889 Stevenson wrote: "And what is far more dangerous, entertaining and being entertained by His Majesty here, who is a very fine fellow, but O, Charles! What a crop for the drink! He carries it too like a mountain with a sparrow on its shoulders."* Bishop Museum

Kalakaua's Victory and Reciprocity

Kalakaua had made his name in the legislature as a champion of the ordinary Hawaiian, outspoken in his condemnation of American influence. Unknown to his countrymen, however, Kalakaua put personal position above political principle. The sugar interests would finance his campaign and in return, if elected king, he would support the American efforts to offer Pearl Harbor as bait for a treaty of reciprocity favoring Hawaiian sugar.

His supporters were persevering, persistent, and economically powerful, with funds far outmaneuvering and out-bribing those of Queen Emma. The election campaign was passionate. A key player for Kalakaua was the banker Charles R. Bishop, who in his mind's eye saw that making massive amounts of money with Kalakaua would carry out his own plans. Kalakaua won overwhelmingly by thirty-nine legislative votes to six.

When Kalakaua's victory was announced at the courthouse, the once overconfident, now despairing supporters of Queen Emma rioted. This mob destroyed part of the courthouse and tossed one of Kalakaua's legislative supporters to his death out an upper window. The standing army had been dissolved after a recent mutiny; the police sent to prevent disorder joined the rioters according to political preference; and the local white militias were reluctant to attack natives. So Kalakaua, Governor of Oahu John O. Dominis (later husband of Queen Lili'uokalani), and banker Bishop (also the minister for the interior), asked the captains of American and British vessels in the harbor to send in their men to restore order. By the next morning everything was quiet. Though all remained calm, the foreign troops stayed ashore for a week. A portentous precedent had been set.

Soon after his enthronement in January 1873, King Kalakaua led the Hawaiian diplomatic mission to Washington DC, and he and his advisors convinced President Grant (who as general during the Civil War had helped crush Confederate sugar) to encourage the US Senate to agree to a treaty allowing Hawaiian sugar to enter the United States free of duties. As inducement, use of Pearl Harbor was offered and accepted.

The Act of Reciprocity came into force in September 1876. Naturalized American-Hawaiian planters and their economic partners had achieved a bond with the United States that was difficult to undo, and to hold fast to their advantage, they now had an additional reason for annexation. So did the United States. Here are the words of the US minister to Hawaii immediately after Kalakaua had left Washington: "The acquisition of the Hawaiian Islands by the United States, sooner or later, must become a national necessity to guard the approaches against hostile attempts on the Pacific States."

Leprosy and Molokai

It was during the reign of Kalakaua that the program to compulsorily gather and send all known lepers to the special isolated settlements on Molokai Island became more intense. The world is aware of the Roman Catholic Father Damien's dedicated ministrations to these unfortunates from 1873 to 1889, but it is less aware of the work of others. Protestant Hawaiians both native and settler, much larger in number than Roman Catholics, held various attitudes toward the praise given Damien during his lifetime and after his death. They could point to the fact that for years before Damien arrived, there had been a Protestant church in the settlement and that a Protestant deacon who was a native Hawaiian had fallen ill with leprosy and lived and ministered in Molokai. There was also a non-leper Mormon elder who conducted church services and lived there, sharing a home with his diseased wife. They also pointed out that there had been earlier visits by Catholic priests long before Damien and that such Protestant and earlier Catholic help went largely unnoticed by the world.

CONTRACTS AND AGENCIES

With the treaty of reciprocity the Hawaiian Islands became unprecedentedly prosperous—if one equates the "Hawaiian Islands" with the native aristocracy, the sugar barons, and the settler business minority.

The Big Five

As sugar increased in economic significance, specialized agencies established quite rapidly. They began to share in

Stealing King Kalakaua's Goldfish, 1885

The American playwright Austin Strong (1881–1957) passed his boyhood in Honolulu. At age four, he daringly stole one of King Kalakaua's prize goldfish from its pond in Kapiolani Park near Diamond Head. It was a sacred fish, a special gift from the emperor of Japan. Below is the climax of Strong's charming short story describing the escapade. In great coincidence, King Kalakaua in his carriage has chanced upon little Austin trudging tiredly along the side of the road leading back to Honolulu and has him sit in the coach. Unknown to the king, his purloined fish sits soggily on Austin's head hidden under his hat!

His majesty began to question me tactfully, trying, as is the way with kings, to put his guest at ease, but the fish was too much on my mind and head. I realized it would soon die if I held my tongue, but if I told, what would be my punishment? Try as I might, I couldn't hold back unmanly tears. The king removed his cigar in concern.

"Are you in pain, Austin?" he asked. I began to shake all over in an agony of indecision. "Won't you tell me what's the matter?"

I heard another and a craven voice blurting out of me.

"Oh, please don't cut off my head!" it cried.

The king replied gravely, "I have no intention of cutting off your head."

Removing my hat, I showed him his gift from the Emperor of Japan. The king raised his hand, the cavalcade came to a halt, again the officer was alongside. The king cried, "Stop at the nearest horse trough. Be quick!"

Away we flew, the king with his arm about me, trying vainly to comfort me as I saw my fish growing weaker and weaker. At last we drew up in front of a native hut. I jumped out and plunged my fish into an overflowing horse trough while the king and his men looked on with polite interest. A native was sent running for a large calabash, and the fish was put in it, his sacred life spared, his dignity restored....

I was rolled home in triumph, fast asleep against His Majesty's protecting shoulder, to be roused by shouts of laughter from my relieved parents... astounded by my royal return....

[The following morning] a smart equerry on horseback, dressed in glistening uniform, dismounted before out gate. He came bearing a large gilt-edged envelope on which was stamped the crown of Hawaii.

It was a royal grant to one, Master Austin Strong, giving him permission to fish in Kapiolani Park for the rest of his days. It was signed "KALAKAUA REX."

—First published in 1944 by the *Atlantic Monthly*.

importing plantation machinery, refining, shipping, marketing, and arranging and making loans. Two agencies, Castle & Cooke and C. Brewer, began to invest shrewdly. Soon they were joined by another business founded by missionaries, Alexander & Baldwin. Other agencies, Theo Davies & Co. and the German Company H. Hackfeld & Co., along with the first three, became part of the "Big Five," the tight circle of companies that quickly took control of much of the economic life of the kingdom.

These five organizations bought up bankrupt and less efficient companies and plantations. To the same end, they sometimes adopted the morally doubtful technique of raising interest rates to put the little man out of business. If a native Hawaiian showed fight and wanted to cling to his land for sugar-growing or some other purpose, he found himself surrounded with large plantations that, with their many connections to other plantations and the agencies, forced him out.

The five gained control of the shipping trade to the west coast, arranged shipping charges for sugar to their own advantage, and again ruined smaller operations. The company headquarters of this cartel soon sat close to one another in downtown Honolulu. (Visitors can still see some of these palatial business premises.) A massive overlap in membership developed among the boards of directors of the Big Five. Families regularly intermarried. Their elegant mansions mushroomed in beautiful surroundings such as the Manoa Valley north of the city, manned and maintained by native Hawaiian and immigrant gardeners and servants.

But there were simmering tensions between agencies and planters. The planters continually claimed they were being overcharged. In 1884 one complained in the *Pacific Commercial Advertiser* that

> It would be a god-send to the planters if the agency system were done away with, unless it is done in a more legitimate manner. This paying for shrinkage, cooperage, cartage, polarizing, large interest, expense of telegram to learn Cuban basis, exchange when against but no credit for exchange when in favor, and not receiving back commission paid to agent in San Francisco, is enough to make any planter hail with joy any change in the handling of sugar that might bring

down expenses from over twenty percent to where they should be. The planters are paying for too many fine residences [of agencies] in Honolulu.

Commercial control became political clout. Still, for more than twenty years, the evolving Big Five faced a worthy opponent in Claus Spreckels.

CLAUS SPRECKELS, SUGAR BARON SUPREME

Easily the greatest and most intelligent of all sugar barons was the self-made German-Californian Claus Spreckels, and he had nothing to do with the evolving Big Five. Seeing more clearly than anyone else, he arrived to negotiate his deals on the same ship that brought the news to Hawaii that the president had finally signed the reciprocity treaty. Plausible and personable—and acting virtually before his competitors were aware of his presence—he had contracted to buy over half of the whole sugar crop to be harvested within the next year for processing in his Californian mill.

The photo shows Claus Spreckels, first row, layered in leis, with a group of friends on a steamer. During his more than 20 years in Hawaii in the late 1800s, Spreckels was the greatest single entrepreneur, controller, and innovator of the sugar industry, a key advisor and and the main economic support of King Kalakaua.
Bishop Museum

Robert Louis Stevenson in Hawaii

One of the most famous authors to have visited Hawaii and written of it was the Scot Robert Louis Stevenson (1850–94), author of such classics as *Treasure Island* and *Kidnapped*. Suffering from tuberculosis from childhood and searching for health in a better climate, he and his American wife, Fanny, and their family chartered the yacht *Casco* in 1888 and sailed the Pacific for two years. They passed five months in the Hawaiian Islands, mainly in Honolulu. Stevenson also toured the Kona District of the western Big Island and Molokai, where he passed eight days in the leper settlement making notes on the life of Father Damien, who had died a short time before. Stevenson later defended Damien against attacks in a famous and pugnacious letter, the "Open Letter to the Reverend Dr. Hyde."

Stevenson studied Hawaiian and he and his wife became firm friends of King Kalakaua and his sister, later Queen Lili'uokalani. They were part of the 'Iolani Palace circle and entertained the "Merrie Monarch" on the *Casco*. Stevenson was also entertained by Kalakaua in the king's more private boathouse, the *Snuggery*. Some fascinating photographs date from these gatherings (see page 160).

Happy times were also spent with his friend, Scots merchant A. S. Cleghorn, and Cleghorn's 13-year-old daughter Princess Kauilani, together under a spreading banyan tree in Waikiki. Just before Kauilani departed for school in Britain, Stevenson wrote the following personalized poem in her red-plush autograph book:

> Forth from her land to mine she goes,
> The island maid, the island rose,
> Light of heart and bright of face,
> The daughter of a double race.
> Her islands here in southern sun
> Shall mourn their Ka'iulani gone,
> And I, in her dear banyan shade,
> Look vainly for my little maid.
>
> But our Scots islands far away
> Shall glitter with unwonted day,
> And cast for once their tempests by
> To smile in Ka'iulani's eye.

The stories in *Island Nights' Entertainments* (1893) with its well-known "The Isle of Voices" and the travel sketches *The Eight Islands* (published posthumously in 1896) all deal with Hawaii. Stevenson's novel *The Wrecker* (1892) grew from a report in a Honolulu newspaper of a shipwreck on Midway Island. He made detailed notes for a major novel to be called *The South Seas* with the theme "the unjust extinction of the Polynesian race by our shoddy civilization," he but died before he could write it. Stevenson ended his short life in Samoa, beloved by the native people as "Tuisitala" (teller of tales).

Alexander & Baldwin were building a seventeen-mile-long irrigation channel to water their plantation on Maui, but most planters concentrated on Oahu. Spreckels also recognized the vast opportunities of Maui. Between 1877 and 1882, he leased or purchased 40,000 barren ac in dry central Maui. The land would reequire massive amounts of water. Undeterred, with his civil engineer Hermann Schussler, he brilliantly diverted immense quantities from the streams on the fertile trade-wind watered northern slopes of the great dormant volcano of Haleakala through marvelous miles-long aqueducts.

Soon after arriving in Honolulu, Spreckels became a close friend of King Kalakaua, who seems immediately to have recognized him as a source of financial backing that could checkmate the missionary-business-plantation-Big Five lobby. To expedite Kalakaua's plans, Spreckels appears to have organized a discrete three-man party for the king and the cattle baron Parker, at which he gave the king $10,000 and lent him (unsecured) $40,000 at 7 percent interest so the king could pay off another royal loan taking 12 percent. Kalakaua needed supporters such as Bishop no longer.

A thirty-mile-long series of tunnels, aqueducts, and channels brought some 50 million gallons of water a day to a huge reservoir of Spreckels's Hawaiian Commercial & Sugar Co. The formerly useless central plain of Oahu between its two great volcanic mountains was now a marvel of economic activity. Today it still is, though about a quarter of it is taken by the towns of Kahului and Wailuku.

Spreckels next spent the then-enormous amount of about $4 million on the world's greatest and most efficient sugar refining factory, and was willing to risk further massive sums. His engineering and technological innovations changed the face of the world's sugar industry. To the traditional three-roller mill, he added two more rollers which, pressing the sugarcane a second time, now captured almost every drop of the juice. To the usual steam power, he added electricity, his mills also having Hawaii's first electric light. He constructed railways to transport cane from the fields and products from the mills. His plantations grew about a third of Hawaii's sugar, and in partnership with W.G. Irwin, he was able to buy up much of the rest. In 1875 about 25 million lbs of sugar a year left Hawaii. By 1890 it would be 250 million.

The brilliant ideas, diligence, careful accounting procedures, and influence with the king of "Herr von Boss" or "His Royal Saccharinity," as his rivals called him, or "Ona Miliona" (owner of a million) as native Hawaiians called him, stirred their enmity. In time he established his own bank, thereby breaking the crushing twenty-six-year monopoly of Charles R. Bishop. Suddenly Bishop was forced to pay higher interest on savings accounts and to reduce his killing rates on loans.

Capping all this frenetic entrepreneurial activity and building upon the government initiatives of the last two kings, in 1881 Spreckels became the real father of Hawaii's tourist industry as well. His Oceanic Steamship Co. brought tourists from the west coast to Hawaii, in particular from San Francisco (Los Angeles was a small town of about 11,000 at that date). So began the enterprise that in the second half of the twentieth century took the place of sugar and became Hawaii's greatest.

King Kalakaua Wins and Loses

Challenges to Kalakaua

Having achieved the reciprocity treaty, King Kalakaua considered his debt to the sugar interests well paid. He then tried to reverse the decline of his native people and to halt for as long as possible the American social, political, and economic advance. To some extent he succeeded, introducing more native cabinet members, worrying the hereditary missionary-business community, and restricting their continual attempts to control or destroy the monarchy. As part of this campaign, he promoted Hawaiian culture, calling for a return of chants and songs and determinedly promoting the hula. (Since 1964 the Merrie Monarch Festival at Hilo on the Big Island, the state's most important resident hula competition, has been named after him.) His opponents and enemies remained largely unchanged and unforgiving; they merely bided their time.

Their opportunity came unexpectedly. Kalakaua was impressed by one Celso Caesar Moreno, who arrived in 1879. Multi-lingual, a former Italian naval officer and civil engineer, and a successful Washington lobbyist, Moreno talked convincingly of schemes to lay cables between California, Hawaii, and China and especially of how to tap into the massive commercial possibilities of China. He also suggested that the king should appoint only native Hawaiians to the cabinet.

The US minister to Hawaii, General J.M. Comly, disliked Moreno (calling him "subtle, crafty, clever"). An important legislative committee rejected Moreno's plans for relations with China, asserting instead that "our interests are with America." A bill to raise a large loan to provide more medical attention for native Hawaiians, which may also have involved a bonus for Moreno, was defeated. Because of cabinet squabbles, Kalakaua sacked everyone and the same day announced their successors, mainly native Hawaiians, which General Comly described as grotesquely unfair. The new cabinet included Moreno, who had only been naturalized that morning and became the new minister of foreign affairs. These moves raised the ire of the king's opponents. Giving Moreno the foreign affairs ministry was an error too, because the diplomatic community united against him. Soon all the king's economic opponents, the US minister, and the French and British consuls collaborated and demanded that Kalakaua dismiss Moreno and the cabinet. Kalakaua resisted for five days, then agreed. But he made a point of writing to their home governments demanding the replacement of the US, British, and French diplomats. Spreckels criticized Kalakaua as a fool to be so manipulated. In huge mass meetings, native Hawaiians who supported the king and Moreno protested that foreigners were compromising their independence.

Perhaps in frustration, Kalakaua announced this was a suitable time for him to leave and take a trip around the world. Princess Lili'uokalani would serve as regent in his absence.

King Kalakua Travels the World

The king left Honolulu in January 1881 accompanied by his aristocratic German valet and two overweight "minders," the Chamberlain Charles Hastings Judd (another son of Dr. Judd) and the Attorney General William N. Armstrong (also son of a missionary). A hundred hula dancers bade him farewell. On behalf of the sugar interests, Kalakaua agreed to discuss in China and Japan their continuing supply of labor.

Kalakaua had a tumultuous welcome in Japan. The energetic young Emperor Mutsuhito, then trying to drag

Japan into the modern industrial world, awarded Kalakaua the Order of the Rising Sun. In return Kalakua instantly and brilliantly invented the "Grand Cross of the Order of Kamehameha" to confer upon Mutsuhito.

Kalakaua also suggested the vague but grandiose idea that the Japanese emperor ought to lead a "Union and Federation of Asiatic Nations and Sovereigns," which would include Hawaii as a sort of counterweight to American and European domination. The magnificent reception the Japanese accorded him also encouraged Kalakaua to suggest a marriage between his niece and the emperor's princely son. The emperor was intrigued by the first suggestion but could do little about it, and his son, already betrothed, diplomatically declined the second—both would have been a direct challenge to US influence in Hawaii.

The Hawaiian royal party visited Peking's (Beijing) port of Tientsin (Tianjin) for a banquet with the Chinese Emperor's Viceroy, then sailed on to Hong Kong to meet the British Governor, to Saigon (Ho Chi Minh City) in French Indo-China (Vietnam), to Bangkok, Thailand, where they were treated to a spectacular regal welcome with river barges and cavalry and a jungle hunting expedition on royal elephants, and then on to British Singapore. Next was a voyage to Calcutta (Kolkata) in British India, from where they crossed the mighty peninsula by train to Bombay (Mumbai). They sailed around the Arabian Peninsula and up the Red Sea to Suez, where they became the Egyptian Khedive's guests in his private train. A Muslim sheik with four wives and several hundred concubines showed them the pyramids. Then on to Italy.

Near London Kalakaua met the Prince of Wales and Queen Victoria in Windsor Castle. On the Continent again, he visited King Leopold of Belgium, the French foreign minister, the governor of Madrid, the emperor of Austria, and the German munitions millionaire Prince William Krupp, whose armaments had helped Prussia to humiliate France and to bring into existence the German Empire. He was also shown the massive Krupp factories. He visited Lisbon and returning to Britain took ship from Liverpool to New York. He chatted with President Chester A. Arthur in Washington DC and by rail journeyed to Kentucky where he purchased some thoroughbred horses. Then it was on to San Francisco, where he looked through the nearby Lick Observatory telescope and prophetically asked if such an observatory might be built in Hawaii. When he returned to Honolulu, he was the world's first reigning monarch to have circled the globe. But his hold on the throne was as unstable as when he departed.

TRIUMVERATE IN CHARGE: KALAKAUA, SPRECKELS, AND GIBSON

Hawaii was politically divided along racial lines, and for some years Kalakaua was able to turn this division to his advantage through his alliance with Claus Spreckels and Walter Murray Gibson. It was Spreckels's money in supporting the king personally through loans and in keeping the country solvent through the massive taxes his sugar and other companies paid to the government that allowed Kalalaua to retain his power.

Walter Murray Gibson, the Natives' Champion

Gibson, the son of English immigrants to the United States was, like a good proportion of the foreigners in Hawaii, something of a mystery. He had various adventures in India and Guatemala, was jailed for being involved in the plots of a Malayan sultan in the Dutch East Indies (Indonesia), and somehow found his way to Salt Lake City in Utah where in 1860 he was baptized a Mormon. As a quasi-missionary he came to the archipelago in 1861, greatly inspired the local mission, and reorganized its funding. Gibson wanted to buy the broad flat saucer of Palawai Basin in Lanai. In November 1861, he confided in his diary:

> There are 10,000 acres of land in this valley.... I hope to influence the government to let us have all of this valley, and most of the island to develop and then we will dig and tunnell and build and plant and make a waste place a home for rejoicing thousands.... I would make millions of fruits where one was never thot [sic] of [in the twentieth century this would occur with pineapples]. I would fill this lovely crater with corn and oil and babies and love and health and... the memory of me for evermore.

Large amounts of money went into purchasing Palawai for a vast Mormon settlement. But reports reached the leaders

Gathering of the Lepers, 1873

Isabela Bird, tiny and tough and the first female fellow of the Royal Geographical Society, rode unchaperoned through some of the least-travelled parts of the Hawaiian Archipelago—to the disapproval of the straight-laced ladies of Honolulu. In this selection from her book, *From The Hawaiian Archipelago: Six Months among the Palm Groves, Coral Reefs, and Volcanoes of the Sandwich Islands*, published in London in 1875, she describes the harrowing gathering of the lepers to be sent to Molokai:

> However, as the year passed on, lepers were "informed against," and it became the painful duty of the sheriffs of the islands, on the statement of a doctor that any individual was truly a leper, to commit him for life to Molokai. Some, whose swollen faces and glassy goggle eyes left no room for hope of escape, gave themselves up; and a few, who, like Mr. Ragsdale, might have remained among their fellows almost without suspicion, surrendered themselves in a way which reflects much credit upon them. Mr. Park, the Marshal, and Mr. Wilder, of the Board of Health, went round the islands repeatedly in the *Kilauea*, and performed the painful duty of collecting the victims, with true sympathy and kindness. The woe of those who were taken, the dismal wailings of those who were left, and the agonised partings, when friends and relatives clung to the swollen limbs and kissed the glistering bloated faces of those who were exiled from them for ever, I shall never forget.
>
> There were no individual distinctions made among the sufferers. Queen Emma's cousin, a man of property, and Mr. Ragsdale, the most influential lawyer among the half-whites, shared the same doom as poor Upa, the volcano guide, and stricken Chinamen and labourers from the plantations. Before the search slackened, between three and four hundred men, women, and children were gathered out from among their families, and placed on Molokai....

of the church in Utah that something was amiss, and after three years a team reached Lanai to audit Gibson's books. They discovered that all the purchased land was in Gibson's name only. He was immediately excommunicated. Most Lanai Mormons then left for La'ie in northern Oahu where the Church of Jesus Christ of the Latter Day Saints thereafter thrived. Today La'ie is the economic and intellectual powerhouse of Mormon Hawaii, with the campus of Brigham Young University and the perennially full Polynesian Cultural center.

Gibson later claimed that his expedient connection with the Mormons was justified by his political aims. He became fluent in Hawaiian, created a slogan, "Hawaii for the Hawaiians," and was elected to the legislature, the only white man to gain such office in Oahu at that date. But he also received bad publicity from the missionary party's Honolulu press. By using a Spreckels mortgage on his Lanai lands and to support his objectives and draw the native vote, Gibson purchased two Honolulu newspapers.

Kalakaua saw something of a Spreckels in Gibson, recognized his business acumen, and appointed him to the cabinet. Soon Gibson was Kalakaua's premier.

Like Gibson, Spreckels became popular with the native Hawaiians because they recognized his genuine desire to help their survival. Spreckels divided his Oahu lands into small sections on which extended families were settled with proper housing. The native Hawaiians shared in the business and were fairly paid. They worked willingly for Spreckels—another counter example to the claim that native Hawaiians were inherently lazy.

Spreckels introduced more capital, employed more native Hawaiians, brought more money into circulation, and generally encouraged more commerce than the rest of the sugar producers combined.

Gibson became the new champion of native Hawaiians, and in the next election he and his supporters were returned with a large majority. Twenty-seven of the candidates sponsored by non-Spreckels business interests had been defeated. Opposition newspapers forecast doom; Gibson's papers argued that the election result merely showed the determination of native Hawaiians to remain independent. Kalakaua formed a new cabinet with Gibson as premier and foreign minister. For some five years he, Gibson, and Spreckels controlled Hawaii, and their missionary-business enemies and rivals simmered in frustration.

'Iolani Palace and Coronation

Kalakaua was dissatisfied with his current "palace," and in 1882 the magnificent new 'Iolani ("Bird of Heaven")

Palace was opened. As a symbol of Hawaii's maturity and as a home suitable for a king, its construction had been ordered by Kalakaua and decried by his opponents as an enormous waste of money. He decided that this was also the time to be crowned.

Kalakaua acknowledged no one, secular or ecclesiastic, as his superior on the islands, so, just as Napoleon Bonaparte had when making himself emperor in 1804, he placed the $10,000 crown on his own head. He then crowned his queen. (The specially commissioned crowns had arrived just in time from Britain.) This coronation took place in 1883 in the elegant little copper-domed coronation stand on the palace grounds, now used as a rotunda for public concerts by the Royal Hawaiian Band. This band's predecessors then began playing coronation music, accompanied by salutes from Hawaiian shore guns and broadsides from US, British, and French ships in the harbor.

A massive *luau* was held for thousands of people. Involving the most exquisite performers from several islands, hula dancing continued until almost midnight. The *Pacific Commercial Advertiser* estimated there were 11,000 people present. Partying continued for days—a marvelous opportunity for the king's opponents to criticize him. The *Planter's Monthly* cried that "the so-called coronation" was "damaging to the property interests and welfare of the country." The *Daily Bulletin* rejected the hula as "heathenism and a disgrace to the age." The *Gazette* thundered that most of the dances were "a deliberate attempt to exalt and glorify that which every pure mind must hold as the type of what is to be kept out of sight, and out of mind as the representative of all that is animal and gross, the very apotheosis of grossness." Kalakaua ignored such opinions.

For more private gatherings of close friends and visitors, Kalakaua preferred his little boathouse, the *Snuggery*, where he, a heavy social drinker, could be more at ease. Even the terminally ill author Robert Louis Stevenson, in Hawaii to improve his health, became a guest there.

Kalakaua enjoyed his leisure, but also supported significant economic developments such as Hawaii's first full-scale railroad, the Kahului and Wailuku Railroad, which opened in 1879. It linked all the main sugar plantations in central Maui and took the products to the Kahului wharves. In 1884 it was extended to Paia farther east, carrying mail as well.

Lacking Judgment and Losing Friends

By this date the sugar industry in the US southern states had revived. The southern planters were pressing their senators to disown the reciprocity treaty with Hawaii. All Hawaiian planters and agencies were deeply worried—all except Claus Spreckels, whose operations were so efficiently run that, unlike the others, he did not need any tariff advantage in the US market.

Because Kalakaua showed little sympathy for their potential bankruptcy, the economically threatened planters cooperated to support anti-Kalakaua candidates in the forthcoming election. Men such as Charles R. Bishop and Charles H. Judd (who had supported Kalakaua to defeat Queen Emma in 1874) gave huge amounts. Their chief editorial support came from Lorrin Thurston of the *Daily Bulletin*. Thurston, grandson of Asa Thurston of the first missionary group, indeed grandson of four missionaries, would later be the key instigator of the coup d'etat. They did well, and their legislators then attacked the government, claiming waste, corruption, negligence.

Unfortunately for Kalakaua, he and Spreckels fell out. The reasons are unclear, but probably had to do with the king's resentment at the economic power Spreckels held over both himself and the kingdom and the sometimes arrogant manner in which Spreckels treated him. As the *Hawaiian Hansard* of 1887 records, a native Hawaiian of the legislature asked pointedly, "Who is in charge of this kingdom, His Majesty Spreckels or His Majesty Kalakaua?" From Spreckels's side, the king's attempt to raise a very expensive loan in London despite a generous offer from the former doubtlessly increased the ill-feeling. In any case Spreckels departed Hawaii in 1886. Kalakaua lost the mainstay of his economic and political life and half of his best advice. As will be explained in the next chapter, his enemies then mounted a coordinated attack aimed at protecting their interests and achieving their aims—and much of their activity was clandestine.

Must-See Sites: Molokai

Always sparsely populated, in pre-contact days it was mystical and mana-shrouded, famous for its fierce human-sacrificing *kahuna*. In 1794 Kamehameha massacred the Molokai warriors and took it into his territories, and here Del Monte had huge pineapple plantations in the twentieth century. There are no high-rise buildings (but instead superb, almost vertical northern sea-cliffs—at 3,600 ft/1,100 m, the highest in the world), no kitsch Hawaiiana, only genuine farmers and ranchers, in fact more farmers than tourists. About 50 percent of the people are of native Hawaiian descent—partly because of the Hawaiian Homelands Act of 1921, which settled many native Hawaiians here. At the insistence of the locals, Maui County, of which Molokai is part, has agreed that tourist development will be confined to the west end and will be low-rise and that the agricultural nature of the island will be retained.

Kaunakakai

The little main town and port, Kaunakakai was put on the world map by the 1935 *hapa haole* (half-foreign) hula song about the legendary "Cockeyed Mayor of Kaunakakai," who does not impress the locals. It is a timeless small town: no traffic lights, false store fronts, no malls. A church steeple is the highest point. Describing sites counter-clockwise around the coast from Kaunakakai we have the following:

The Drive to Halawa Valley

From Kaunakakai, the road east along the south coast is one of Hawaii's most attractive drives, nestled under the mountains of eastern Molokai. Pretty little churches such as St. Josephs built by Father Damien, masses of tropical flowers, forests, and ancient fishponds such as 'Ualapu'e speckle the journey. The road ends in magnificent, amphitheater-shaped Halawa Valley. There are overlooks about 750 ft (230 m) up prior to entering. There are also ruined *heiau* in the undergrowth, and at the far end of the valley waterfalls cascade. Probably Molokai's first settlement was here, from the 600s, with taro cultivation for perhaps a thousand years. The 1946 and 1957 tsunamis forced virtual abandonment, but once again farmers are living here.

Molokai Sea Cliffs on the Pali Coast

At the eastern end of the north coast are probably the highest and perhaps the most beautiful sea cliffs in the world, higher even than

Kauai's striking Na Pali coast. Access is by plane, helicopter, boat (from Halawa Bay en route to Kalaupapa), or kayak. Wailau and Pelekunu Valleys, nestled among the cliffs, have superb ribbons of silver waterfalls running from verdant upper reaches.

Kalaupapa Peninsula and National Historical Park

Built by volcanic action at the base of the great cliffs after the rest of the island was formed, the peninsula is very isolated and enormously beautiful. Its history is poignant: It has been a leprosy settlement since 1866. At first food and medicine were in short supply and banishment there was a virtual death sentence. Relocation of the settlement from Kalawayo to more sheltered Kalaupapa and the dedication of Father Damien improved matters. Damien's body was interred in St. Philomena Church yard before being returned to his native Belgium in 1936.

Because the disease can now be cured, the former patients who continue to live there do so voluntarily. The park serves as a memorial. Hikers and riders on mules can pick their way down the cliff of the famous precipitous Kalaupapa Trail, with its 26 switchbacks and extraordinary views.

NEW ARRIVALS AND POPULATION SHIFTS

A strange relationship between native Hawaiians and sugar soon became apparent: Their population continued to decline as the sugar industry grew. It had fallen from approximately 300,000 Hawaiians at European contact to about 45,000 by 1875. Although population decline had nothing directly to do with sugar, in seizing huge swathes of land and in changing radically the racial, social, political, and economic climate of the islands, the industry contributed importantly to the malaise of the native people.

The proportion of native people involved in agriculture, trade, and industry continued to decrease, but the claim about natives not working on plantations has been greatly exaggerated: In 1873 over 50 percent of healthy male Hawaiians were working on plantations. But a declining Hawaiian population meant that a growing sugar industry would soon be short of labor.

Asians Arrive to Work the Plantations

As early as the mid-1800s, businessmen in the islands were concerned about the issue of labor and made a concerted effort to find a source of such labor for the canefields. At first this effort was directed to other Pacific islands, but this source proved barren. To regulate future contract labor, the legislature passed an act titled "For the Government of Masters and Servants," allowing punishments such as flogging and jail for laborers who broke their contracts. "Imported" laborers were in effect indentured servants, subject to harsh working conditions and severe punishments. The law's first real application came with the arrival of a shipload of Chinese workers in 1852 on five-year contracts. Not everyone greeted them warmly. As early as the end of the 1850s, the *Pacific Commercial Advertiser* complained of Chinese bringing "insecurity to life and property.... The thoughtless importation of coolies a few years ago, because they were cheap labor, is now producing some lamentable fruit in the shape of burglary and murder."

Despite such reactions, the solution to the labor shortage became the increasing importation of Asians in tens of thousands—at the same time making native Hawaiians even more strangers in their own country. (The sugar industry also needed imported labor to counter the continual drain of laborers away from the plantations into the towns.) Chinese continued to arrive and by about 1865 outnumbered Americans and Europeans together. Though Chinese merchants usually assimilated smoothly, not disturbing the social hierarchy, the laborers tended to have a rougher transition. Many struggled under the gruelling conditions, and often workers returned to China or moved into the towns immediately after their contracts expired. So a Chinatown formed in Honolulu, and by the mid-1880s about 60 percent of business licenses in the town were held by Chinese.

Fear of the rising number of Chinese in the islands developed, and in response to pressure from the United States, which had passed a Chinese Exclusion Act in 1882, and not wanting to lose its preferential sugar treatment there, the Hawaiian government passed its own act in 1888. By this time there were about 45,000 Chinese on the island.

To maintain the plantation workforce, from 1906 tens of thousands of laborers from the new US possession of the Philippines were employed. They were the last of the large-scale foreign immigrant groups to arrive in the islands. Hawaii State Archives

The first shipload of Japanese peasants arrived in 1868. By the 1880s, worried about its overpopulation, the Japanese government began to encourage large-scale emigration. Though many returned home, eventually 180,000 Japanese would move to Hawaii as contract labor. The plantation owners welcomed them because they worked hard. As they came to feel more at home in Hawaii, many Japanese men organized so-called mail-order brides. Others married women of different nationalities, contributing to the islands' racial "melting pot."

The plantation owners had their own racially motivated agenda, and, to maintain a racial balance favorable to themselves, began to encourage the importation of Europeans: Portuguese, Norwegians, Germans, and Galicians (from what is now mainly northern Romania). Mostly this effort was without success because the wages were lower than those to which the Europeans were accustomed. However, some thousands of Portuguese came, almost all from the Portuguese Atlantic islands of the Azores. (They brought their ukuleles too, which became a key feature of Hawaiian music.) They were willing to work for wages lower than those other

Europeans accepted—but still much higher than those paid to the Asians. Closer to the racial background of the plantation owners, the Portuguese were often given the job of overseers, called "lunas."

Filipinos would in time become the main sugarcane workers. All such immigrants would contribute to the eventual multicultural nature of Hawaii.

8

Coup d'Etat and Annexation to the United States

The Bayonet Constitution

Hawaiian League

Lorrin A. Thurston and Sanford B. Dole became the leaders of the small but aggressive opposition in the 1886 assembly. In debate Thurston delighted in trying to embarrass the king. As recorded in the 1886 *Hawaiian Hansard*, according to one of the native Hawaiian members, Thurston, "talked very loudly and gesticulated violently. It was perhaps a peculiarity of the honorable member that he could not speak in any other way. The clenching of his fists was very significant." Early in 1887 Thurston, Dole, William R. Castle, and others formed the secret "Hawaiian League," which eventually numbered over 400 (with a handful of mixed-race Hawaiians but no Asians)—by which time it was hardly secret. The league wanted the king to agree to a constitutional monarchy, "to reign not rule" as they put it— or else. But their concept of "constitutional monarchy" was only half-way to that of modern Britain or the Netherlands or Australia. The legislature was to be elected by a minority based on race, which would be achieved through financial restrictions and language tests for voters. Dole's home was host to the group's secret meetings, and Thurston wrote the league's rules.

When legal efforts failed to persuade the king to change, the league decided it might have to use the already existing "Honolulu Rifles," a company of the most physically fit annexation-minded members of the missionary-business community, to force Kalakaua to repudiate Lot's constitution of 1864 and to implement theirs. The 200-man Rifles were well drilled by the magnificently bewhiskered Colonel Volney Ashford.

An American and European volunteer militia company, the Honolulu Rifles played a key part in the revolts and constitutional changes of the late 1800s. Here Captain Clarence W. Ashford stands behind Lieutenant C. J. McCarthy and Lieutenant A. W. Carter. Hawaii State Archives

(Impetuous, he believed their aims could be accomplished in a trice by shooting the king, establishing a republic, and filling the cabinet with league members.)

Then, early in June 1887, a scandal broke over the king's head, precisely what the league was waiting for. Opium had entered the kingdom with the first Chinese laborers, and the traffic expanded geometrically. To control it, in 1860 the government issued a license to sell the opium and awarded this to the highest bidder. Later opium was made illegal, but smuggling and corruption took over, and Kalakaua legalized it again in 1886, by which time the cost of the license was enormous. The scandal broke when Aki, a Chinese businessman who was trying to outmaneuver his rivals, stated that under the advice of Junius Kaae, the registrar of conveyances, he had secretly given Kalakaua $71,000 for the license in several installments for which he had received no receipt. However, the cabinet awarded the license to another dealer for $80,000. Aki said his money was not returned. Kalkaua remained silent. The anti-Kalakaua press seized upon the story, printing relevant affidavits, and to the league's delight most people seemed to believe it. A second scandal erupted at about the same time.

To strengthen themselves against the great powers, especially the United States, Kalakaua and Gibson had tried for several years to form a kind of confederation of Pacific Islands. (They were over a century ahead of their time; the leaders of the many now-independent Pacific island countries have discussed this very idea, and organizations for cooperation have existed for decades.) In July 1880 in a dispatch to the US secretary of state, the US minister to Hawaii claimed that Kalakaua "was inflamed with the idea of gathering all the cognate races of the Islands of the Pacific into a great Polynesian Confederacy, over which he will reign." In 1883 Gibson sent a resolution that opposed all future annexations by great powers in the Pacific. His "Hawaiian Protest" was delivered to twenty-six governments. Some of the replies were caustic. Undeterred, he sent a similar note in 1885.

In 1883 Kalakaua and Gibson attempted but failed to establish Hawaiian protectorates over the New Hebrides (today Vanuatu) and the Gilbert Islands (now Kiribati). The league seized upon this diplomatic disaster, claiming that it was obvious that the king and his government were not only deeply corrupt but also equally incompetent. Later plans to connect with Tonga and to develop a confederation with Samoa went awry and were a calamity for relations with the United States, Britain, France, and Germany, all of which had designs upon one island group or another.

The Bayonet Constitution

On June 30, 1887, a large public meeting was held in very undemocratic surrounds at the armory of the Honolulu Rifles, with Rifles militia lined up outside. Dressed in the Rifles uniform, Lorrin Thurston addressed the meeting. There were few native-Hawaiians present and a complete absence of the tens of thousands of Asians. It was agreed that Kaae be sacked and Aki's money returned, but more important, that Gibson be dismissed, a new cabinet appointed, and most of all that Kalakaua must agree to a new constitution that favored the white population and landowners and ensured that cabinet, not king, would rule.

The Hawaiian League had a draft of their constitution ready by July 6, and a deputation presented it directly to King Kalakaua. He knew spies watched his every move, worried that he might be assassinated, and had good grounds for believing that rejection would bring a coup d'etat backed by the Honolulu Rifles. There exists a striking description of the encounter, written by Clarence Ashford, attorney general, officer in the Honolulu Rifles, and a member of the league:

> The cabinet proceeded in a body to the Blue Room of the Palace for the purpose of submitting [their constitution] to the king.... [There was]... a thundercloud on his brow, that bespoke no pleasant prospect ahead. The document was read to His Majesty, who listened in sullen and somewhat appalling silence.... [Debate] proceeded until about sundown of that long summer day. The King argued, protested, inquired as to the effect of certain phases of the changes... and for considerable periods appeared to be gazing into space and weighing the probabilities of success in the event of a refusal [to sign].... I have spoken of the thundercloud which rested upon his brow... the sullen and forbidding countenance which

he then presented. But at the end, all... dissolved into a smile, as sweet as seraphs wear, as, with apparent alacrity, the King reached for a pen and attached his signature to that instrument whereby he was reduced from the status of an autocrat to that of a constitutional Sovereign.

Lorrin A. Thurston (1858–1931), a lawyer, was the key figure in planning and carrying out the 1893 coup d'etat against Queen Lili'uokalani. He became a very successful businessman, owner and operator of the Honolulu Advertiser. *He encouraged tourism and plantation industries. His interest in science was shown in his support of Professor Jagger's volcano studies, and his exploration of the now famous Thurston Lava Tube near Kilauea Volcano on the Big Island.* Hawaii State Archives

The Adventures of Kamehameha's Statues

In 1878 the Hawaiian legislature allocated $10,000 for a sculpture of Kamehameha I, and the Boston sculptor Thomas R. Gould earned the commission. His cast was converted into bronze in Florence, Italy, and dispatched to Honolulu by ship from Bremen, Germany. In late 1880, the ship and its statue sank very close to the British Falkland Islands in the far South Atlantic. Fortunately, the hardy, practical Falkland Islands settlers were able to reclaim Kamehameha from the sea and haul him ashore.

A passing British ship's captain then carried the statue all the way around the Horn and on to Hawaii by March 1882. The Hawaiian government purchased it and it went to Kamehameha's birthplace, the district of Kohala on the Big Island. Here in May 1883, King Kalakaua ceremoniously unveiled bronze Kamehameha in glorious helmet and feather cloak.

But meanwhile, believing the first statue lost forever, Hawaiians paid for a replica. It arrived in January 1883, two months before the unanticipated appearance of the rescued Falkland Islands bronze. Identical in every way to the statue that was supposedly lost, a great team of horses dragged it to where it had been planned to replace the original, outside Ali'iolani Hale (then Honolulu's most regal and important government building). King Kalakaua unveiled it as well. So, fickle fortune provided Hawaii with two statues of the founder.

Outside Ali'iolani Hale the slightly younger replica stands, usually garlanded with long and elaborate leis, the most photographed manmade object in the islands.

The constitution became known to native Hawaiians and to history as the "Bayonet Constitution"—because of the "standover" tactics of the Hawaiian League. The monarch's authority was much reduced: Cabinet appointments had to be approved by the legislature, the royal veto could be overridden by a two-thirds vote, and the upper house, the House of Nobles, became elective. The oligarchical aspect was achieved by voting restrictions. Two-thirds of native Hawaiian voters were disenfranchised because the constitution restricted the vote to owners of taxable property worth $3,000 a year or earners of considerable incomes. The constitution then gave a vote to foreigners who lived in Hawaii, even if not naturalized, as long as they met the property/income qualification. Some 99 percent of Asians were disenfranchised because voters needed to be able to read and write Hawaiian, English, or some other European language. Meanwhile, the Honolulu Rifles patrolled the streets.

To save himself, Kalakaua also had to dismiss Gibson, already terminally ill with tuberculosis. Thurston and three other members of the league made up the new cabinet. Claiming he was worried about being shot, Thurston wrote in his memoirs a confession that might have come out of the Wild West: "In the light of Kalakaua's very obvious dislike of me... during the entire three years of my cabinet incumbency, I carried a loaded six-shooter in my coat pocket whenever I had to go to the Palace alone. If the King made any attempt to take advantage of his official immunity for assault on me, I should be in a position to counter, without waiting for an official indictment."

Following years of accusation and insinuation from his enemies, Gibson was charged with "high crimes and misdemeanours," specifically with embezzlement of government funds. Careful examination of the books showed he was innocent. The Honolulu Rifles then marched Gibson to the wharf, where Volney Ashford threatened to hang him from a yardarm before being restrained by Thurston and others. Soon Gibson was on a ship sailing for San Francisco. Even there his tormentors would not let him alone. In a trumped-up affair, he was sued in his absence for breach of promise of marriage (he had been a bachelor for 40 years!) by a travelling book saleswoman. The court awarded her the then-enormous sum of $8,000. Her attorneys were Lorrin Thurston, William McKinley, and William Smith—leading members of the league. Gibson died within the year. Under the new rules, Thurston's Reform Party won easily at a special election. Opium was once again made illegal.

Hawaiian Rebellions
The Reform cabinet learned of a plot by Robert W. Wilcox to overthrow the Bayonet Constitution, so they exiled him

to California. Returning, he organized an unsuccessful revolt in 1888. Early in 1889, Wilcox achieved another, poorly organized, armed rebellion with about 80 red-shirted followers who captured 'Iolani Palace and government offices. Thurston's cabinet placed their own troops on strategic buildings, and gunfire was exchanged throughout July 30. Seven Wilcox men were killed and twelve wounded, and Wilcox surrendered. A native Hawaiian jury found Wilcox not guilty of conspiracy by nine to three—he said he had Kalakaua's approval, which Kalakaua denied. Then he suddenly became anti-monarchist and began noisily advocating a republic.

In November 1889, A. P. Carter, the Hawaiian minister to Washington, was prescient in his dispatch to King Kalakaua:

> I have always been opposed to their [US troops] landing, even for drilling, but they have been allowed to so long that they would probably do it whether we wished or not, and it rests with every naval commander to do as he pleases and help which side he pleases.... If a revolution were started against the throne to establish a republic or for any other purpose, they might land and prevent the defence of the throne, all this I think is wrong. I do not think we can get them to agree not to land... but I would try to get them to agree never to land except when the Government was in danger and then only to sustain the Government which is a monarchy.

Fleeing the political hot-house and advised by his physicians to rest, Kalakaua sailed to San Francisco aboard the *USS Charleston* as a guest of the US government. Instead of resting he reveled in, as he wrote, "receptions, balls, dinners, [and] Masonic initiation..." Three weeks later in January 1891, he was dead from a stroke. His closest living relative, his sister Lili'uokalani, succeeded him. She had ruled as regent while Kalakaua was in the United States and on several other occasions when he had been overseas.

Coup d'Etat by American Businessmen
Queen Lili'uokalani
Lili'uokalani was intelligent, well educated, well travelled, musically talented (she composed much fine music,

including the poignant farewell "Aloha 'Oe" now known around the world), and convinced of Christian teachings. She was 52 when she ascended the throne in January 1891. She had a complex personality and was sometimes inconsistent, and she believed her brother had yielded much too easily. Her husband, the American John O. Dominis, died soon after her enthronement, leaving a massive gap in her personal life. None of the four members of her first cabinet had any missionary connections.

Lili'uokalani was soon presented with a large petition of mostly native Hawaiian voters asking her to reject the Bayonet Constitution. Though she wanted to restore royal authority, this was more easily said than done, because so much politicking and plotting was going on out of sight, while fully in sight was the United States' new policy of always maintaining a warship in Hawaiian waters. To support the queen's authority and to warn off other great powers were the two justifications given for its presence.

Unluckily for the new queen, the sugar interests in the American south had won, and in April 1891 the McKinley Act went into effect, ending special treatment for Hawaiian sugar. These changes occurred less than four years after the Hawaiian reciprocity treaty had been renewed for seven years. Hawaiian ministers to Washington protested in vain. With so much of the economy depending on the prosperity of sugar, the kingdom was in deep trouble.

Difficult economic times merely strengthened the belief of native Hawaiians that a strong decisive monarchy was necessary. The league members' Reform Party that had forced the Bayonet Constitution lost the 1890 elections, and the new government disbanded the Honolulu Rifles. League members were pessimistic about the elections of 1892. From their viewpoint, economic and political stability could come only with annexation to the United States. Many members of the former Honolulu Rifles met informally and kept their uniforms and weapons. In the legislature Wilcox derided the queen: "I do not wish to be governed by dolls. I believe no woman ought to reign. They have no brains." Honolulu was rife with gossip about revolts, annexation, republics, and republics as a prelude to annexation.

The queen is shown upon the Hawaiian throne in the throne room of 'Iolani Palace, Honolulu, shortly after her accession in 1891. Hawaii State Archives

An Imprisoned Queen's Prayer

Imprisoned in 'Iolani Palace by the leaders of the republic, Queen Lili'uokalani composed the following prayer:

> Your loving mercy
> Is as high as Heaven.
> And your truth
> So perfect.
>
> I live in sorrow
> Imprisoned.
> You are my light
> Your glory my support.
>
> Behold not with malevolence
> The sins of man
> but forgive
> And cleanse.
>
> And so, O Lord
> Protect us beneath your wings
> And let peace be our portion
> Now and forever more.

During her lifetime, the queen also composed about 150 pieces of music, including hula. Listen to the Galliard String Quartet version of Queen Lili'uokalani's haunting "Aloha 'Oe" (Farewell to Thee) at www.pbs.org/wgbh/amex/hawaii/legacy.html.

Conspiracies Against the Queen

Early in 1892 Thurston, Dole, and a small number of other like minds formed another secret organization, the Annexation Club. Thurston was about to undertake an American business trip and decided to place Washington DC on his itinerary to test the amount of support a Hawaiian settlers' plea for annexation might receive from President Harrison's administration.

In his *Memoirs of the Hawaiian Revolution* published posthumously in 1936, Thurston writes that the US Secretary of State James G. Blaine said that the subject of annexation was of the utmost importance and that he should therefore call upon the secretary of the navy to arrange a meeting with President Harrison. Thurston continues:

> We went to the White House. Mr. Tracy had me wait in an outer room while he spoke with the President. [Tracy then stated that] "the President... authorizes me to say to you that, if conditions in Hawaii compel you to act as you have indicated, and you come to Washington with an annexation proposition, you will find an exceedingly sympathetic administration here." That was all I wanted to know.

Blaine then sent John L. Stevens as minister to Hawaii. Blaine and Stevens had been friends and shared the same political aspirations for about forty years. Both wanted annexation.

During Thurston's absence, the Hawaiian election had produced a legislature with several roughly equal struggling factions. The legislative session of 1892 was contentious. The queen appointed four cabinets in turn, but each was soon rejected by the legislature for sheer politicking as much as matters of principle. Determined to protect their sugar economy and to confirm their position of social and economic dominance in a sea of Hawaiians and Asians, the settlers of the Annexation Club hoped to maneuver a pro-annexation cabinet into office and then force an American annexation bill through the legislature. If these actions were not successful, they hoped the queen would provide them with an excuse to accuse her of unconstitutionally proclaiming a new constitution. They would then carry out a coup d'etat.

The Queen Tries to Change the Constitution

After closing the final legislative session of 1892, Queen Liliʻuokalani returned to ʻIolani Palace for an appointment with another recently appointed cabinet. She asked them to agree to a new constitution that she had written and which had been formally presented to her by a deputation of native Hawaiians. It would restore the royal prerogatives largely to those of the 1864 constitution. Though she knew this constitution would be bitterly opposed, she believed it was in the best interests both of the native people and the country generally.

The cabinet members, aware of the increasing possibility of a coup, were deeply troubled. They advised the queen not to proclaim the constitution for the time being. Dismayed by their lack of support, she agreed to a postponement.

She then spoke to her supporters, indicating "that your wishes for a new constitution cannot be granted now, but will [her Hawaiian words can be variously translated] some future day/sometime/in a short time." Two days later, she and her cabinet made public a notice specially given to the United States minister, Stevens, and all other foreign diplomats that stated that any changes to the constitution would now be sought only by methods allowed for in the Bayonet Constitution.

But mere talk of constitutional change was enough evidence for the Annexation Club to act, establishing another organization led by Thurston, the "Committee of Safety." All except one member were drawn from the Annexation Club. They decided on a coup d'etat to establish a provisional government.

The queen and her advisors were aware that a conspiracy was afoot. The US Minister Stevens had had discussions with the plotters. He shared their aims. So when requested, he refused to protect the queen against any armed insurrection. Some of her supporters then urged her to declare martial law and use her loyal Hawaiian troops to arrest the Committee of Safety. It seems she feared bloodshed and fatefully hesitated.

Meanwhile no such reservations worried the Committee of Safety, who sought the views of G. C. Wiltse, captain of the US warship *USS Boston*, and of Minister

Stevens. Both agreed that US forces would land to protect American lives and property if necessary. Thurston and the Committee of Safety claimed that the queen herself had committed a revolutionary act.

Consul, US Navy, and Coup d'Etat

Lili'uokalani underestimated the determination of her opponents. Within two days, the Committee of Safety (six American Hawaiians, five Americans, one Briton, and one German) asked Stevens to support them in crushing what they called a royal revolt:

> We the undersigned… represent that in the view of recent public events in this kingdom, culminating in the revolutionary acts of Queen Lili'uokalani… the public safety is menaced and lives and property are in peril, and we appeal to you…. We are unable to protect ourselves without aid, and therefore pray for protection of United States forces.

Shortly after delivering the letter, the plotters decided they required more time to prepare. But they had "prayed for protection," and Stevens was not going to miss this opportunity. In the afternoon of January 16, 1893, the captain of the USS *Boston* sent into the peaceful town of Honolulu two pieces of artillery and about 160 marines supplied with haversacks, canteens, and double cartridge belts full of ammunition, as well as a hospital corps, "for the protection of the United States legation and United States Consulate, and to secure the safety of American life and property." The British minister to Hawaii does not appear to have thought there was any such emergency, but he was neutralized politically because there was then no British warship in Honolulu Harbor, a crucial fact of which Stevens was well aware.

A handful of marines were stationed at the US Consulate near the port; a detachment marched up Nu'uanu Street to the office of Stevens, and the remainder went to Arion Hall near Ali'iolani Hale (which stored government archives and cabinet records) and 'Iolani Palace. Meanwhile, the "finance committee" of the plotters began collecting guns and ammunition. The cabinet ministers asked Stevens to withdraw the US troops. Stevens told them to put their request in writing, then kept the troops ashore. Now that the American forces were in Honolulu, the Committee of Safety's forces took over the police station (but only after the queen had ordered Charles Wilson, her marshal of the kingdom and chief of police, and his 270 police to surrender) as well as 'Iolani Palace and Ali'iolani Hale—which they made their headquarters.

Thurston composed the declaration of overthrow:

> [The constitutional situation has] regretfully convinced an overwhelming majority of the conservative and responsible members of the community that an independent, constitutional, representative and responsible government, able to protect itself from revolutionary uprisings and royal aggression is no longer possible in Hawaii under the existing system of government.... It is firmly believed that the culminating revolutionary attempt of last Saturday [the queen's actions] will unless radical measures are taken, wreck our already damaged credit abroad and precipitate to our final ruin our already overstrained financial condition; and the guarantees of protection of life, liberty and property will steadily decrease.... [So the monarchy must give way to a provisional government] to exist until terms of union with the United States of America have been negotiated and agreed upon.

The "provisional government," as the tiny group of rebels called themselves, declared martial law. By the night of the January 17, Stevens had already recognized the provisional government as the de facto government of Hawaii. Lili'uokalani yielded, but only, she said, "until such times as the Government of the United States shall, upon facts being presented to it, undo the action of its representatives and reinstate me." Lili'uokalani doubtless had the 1843 precedent of Paulet and the British government in mind. In fact it would be the year 2002 before a woman would again be leader of Hawaii.

On February 1, Stevens ordered the US flag raised above the government building and formally stated he had placed the "[Provisional] Government of Hawaii under the United States protection." In short, Hawaii had now become an American protectorate. His pretexts were that the provisional government said it feared unrest and had

American Minister to Hawaii John L. Stevens played a crucial role in the overthrow of the monarchy. Hawaii State Archives

alerted its forces and had asked him to raise the American flag to make public his support. Stevens wrote to the state department, "The Hawaiian pear is now fully ripe and this is the golden hour for the United States to pluck it."

Three pieces of diplomatic correspondence several weeks after this date reveal the close relationship between Stevens, the coup leaders, and the American government, the first from American President Benjamin Harrison to Sanford Dole, the second from Stevens to the acting US Secretary of State John W. Foster, the third from Stevens to Walter Q. Gresham, the US secretary of state.

> Benjamin Harrison, President of the United States of America, To His Excellency, Sanford B. Dole, President of the Provisional Government of the Hawaiian Islands.

WASHINGTON, March 1, 1893.

GREAT AND GOOD FRIEND: I have received your letter of January 24, 1893, by which you inform me that the Provisional Government of the Hawaiian Islands has been quietly and peaceably established under a proclamation formally and publicly made at the door of the Government building in Honolulu, on the 17th day of January, 1893....

I am pleased to note the expression of your earnest desire to maintain and strengthen the strong friendship which has for so many years existed between the United States and the Hawaiian Islands, and to assure your excellency that I shall omit no effort which may conduce to the accomplishment of a purpose which I so heartily desire.

May God have your excellency and the people of the Hawaiian Islands in His wise keeping.

Your good friend,
BENJ. HARRISON.

Mr. Stevens to Mr. Foster.
UNITED STATES LEGATION,
Honolulu, March 1, 1893.

SIR: My telegram preceding this dispatch informed the Department of State that quiet... in political and business affairs prevailed throughout the islands. Our qualified protectorate appears to work favorably. It not only tends to increase American and annexation sentiments, but it also operates to prevent foreign complications.... [T]he English Minister here... is very desirous of bringing about a state of things to afford a pretext for landing English marines and sailors, and to bring about a tripartite management of Hawaiian affairs. Hence his efforts to secure the Japanese commissioner to his design....

I still hope to separate the Japanese commissioner from the English minister.

I am, sir, etc.,
JOHN L. STEVENS.

Mr. Stevens to Mr. Gresham.
UNITED STATES LEGATION,
Honolulu, March 15, 1893.

SIR: ... It is necessary for me to state as accurately as possible the practical working of the qualified and restricted protectorate which the United States officials are exercising here.... This restricted protectorate has proved more necessary and beneficial than was fully perceived when assumed.

... [T]he English minister... was bitterly dissatisfied that I had acted independently of him, landing the men of the Boston when they were imperatively needed, while there was then no British vessel here.... [But] the prompt American action had given so much moral support to the new Hawaiian Government that neither the Government nor the United States officials here would consent to any temporary dual or tripartite arrangement as to Hawaiian affairs....

There is no doubt that but for our protectorate, restricted as it is, the British minister would have insisted on the same right to land troops that he had formerly exercised here, while our action of February 1 [i.e., proclaiming a protectorate] and of the days preceding closed the door against complications, [and] saved the Provisional Government from foreign pressure, leaving the United States complete master of the situation....

I am, etc.,
JOHN L. STEVENS.

When Thurston, the real leader of the coup, declined to be president, Dole reluctantly agreed to assume the position. In fact, prior to the coup, Dole had made the moderate suggestion to the Committee of Safety that though the queen should be deposed, the monarchy ought to be retained, and Princess Kaiʻulani should take her place. Meanwhile, a regency should be implemented until Kaiʻulani's majority. His idea had been strongly rejected. The provisional government moved into ʻIolani Palace (the "Executive Building" they called it). Most of the palace furniture was sold off at a series of public auctions between 1895 and 1903. Since its restoration in 1978, a worldwide search has regained many of the lost pieces of furniture, recovered in places as far scattered as Kansas and Ireland.

Then the Democrats took office in the White House. When the annexation delegation that the provisional government had organized reached Washington, it received a cool welcome. The new president, Grover Cleveland, sent James H. Blount to Honolulu to get the facts. His words would be "paramount," said Cleveland. Blount was courteous but tight-lipped, becoming known in the town as "Paramount Blount" and "Minister Reticent." His report was a devastating critique of the coup d'etat and the US naval involvement. But he had not interviewed the provisional government.

The provisional government had proclaimed a new constitution that erected stringent qualifications for voting and political office. No Asians and few native Hawaiians could vote or run for the legislature. This was a constitution by fiat, by dictate. The coup leaders were afraid to put this constitution to a vote, so it was unapproved even by the votes of the general settler community. The provisional government had supposedly risen against the queen for wanting to alter the Bayonet Constitution by proclamation, and now, claiming special rights to liberty and property, they were doing precisely that. At least the provisional government did not maltreat or murder its opponents.

After receiving Blount's report, President Cleveland made a December 1893 speech to Congress that rejected the actions of the rebels. Cleveland said that this project to annex Hawaii "was one which was zealously promoted by the Minister representing the US in that country [Stevens]. He evidently had an ardent desire that it should become a fact accomplished by his agency and during his ministry." Cleveland also said that "if the Queen could have dealt with the insurgents alone her course would have been plain and the result unmistakable. But the United States had allied itself with her enemies...." As Lili'uokalani wrote in her book published in 1898: "If we did not by force resist their [the rebels'] final outrage, it was because we could not do so without striking at the military force of the United States."

Some have said it was also "mission accomplished"; as in the old saying, the missionaries had come to do good and in fact had done well. A hundred years later in 1993, Rev. Paul Sherry, president of the United Church of Christ of the United States, apologized to native Hawaiians for the

Princess Kauilani Pleads in Washington

Born in 1875, Princess Kauilani grew up at Ainahou, her home in Waikiki. The grounds stretched from close to the beach to what is now Tusitala Street near the Ala Wai Canal and possessed a famous banyan tree under which she played.

On January 18, 1893, while studying in England, she received a telegram from Hawaii reporting the overthrow of her aunt, Queen Lili'uokalani. Appalled, at the age of seventeen she decided to leave her school to sail to New York to try to persuade the US government to restore Hawaii's sovereignty. In New York Harbor before a massive crowd and many reporters, she read a prepared statement that challenged the usurpers: "Today I have the strength to stand up for the rights of my people. Even now I hear their wail in my heart.... I am... strong in the strength of 70 million people who in this free land will hear my cry and will refuse to let their flag cover dishonor to mine!"

Many newspapers printed favorable reports. Sympathizers followed her. She met the new president, Grover Cleveland, in Washington soon after his inauguration. Cleveland wanted justice for Hawaii. Kauilani attended benefits, gatherings, and dinners. By the time she returned to school in Britain, she believed her mission had succeeded.

It was not to be. Within a few years Congress moved rapidly toward US annexation. Aware of this distressing trend, Kauilani returned home to be with her beloved Hawaiians. A year later, out riding, she became drenched in a thunderstorm, contracted a rheumatic illness, and died soon after, aged twenty-three. For many native Hawaiians, her unexpected death was a symbol of the death of their country as well.

important long-term part played by his church in the overthrow of the monarchy.

A Few Disastrous Words?

Cleveland soon sent a new minister to Hawaii, Albert S. Willis. He had instructions to reinstate Lili'uokalani if she would agree to amnesty for all who had participated in the revolt. If she agreed, he was to inform the provisional government of President Cleveland's intention and ask it to reinstate the queen. If either Queen Lili'uokalani or provisional government refused, he was to inform Washington and wait for instructions. Cleveland gravely underestimated both the deep affront the queen had received and the profound resolve of the provisional government.

Willis met the queen on November 13, 1893, apologized for US intervention, and asked her if she would grant amnesty to Thurston, Dole, and the others. But she certainly did not want this "dishonorable... lot of adventurers," as the American secretary of state called them, to remain in Hawaii. Unfortunately for herself and for the future of the Hawaiian kingdom, it seems that the queen did not immediately agree to amnesty. In a moment's passion the word "beheading" may have been used, though Lili'uokalani denied doing so and it had never been a formal Hawaiian punishment. Still, the queen's diary entry is in general agreement with Willis: "I told him that our laws read that those who are guilty of treason shall suffer the penalty of death, and their property confiscated to the government. If any amnesty was to be made, it was that they should leave the country forever...." There was of course nothing unusual about punishing treason with death, the penalty throughout the world since early times. Soon after Kalakaua ascended the throne a treason trial had sentenced the accused to death, though this sentence was later commuted to ten years in prison. But a few hasty words can change the course of history. We shall never really know what was said, but Willis decided he needed to refer the whole case back to Washington. Meanwhile, a worried provisional government got ready to repel by armed force any US invasion aimed at restoring Lili'uokalani.

Having received new instructions, Willis met the queen again on December 18. She accepted President Cleveland's terms of amnesty. The next day he met the provisional government and asked them to restore the queen. He received no immediate answer. But around midnight on December 23, Dole personally handed him a detailed refusal in eighteen typewritten pages that went so far as to claim they had not needed American help and blamed the American representatives for landing the troops. "We have done your government no wrong," the document stated. "Our only issue... has been that, because we revered [American] institutions of civil liberty, we have desired to have them extended to our distracted country." This was not what Willis had expected.

Letters of criticism and charges were exchanged between the two governments, but the United States was now in a difficult situation. Not only had its representative (Stevens) acknowledged the provisional government's legitimacy, but other governments such as that of Britain had now also done so. To restore the queen, the United States would have to make war upon the provisional government of Hawaii.

Matters were becoming politicized; President Cleveland was finding it an embarrassment; and in January 1894 the whole issue was turned over to US congressional committees (and their long delays). But timing is everything in politics, so suppose Lili'uokalani had agreed to amnesty on November 13. After all, one of Blount's first actions had been to lower the American flag and order the US marines back to their ship; US Secretary of State Walter Gresham had advised President Cleveland that in the name of justice the monarchy ought to be restored; and Rear Admiral John Irwin, the US naval commander in the Pacific, had been expecting orders to land US troops and remove the provisional government.

With deliberate symbolism, on July 4, 1894, Dole proclaimed that the Republic of Hawaii had been inaugurated with himself as president. It was not a genuine republic, but a change in name only. As the attorney general admitted, "These islands are totally unfit for an ideal republic. In general terms the problem to be solved is, how to combine an oligarchy with a representative form of government so as to meet the case." And in a massive example of government theft, the remaining vast government and crown lands (the queen's lands) were all declared to be the property of the republic, and approved private owners bought significant amounts of such lands.

The United States Congress procrastinated and came to no conclusions except to censure Stevens years later. Senate hearings blamed the queen, though not all members of the committee agreed. No action was recommended.

The five members of the cabinet of the Republic of Hawaii, promulgated by the provisional government, 4 July 1894. From left: Samuel A. Damon, minister of finance; Ernest A Mott-Smith, minister of foreign affairs; President Sanford B. Dole; Alexander Young, minister of the interior; Henry E. Cooper, attorney general. Hawaii State Archives

There would be no restoration of the Kingdom of Hawaii, but for the time being no annexation either.

Counter Revolt by Royalists Including the Princes
When all peaceful attempts to restore the kingdom failed, royalists organized a counter coup. The republic learned of these plans. When on January 6, 1895, they sent police and volunteers to search for weapons, shots were fired at them and one man fatally wounded. The royalists were led by Robert Wilcox, who had now rejected his recent Republican persuasions. The republic's militias forced the poorly

organized royalists back to Diamond Head. Among their number were Lili'uokalani's two sons, Prince Kuhio and Prince Kawananakoa. The royalists retreated into the valleys behind Honolulu. Here they were attacked, some killed, and in a little over a week most had surrendered.

On January 16 the queen was arrested, taken from her house in Washington Place (now the governor's residence), and confined to an apartment in the palace. Some weapons and ammunition had been discovered in her garden. One hundred and ninety-one royalists were tried before a "military commission," five sentenced to death and others to long prison sentences. In fact within a year, all were freed, the foreign nationals who were Americans and Britons being told to depart the islands. Prior to the trials, Lili'uokalani abdicated—a "forced abdication" she said—in the hope of saving her supporters from the death sentence. She too was tried for treason under her married name of Lili'uokalani Dominis. She was sentenced to five years' hard labor and fined $5,000, but was in fact confined in the palace until November 1896—though the republic kept her money and her jewelry was sold.

While Queen Lili'uokalani was taken under arrest by the republic, Albert F. Judd, Dr. Judd's son, the republic's chief justice, entered the queen's house and seized all her records. These included the constitution petition that had been presented to her by the voters. Her records were never returned but guarded by the republic, first by Albert F. Judd, then by his sister's son George R. Carter, and not made public until 1924, more than six years after her death. She had never been permitted to see her records again.

ANNEXATION TO THE UNITED STATES

With the election of Republican William McKinley as president, the leaders of the Hawaiian republic renewed efforts to achieve annexation. The queen's enemies meanwhile had not been idle, but had worked hard at discrediting her name in the United States. The most scurrilous of these was Rev. Sereno Bishop, the Hawaiian correspondent of the United Press and contributor to eastern newspapers, who had changed from her enthusiastic supporter, extolling her, "gracious demeanor, her good sense and fine culture," to an unprincipled enemy. Now an annexationist, Bishop damned her as a savage, according to the *New York Independent,* with such lines as: "The queen allows herself to be influenced by ignorant kahunas, heathen sorcerers... she encourages the lascivious hula... she makes regular sacrifices to the volcano goddess Pele..."

Native Hawaiians did not want annexation. In 1897 they sent two huge petitions signed by virtually every native Hawaiian to Washington protesting against annexation. In the United States itself there was fierce pro and con debate, with both sides making liberal use of words like "duty," "honor," and "destiny." The "pro" lobby included "manifest destiny" men such as Henry Cabot Lodge, Teddy Roosevelt, and Alfred T. Mahan; the latter wanted a worldwide US Navy and Hawaii was a key place in his scheme. Helped by the spirited lobbying in Washington of the queen and four native Hawaiian delegates, the first submission to Congress early in 1898 of a bill of annexation was rejected.

But capture of the Philippines from Spain during the Spanish–American War of 1898 changed the attitude of many. The Hawaiian Islands were now seen as an important strategic site en route. In a political climate of colonialist expansion, opponents of annexation became a minority. So, despite Speaker Reed's six weeks of procedural obstruction in the house and a sixteen day anti-annexation filibuster in the Senate, annexation was approved late in 1898. Congress voted 209 to 91, the Senate 42 to 21. President McKinley was now effusive, convinced that annexation was:

> No new scheme.... Union despite successive denials and postponements has been merely a question of time. While

its failure in 1893 may not be a cause of congratulations, it is certainly a proof of the disinterestedness of the United States, the delay of four years having abundantly sufficed to establish the right and the ability of the Republic of Hawaii to enter, as a sovereign contractant, upon a conventional union with the United States.... Under such circumstances annexation is not a change. It is a consummation.

Hawaii formally became an American territory in 1900. The official ceremony of annexation was scheduled for 'Iolani Palace, August 12, and declared a holiday. Leading native Hawaiians such as Queen Lili'uokalani, Princess Kauilani, and Prince Kuhio boycotted it. In handing over the territory, President Sanford Dole stated: "I now in the interest of the Hawaiian body politic and with full confidence in the honor, justice and friendship of the American people, yield up to you... the sovereignty and public property of the Hawaiian Islands." The American admiral L. A. Beardslee, who was present, commented, "The band of Hawaiian damsels who were to have lowered for the last time the Hawaiian flag, as the government band played for the last time officially the *ponoi* [national anthem], would not lower it. The band also refused to play the *ponoi*, and loud weeping was the only music contributed by the natives."

After annexation, what remained of the vast crown and government lands were ceded to the United States federal government, becoming known as the "Ceded Lands." It is these that modern sovereignty activists say should form the independent or semi-independent native Hawaiian nation.

As they had anticipated, annexation proved good for the Big Five business community. An intermarried, elite group of *haoles* (native name for Caucasians), mostly Americans, a few of British descent, by 1901 they owned most of Hawaii's private land, businesses, cattle ranches, and plantations. They had the largest houses in Honolulu and made sure to keep up appearances: In 1899 one of their number, Henry P. Baldwin, purchased Hawaii's first automobile.

Government of the Territory
In April 1900 President William McKinley signed into US law the Organic Act to provide a government for the new

territory of Hawaii. It would remain the form of government for almost sixty years.

The US federal government took control of immigration, customs, the post office, and the higher courts. As with US states, there were to be an elected, 30-member house of representatives and a 15-member senate. Unlike US states, the governor and secretary of the territory were to be appointed for four-year terms by the US president as were all the higher court judges. With the approval of the senate, the governor would appoint all administration posts such as the heads of the several departments. He also had complete power of veto over all legislation, could not be impeached, and had the authority to place Hawaii under martial law. His power over Hawaii was greater than that of a president over the United States.

A single delegate would be elected to represent Hawaii in the US House of Representatives. He could introduce legislation and inform Congress of Hawaiian concerns, but he could not vote on any congressional bills—not even on bills dealing with Hawaii. The US Congress could amend or invalidate any legislation passed by the territorial legislature.

At annexation, all citizens of the Republic of Hawaii as well as all native Hawaiians were made citizens of the United States (though they could not vote in federal elections). Because most Asians had been excluded from the republic's citizenship, they did not now become US citizens either, so citizens were in a minority.

Political, social, and business connections in Washington DC ensured that Sanford B. Dole was now made first governor of the territory. His appointment meant that the same oligarchy that established the republic filled other appointive offices and so continued to control the new territory. The attorney general and four others in Dole's new administration were his relatives.

The US Census of 1900 established the following population of the territory (in round figures; note that officials at the time distinguished between native Hawaiians of full blood and less than full blood, and that, according to contemporary prejudices, Portuguese were distinguished from other Europeans):

Native Hawaiians 30,000
Part-Hawaiians 10,000
Caucasians (excluding Portuguese) 9,000
Caucasians (Portuguese) 18,000
Orientals (Chinese) 26,000
Orientals (Japanese) 61,000

First Territory Election and Congress

Dole and his Republican Party already controlled the executive, and most native Hawaiians and part-Hawaiians wished to support neither them nor the Democrats. They established a third party, the Home Rule or Independent Party. Its spokesman was Robert W. Wilcox. Given that men of Hawaiian stock formed the largest block of voters among residents, the Home Rule Party easily won the first territorial election. Wilcox was elected first occupant of the politically limited office of delegate to the US House of Representatives. Nevertheless, supporting Hawaiian issues, he served outstandingly from November 1900 to March 1903 and died soon after.

The Organic Act had stipulated that the business of the territorial congress would be conducted in English, but in high dudgeon most native Hawaiian representatives ignored this rule and spoke Hawaiian. So Dole was governor, but, continually opposed by native Hawaiian legislative members, he remained ineffective. In 1903 he willingly accepted the offer of another appointed position as justice in the Hawaiian District Court and resigned from the governorship. For an American politician, his career had been a paradox—though twice made a president and once a governor, he had never been elected to these offices. His successor, George R. Carter, appointed by the expansion-minded President Theodore Roosevelt, was the nephew of Albert F. Judd.

Must-See Sites: Honolulu

The state capital and metropolis has many worthy destinations. Visit www.co.honolulu.hi.us for the city and county of Honolulu and www.visit-oahu.com for the Oahu Visitors Bureau.

Ali'iolani Hale

One of Honolulu's elegant landmarks on Queen Street behind 'Iolani Palace was designed by Australian architect Thomas Rowe and opened in 1874 as a symbol of Hawaii's prosperity. Planned as a palace for the monarchy, the more pressing needs of legislature and supreme court took precedence. In front, the famous statue of King Kamehameha I was unveiled in 1883. Here in 1893 the provisional government declared itself and made its headquarters. The state supreme court meets and the Judiciary History Center is also sited here.

Aloha Tower

This 184 ft high (57 m) square tower with dome, built near Honolulu Harbor in 1926 close to where John Young built the old fort, was for decades the city's best known landmark, and its balconies still provide some of the best views. A chic eating and shopping center thrives below with regular live Hawaiian entertainment.

Hawaii Maritime Center

Operated by Bishop Museum at Pier 7 near Aloha Tower, the Hawaii Maritime Center has exhibits of Hawaiian ocean culture from the birth of the volcanic islands and Polynesian voyages to the arrival of European explorers and whalers. Kalakaua Boat House has interactive exhibits on Hawaii's whaling, the history of Honolulu Harbor, Clipper seaplanes, and surfing and windsurfing. Next door is *Falls of Clyde,* built in 1878, a four-masted square-rigger that brought tea from China to the US west coast and is now a museum. Also moored when not in use is *Hokule'a,* the famous working reproduction of an ancient Polynesian double-hull voyaging canoe.

'Iolani Palace

Completed in 1882 on the site of a small predecessor, this is the United State's only royal palace. Downstairs galleries display royal jewelry, kitchen, and offices of the monarchy. The matching gift shop is the former 'Iolani Barracks, which housed the Royal Guard. The palace is now a US National Historic Landmark.

Kawaiaha'o Church

This 14,000-coral-block house of worship, completed in 1842, witnessed the coronations, weddings, and funerals of generations of Hawaiian royalty. Its blocks were quarried from reefs offshore at depths of more than 20 ft. Interior woodwork was cut from Koʻolau Mountain forests just north of Honolulu. The upper gallery exhibits paintings of royalty. Graves of missionaries, early converts, and the quaint little mausoleum of King Lunalilo stand in the yard.

St. Andrew's Cathedral

Begun in 1867 with its foundation stone laid by Kamehameha V, this one-time Anglican, now Episcopal, cathedral with its arched cloisters was the brainchild of King Alexander (Kamehameha IV) and Queen Emma. Emma went to Britain to raise funds and find an architect. A wall of stained glass was incorporated in 1958.

Mission Houses Museum

Housed in three modest buildings including the early printing house, this museum displays the nineteenth-century history of cultural encounter between missionaries, other foreigners, and native Hawaiians. It is the oldest collection of Western-style buildings in Hawaii.

The State Capitol

Completed in 1969 next to ʻIolani Palace, the Capitol is an imposing modern structure supported by huge palm-like pillars and a large open-air courtyard. The upper-story senate and house chambers are shaped to resemble volcanoes. Before the entrance is a modern statue of Father Damien and behind the exit a traditional statue of Queen Liliʻuokalani.

9

American Territory

Social and Economic Developments

Chinatown Plague and Fire

As time passed, substantial numbers of Japanese and Chinese people settled in Honolulu and other towns as laborers or domestic help or began businesses of their own—mostly to meet the needs of their own ethnic group, as in special foods. At the turn of the twentieth century, Honolulu's population of about 30,000 was more than half Asian. Much of this population was clustered in Chinatown, in an area much the same as today's Chinatown, together with considerable numbers of poor native Hawaiians. It was a crowded and unhealthy place—cesspools often existed directly underneath habitations.

Apparently brought by rats from a visiting ship, bubonic plague hit Chinatown in December 1899 with five deaths. Authorities began inspections of all premises, exterminating rates, closing schools, disinfecting potential carriers, spreading lime, and quarantining Chinatown Many structures were condemned and destroyed. Workers from Chinatown had to pass through a disinfecting station. Rather than be exposed to the accompanying indignities, many workers chose to remain in the quarantined area, and suddenly Honolulu was short of key labor.

When many additional cases of plague were reported, more stringent measures were adopted. There was now a full quarantine of Honolulu Harbor. Supervised by the fire department, the controlled burning of condemned buildings began. However, on January 20, 1900, a strong wind blew the fires out of control. Like Moscow, London, Chicago, and other famous cities throughout history, Honolulu had its own great fire. Water pressure inadequate to stop it, fire raced rapidly through the mostly wooden houses and stores. The structure and twin steeples of landmark Kaumalapili Congregational Church (built in 1837) were quickly engulfed as was the area's fire station. The church was rebuilt some blocks away on Kalihi Corner (now opposite the fish market) and remained the ordinary man's church, in contrast to the wealthy business and elite congregation of Kawaiaha'o Church.

Chinatown was razed. Though there was no loss of life, the fire destroyed the dwellings and businesses of more than 4,000 people. Some of these people believed the spread of the fire, confined almost entirely to Chinatown, could scarcely be an accident, though they could not prove their claims. When the quarantine was lifted, about seventy plague victims had perished. The federal government allocated a very inadequate million dollars to rebuild Chinatown. The inhabitants returned and rebuilt anyway.

The same year, something similar happened on Maui. A major outbreak of plague in the port of Kahului forced authorities to burn down the oceanfront Chinatown and erect rat-proof fences.

Sugar and Labor

In time the Big Five began to take over everything connected to sugar: plantation insurance, downtown Honolulu buildings, and people's homes, as well as loans for construction and general banking. They controlled the merchandizing for not only packets of sugar but all kinds of food through retail stores and wholesale outlets. They moved merchandise by rail and road across the islands and controlled inter-island shipping of passengers and products as well as shipping between the islands and California.

To work the plantations, a few hundred African Americans came to the islands in 1900. The first of several thousand Puerto Ricans arrived in early 1901, exchanging poor conditions at home for equally awful ones in Hawaii. But such small numbers were little use for the plantation owners. To maintain the plantation workforce from 1906, laborers from the new US possession of the Philippines were imported in large numbers. From the beginning in 1852, about 400,000 plantation workers had been imported into Hawaii by the early 1930s. Until the end of World War II, the sugar industry was the giant of Hawaii. Though the number of plantations decreased, overall acreage under sugarcane greatly extended.

In 1905 the Big Five had purchased a California sugar refinery. During World War I, in 1917, the US Trading-with-the-Enemy Act seized H. Hackfeld, a German company and one of the five, valued at $15 million, and reallocated its assets to a newly created company, American Factors Limited. Though there were about 600 stockholders, the other four giants, together with H. P. Baldwin Ltd. and Welch & Co., appropriated most of the stock, and the increasingly powerful Matson Navigation Co. itself integrated with the Five. The labor force doubled to about 50,000 and sugar production grew by about 300 percent to more than a million tons a year. By 1910 plantations owned by the Big Five produced 75 percent of all sugar. By 1933 this number had risen to 96 percent.

Sugar Strikes

In 1909 about 5,000 Japanese laborers went on strike. Given the divide of nationalities and rule strategies of the plantations, all early strikes were confined to single nationalities. There was even a pecking order among the groups. The main reason for the strike was that the Portuguese workers were paid 33 percent more than the Japanese. The Japanese complained:

> It is not the color of the skin or hair or the language he speaks or manner or custom that grow cane in the field. It is labor that grows cane and the more efficient the labor the better the crop... [W]e demand of higher wages of planters in the full confidence of the efficiency of our labor and... confidence in the planters' sense of justice....

Strike breakers (mostly Filipinos) were taken on at twice the Japanese rates, strikers were evicted from their plantation houses, and the strike failed. A second Japanese strike in 1920 had the same result.

The difference was that the planters claimed the 1920 strike was a conspiracy to "Japanize" the territory, whereas they wanted to "Americanize" it. If the Japanese succeeded, editorialized the *Star Bulletin*:

> ... Hawaii would be as thoroughly Japanized so far as its industrial life is concerned, as if the Mikado had the

Ikua Purdy, Cowboy Champion, 1908

Ikua Purdy, the *paniolo* (cowboy), was born on Christmas Eve in 1873 in the cowboy town of Waimea on the Big Island. In 1908 he astonished the American West with his prowess with the *kaula ili* (rawhide lariat) when he won the World Roping Championship in Cheyenne, Wyoming. As Hawaii's most famous *paniolo*, his riding and roping skills were extraordinary.

Ikua was a great-grandson of John Palmer Parker, the American who founded the Parker Ranch. He had royal blood too, because his grandmother, Parker's wife Kipikane, was a granddaughter of Kamehameha I.

Ikua learned his cowboy skills as he worked on the grasslands and upland forests of Waimea and the great snowcapped volcano Mauna Kea. The rancher Eben Low was very proud of his *paniolos* and sought an invitation to compete in the 1908 Frontier Days World Championship in Cheyenne. The invitation read: "Bring your saddle and lariat; horses will be provided at the rodeo."

Though no one expected them to win anything, the Hawaiian-speaking *paniolos*, with their spectacular hat bands, strange saddles, and bright clothing, were instantly the talk of the town. Showy as they might have been, such outlandish riders could not be taken seriously, especially as they were not even riding their own horses.

But Ikua roped his steer in fifty-six seconds flat, leaving the competition open-mouthed. The Wyoming hosts were dumbfounded because they were ignorant of the fact that Hawaii had developed a cowboy culture very early. After all, Captain George Vancouver brought cattle as gifts to King Kamehameha in 1792, the first horses arrived in Hawaii about 1804, and Parker and Kamehahmeha III invited *vaqueros* to the islands in 1832 to teach Hawaiians how to ride and rope wild cattle. By 1834 Hawaii had fully competent cowboys.

In contrast, even in Texas cattle rearing was only a minor part of the economy until after the Civil War. Hawaii was way ahead of the Wild West. Hawaiian Cowboys predate those of Wyoming by at least forty years.

Ikua returned to Hawaii famous and worked another thirty years, mostly as foreman on the Ulupalakua Ranch in Maui. He was honored in many songs. Ikua Purdy died at age 71 on July 4, 1945, and is buried in the rich green curving upcountry of Ulupalakuai.

> power to name our governor.... Is Hawaii to remain American or become Japanese?... The American citizen who advocates anything less than resistance to the bitter end against the... Japanese agitators is a traitor to his own people.

But the problem was sugar growing. The planters wanted and perhaps needed cheap labor. But only Asian peasants would work for such wages. The US commissioner general pointed out that "[e]ither the planters are insincere in their declared desire to Americanize the islands, or else their efforts are at cross purposes with their ambitions." Interestingly, a new kind of Asian-Americanization was occurring anyway. In the year of the above newspaper quotation, the *nisei* (people of Japanese descent born in the US and so US citizens by birth) totaled merely three voters in a hundred; six years later they were eight; and by 1936 they were twenty-five percent of all voters.

In all, over 100,000 Filipino males would also come. They filled the bottom rung of the social ladder and did not integrate as well as the other Asians, and a large proportion returned home after completing their contracts. Though the Filipinos were often divided among themselves (Tagalog versus Ilocano versus Visayan), they acquired a dynamic, able, aggressive leader in Pablo Manlapit, and he encouraged them to strike at the same time as the Japanese. Racial tensions prevented coordination, however, and the Filipinos failed too. Though the owners refused to increase wages, they agreed to improve working conditions.

Encouraged, Manlapit led another strike of 3,000 Filipinos in 1924 on Kauai. The owners tried the same tactics, but this time the Filipinos had armed themselves with machetes and clubs and they stormed against the hired strike breakers. Struggle erupted into riot; the governor, Wallace R. Farrington, called in the police and the National Guard and four police and sixteen strikers were killed. The strike had failed and Manlapit was made the scapegoat and deported.

The Changing Labor Union Scene
The National Labor Relations Act became law in 1935. This was the first time in American history that workers gained real power to unionize and use collective bargaining

to improve conditions. As a result, in 1937, the third strike by Filipino sugar workers, now about two-thirds of all plantation labor, succeeded and they gained a fifteen percent raise.

Although in 1937 the US Supreme Court upheld the constitutionality of the Labor Relations Act, Hawaiian employers continued their strong resistance to unions in the special conditions of Hawaii.

In 1937 the Filipino sugar workers went on strike for 86 days on Maui. The union won a small wage increase and recognition. This was the last strike based on an individual racial group. Henceforth, strikes crossed national lines and were more class-based. "Know your class and be loyal to it" became the theme of future strikes. One of the early union organizers to settle in Hawaii was Jack Hall, a veteran of the bitter 1934 San Francisco maritime strike. He would become a powerful post-war figure.

In 1938 the International Longshoremen and Warehousemen's Union (ILWU) gained control of much of the wharf-front unionism in Hawaiian ports. In a test of the 1935 act, the ILWU, the Honolulu Waterfront Workers' Association, and two other unions organized a united strike against the monopolistic Inter-Island Steamship Company, which was backed by Castle & Cooke and Matson Navigation Company. Potentially, the strike could have been as devastating to Hawaii's economy as later strikes were, because the shipping company controlled so much of Hawaii's trade. In fact, in 1942 when Japanese strategists were considering plans to blockade and invade Hawaii, they studied the way waterfront strikes had restricted Oahu's food supply.

Union and management talks stalled. The company employed strikebreakers to take a ship from Honolulu to Hilo, the main town on the Big Island. Some hundreds of strikers and supporters bearing sticks and clubs marched down Kuhio Road to meet the ship on the pier. Alerted by the company and waiting for them were forty local armed police. To halt the strikers, the police first used hoses, then tear gas, then shotguns, injuring fifty strikers, both men and women. Though no one was killed, it was nasty business and unionists commemorate the incident as the "Hilo Massacre" or "Bloody Monday." It strengthened labor solidarity, but within a few months funds were short and the strike was broken. With many police and strikers related in a small town such as Hilo, the bitterness was intense. On the fiftieth anniversary, a monument was erected.

In July 1940, a harsh dock strike broke out on Kauai and lasted nearly 300 days. Again the community was deeply divided.

POLITICAL DEVELOPMENTS

In 1901 the Republicans engaged in a superb piece of political maneuvering. Annoyed by Wilcox's success, leaders of the Big Five such as Henry Baldwin convinced the handsome son of deposed Queen Lili'uokalani, Prince Jonah Kuhio, to accept nomination as the Republican candidate for delegate to US Congress. As in the past, many native Hawaiians followed this royal example and joined the Republicans, for that party appeared to be the path to political influence and success. The Home Rule Party was seriously weakened, the native vote split, and at the second territorial election in 1902, Prince Johah defeated Wilcox and a Republican Party state Congress was elected. Republicans now controlled the territorial executive and legislative branches of the government. By 1912 the Home Rule Party ceased to exist.

Prince Jonah seems to have believed that by cooperating with the Republicans he would be in a position to improve the lot of his people and to reclaim some of their lost lands, and over the years the personable aristocratic Jonah made a marvelous ambassador for Hawaii and its elite in Washington. But he was under a deep misapprehension—little came in the way of quid pro quo for his native Hawaiian people. The political power Prince Jonah had been unable to manipulate was based on economic power, and the same general clique or caste continued to run Hawaii. As one of them, Attorney General of Hawaii Edward P. Dole, said in a report to Congress, "There is a government in this Territory which is centralized to an extent unknown in the United States, and probably almost as much centralized as it was in France under Louis XIV."

The Big Five maintained lobbyists in Washington so their business views would prevail. Their largest shareholders and top executives controlled the Hawaiian Republican Party. They also controlled the newspapers, and from the late 1920s the radio stations. Showing how genealogy ruled, every Big Five board had at least one direct descendant of a missionary. At one stage on the board of Alexander & Baldwin there were six: William Alexander, Henry A. Baldwin, F. F. Baldwin, William O. Smith, A. C. Castle, and J. P. Cooke. By his death in 1922, even Prince Kuhio's own strong hopes of being appointed Hawaiian governor had come to nothing. That position was a perquisite handed out by the US president to loyal party supporter friends and acquaintances.

Son of Queen Lili'uokalani, Prince Jonah Kuhio fought for the royal and native cause in the 1890s revolts against the settler government and was captured and jailed. Later, for two decades, he became the immensely popular elected Delegate of Hawaii to the US Congress. Hawaii State Archives

Counties and City

Prince Jonah Kuhio's biggest triumph began in 1904 when he and his supporters campaigned for "home rule" in the form of local government through counties. The appointed governor, George R. Carter, who had just replaced Dole, was opposed to the idea for it weakened his power, but Kuhio and the legislature triumphed. So from mid-1905, there were five counties in the territory: Kauai (Kauai and Niihau Islands), Oahu (Oahu Island), Maui (Maui, Molokai, Lanai and Kahoolawe Islands), Hawaii (the Big Island), and Kalawao (the leper settlement on Molokai). Counties were allowed to assess land values and charge a land tax to generate revenue. The new bureaucracy created hundreds of jobs for native Hawaiians.

In 1908 the growth of Honolulu encouraged the formation of a special new entity. The former County of Oahu became the City and County of Honolulu and the office of mayor was established. This arrangement still exists. The other counties would not gain mayors until 1969.

Hawaiian Homes Commission Act

In 1920, under Kuhio's sponsorship, the US Congress passed the Hawaiian Homes Commission Act. The act allocated approximately 200,000 ac of homestead lands, located on Oahu, the Island of Hawaii, Kauai, Lanai, and Molokai, for residential, agricultural, and pastoral homestead 99-year leases for native Hawaiians (with at least 50 percent native blood). Still, this was only a fraction of the millions of acres of "Ceded Lands" (crown and government lands) acquired from the Kingdom of Hawaii via the republic when the United States annexed Hawaii. Partway through the preliminary discussions, Governor McCarthy said:

> I have my doubts as to whether the Act will do all that is claimed, but I am strongly in favor of it and I am willing to give it all the support I can. If it works it will be the best thing that could possibly happen to the Hawaiians and also to the Territory at large. Should it fail the Hawaiian people will have only themselves to blame.

The claim in the governor's last sentence is scarcely acceptable. The best of the Ceded Lands, already in private hands or leased to the sugar plantations, were not included.

Much of the available land was poor. The very first homesteading village, on Molokai, failed when the wells soon drew brackish water.

Commonly, administration of the act has not followed the intentions of its framers and Home Lands have been leased to big business to pay for the administration of the program. Parker Ranch, for instance, has leased about 30,000 ac of Home Lands. County, state, and federal (mainly military) authorities have also taken large swathes of designated Home Lands. The number of leases awarded since 1920 totals only 7,200. At the end of 2004, the waiting list of applicants was over 20,000, including some 12,000 for residential land, with about 6,500 native Hawaiian families on some 30,000 ac of Home Lands.

Military Developments

By the time of annexation, the first (temporary) US Army post had already been established at Camp McKinley near Diamond Head to billet troops travelling to the Spanish-American war in the Philippines. A series of small forts was then built to protect Honolulu Harbor and Pearl Harbor. The coral obstructing the entrance to Pearl Harbor was removed, and beginning in 1902 a 600 ft wide, 35 ft deep channel was dredged. Many US and foreign ships visited. In 1908 a famous flotilla painted white called in enroute to New Zealand and Australia, where it was received with immense enthusiasm and dubbed the Great White Fleet. Construction of a true naval base began at Pearl Harbor in 1909. Schofield Barracks in the center of Oahu opened in 1909 for the Fifth Cavalry. Later installations included Wheeler Field for army aircraft near Schofield in 1922, as well as Ewa Marine Corps Air Station, Bellows Field, and Kaneʻohe Naval Air Station.

World War I

In August 1914, World War I broke out in Europe and elsewhere. The first Allied victory of the war was in fact in the Pacific, several thousand miles southwest of Hawaii, when German Samoa was captured for the British Empire by the troops of New Zealand.

Though a long way from the conflict, Hawaii was still affected. Big business benefited when sugar prices rose

Puerto Ricans Work Hawaii's Plantations

In a fact little known outside Hawaii and their own island, several thousand Puerto Ricans migrated from the Caribbean to Hawaii. Just as Hawaii had been annexed by the United States in 1898, so had their country.

The first of them, 114 men, women, and children lured by false promises of well-paying jobs and good conditions 6,000 mi away, set out in November 1900 to work on Maui. They had worked on coffee plantations destroyed by hurricane in 1899, and they travelled on an appalling journey with water and food shortages. They crossed the Gulf of Mexico in crowded steamships, travelled from New Orleans to San Francisco by slow train across the dry southwest, then sailed to Hawaii on even more crowded ships. Many abandoned the journey—only 56 arrived, exhausted. Poor conditions in Puerto Rico became almost slave conditions on the Hawaiian sugar plantations— just "trabajo y tristeza," work and sorrow.

By 1902, Puerto Ricans worked on 34 plantations on various islands. There were four clerks, eleven lunas, fifteen railway laborers, nine mill hands, and what the planters really wanted, 1,734 field hands and laborers. In time, more than 5,000 Puerto Ricans made the journey to Oahu, Maui, and the Big Island. Despite brutal conditions and being forced to buy food and goods from the owners, most stayed on the plantations to work, many perpetually in debt. Younger and more enterprising members moved to California.

Those who stayed integrated into the community and inter-married with other races. Still, a Puerto Rican presence continued and continues to exist. They sustained their heritage of food, dances, and religion, and much of these traditions has been absorbed into the broad Hawaiian multicultural stream—the Puerto Rican rhythms in Hawaiian music, for instance.

considerably. About 200 young male Hawaiian residents of British ancestry soon departed for Britain or for other British countries such as Canada to join the armed forces. Though the United States did not enter the war on the Allied side until April 1917, over several years the involvement of American troops became increasingly likely, and about 10,000 Hawaiian citizens served either in

Somerset Maugham on Honolulu, 1916

The famous novelist and short-story writer Somerset Maugham was a British secret agent during World War I. Around the middle of 1916, en route to Russia, he passed through Honolulu, the title of the story from which this extract is taken:

> The shops are filled with all the necessities of American civilization. Every third house is a bank and every fifth the agency of a steamship company.
>
> Along the streets crowd an unimaginable assortment of people. The Americans, ignoring the climate, wear black coats and high, starched collars, straw hats, soft hats, and bowlers. The Kanakas [native Hawaiians], pale brown, with crisp hair, have nothing on but a shirt and a pair of trousers; but the half-breeds are very smart with flaring ties and patent-leather boots. The Japanese, with their obsequious smile, are neat and trim in white duck, while their women walk a step or two behind them, in native dress, with a baby on their backs. The Japanese children, in bright-colored frocks, their little heads shaven, look like quaint dolls.
>
> Then there are the Chinese. The men, fat and prosperous, wear their American clothes oddly, but the women are enchanting with their tightly-dressed black hair, so neat that you feel it can never be disarranged, and they are very clean in their tunics and trousers…. Lastly, are the Filipinos, the men in huge straw hats, the women in bright muslin with great puffed sleeves.

National Guard military units or travelled to the mainland to join up. 102 were killed.

For the three years prior to direct US involvement, the arrival of German vessels seeking shelter in neutral US waters generated excitement in Honolulu. In October the German gunboat *Geier* and its coaling vessel were given three weeks to make repairs before they were required to depart. Meanwhile the Japanese battleship *Hizen* (Japan was on the Allied side in World War I) patrolled just outside the three-mile limit ready to sink the *Geier* immediately once it departed port. Knowing they were outgunned, the Germans refused to leave, and the *Geier* was seized by the United States. When the United States entered the war, the German crew sabotaged the ship and were then interned on the US mainland.

As in mainland US, the government issued "liberty loans" and special savings stamps to generate war funds. Hawaii observed meat-less, wheat-less, pork-less days and dug school and home gardens to supplement food stocks. "Banana bread" became a popular addition to the normal diet.

Despite Japan's support and importance as a trading partner, formal naval limitation agreements in the 1920s, and Taisho democracy in Japan itself in the 1920s and early 30s, the US government remained wary of Japan's increased military and naval power. It therefore maintained a large Pacific fleet based in Pearl Harbor and the Philippines.

ROARING TWENTIES AND DEPRESSING THIRTIES

The "Roaring Twenties" hit Hawaii like everywhere else in the Western world, though perhaps more muted than in mainland US. The use of motorcycles and automobiles increased (though traffic lights didn't arrive until close to World War II). Electrical appliances such as vacuum cleaners and refrigerators became available, though only for the wealthy. Crazes like jazz and controversial new dances like the Charleston and Turkey Trot arrived, and many middle class homes had a *pianola,* or piano. New fashions proliferated, such as flat chests and cloche hats. Radio stations thrived and in the late twenties so did films with sound, or "the talkies." Bathing beauty contests began.

Civil aviation burgeoned, with the first commercial flying school in Honolulu in 1921. In 1927 James D. Dole (a relative of Sanford Dole), of the mighty pineapple company, announced a race from California to Oahu, the "Dole Derby," with a first prize of $27,000 (worth millions now). Eight planes competed, two finished, and appallingly, of the sixteen pilots and navigators, twelve perished at sea. But this was 1927, the public still regarded flying as dangerous anyway, and Dole managed to avoid adverse publicity.

In 1928 Hawaii became a stop-over in the first-ever cross-Pacific flight by the Australian pilot Charles Kingsford-Smith from Oakland, California, to Brisbane, Australia. He was accompanied by an Australian navigator and two American crewmen.

A lone worker is shown with his horse-drawn plough in the vast pineapple fields of the Hawaiian Pineapple Company in the volcanic Palawai ("Pond Scum," after the early morning fog) Basin in Lanai, now largely deserted. Lanai's highest point, Lanaihale, rises in the background.
Castle & Cooke Resorts

Then the 1929 Wall Street crash hit Hawaii along with the Depression, although as usual the economic changes were delayed and less devastating than in mainland US. Resources shrunk and unemployment grew, as did bankruptcies and people on relief, and construction almost ceased. Tourism also dropped radically. Lawrence M. Judd, a grandson of Dr. Judd, had been appointed governor of Hawaii a few months previously by President Herbert Hoover. Like his counterparts elsewhere, he became the victim of the economy rather than a controller and found himself hamstrung.

But the United States still needed its sugar, and though sugar prices dropped and some plantations lowered wages and instituted shorter hours and dismissals, the sugar economy improved after the low point of 1932. Hawaiian unemployment was also lessened when some thousands of Filipinos on contracts returned to their homeland in 1932 and 1933.

The situation was very different with pineapples. In 1922 Dole had purchased all but a few hundred acres of the island of Lanai from the cattle rancher Henry Baldwin, and soon integrated all aspects of the industry. Lanai grew a significant proportion of the world's pineapples. These were a luxury item, and soon mainland grocers were unable to sell their stocks. By the end of 1931, the Dole Co. had about three million cases of tinned pineapples in its warehouses and tens of millions of plants in the fields, most destined to rot. Dole's Hawaiian Pineapple Co. retrenched, suspended dividends, reorganized, and Castle & Cooke became the majority shareholders. Such changes, together with cooperation among planters and a new procedure to extract pineapple juice, allowed the company to show a profit in 1934.

Hawaii's Japanese

In 1924 the US government passed a law that excluded further Japanese immigration into the United States. Though the Japanese were the largest racial group in Hawaii in the 1920s, they represented only a few percent of registered voters. But by working and studying hard and gaining in prosperity, they became the largest racial voting block by the mid-1930s. Because the powerful Caucasians

Thalia Massey "Abduction," a Racial Allegory, 1931

In September 1931, Hawaii was rocked by a spectacular alleged rape and abduction. This was the era of Prohibition, the banning of all alcohol in the United States, and Prohibition of course applied to US territories. But the locals in Hawaii produced a strong illegal alcoholic concoction from the *ti* plant, which was openly consumed, especially on Saturday night.

Thalia Massie, 21, wife of a submarine lieutenant based at Pearl Harbor and daughter of a wealthy East Coast family, had been partying with her husband's Navy friends, most of whom she disliked, at the Ala Wai Inn near the canal at the west end of Waikiki. After an altercation with one of her group whose face she slapped, she walked alone down the road toward Ala Moana. An hour later she staggered into the road, stopping a car driven by white men with the story that she had been beaten by five or six young Hawaiian "boys." Her jaw was broken and her face was bruised, but she did not want to contact the police. The driver took her home and when her worried husband found her, she said she had been beaten and raped. He phoned the police and took her to hospital.

Within 24 hours, five young suspects had been arrested on an entirely unrelated minor assault across town, a long way from where Massie had been. (In the hospital Massie had heard their arrest being discussed on a police radio, and she soon produced a much more detailed description of her case and claimed attackers—even the car's number, which she had never before mentioned.). Having failed to discover any other suspects, the police conveniently assumed these must also be the Massie five. Two suspects were Japanese, two Hawaiians, the fifth Chinese-Hawaiian. Though they strenuously denied involvement with Massie, three had prison records. Except for Massie's claims, there was no evidence that they were involved. On none of the bodies or clothes of the suspects (or of Massie) was there any evidence of sexual activity. Still, the newspapers assumed their guilt.

Evidence was so conflicting that the jury could not agree, a mistrial was declared, and the suspects were allowed out on bail. Powerful people in the community pushed for another trial. Meanwhile, several sailors kidnapped one of the five, the Japanese Horace Ida, and in an unsuccessful attempt to have him confess, beat him unconscious in an isolated cane field. Honolulu was in a racial frenzy, and thousands of miles from the evidence, the mainland press had long ago found the five guilty.

When a retrial looked unlikely, Massie's mother, Mrs. Grace Fortescue, who had arrived on the first available ship, concocted a plot with Massie's husband Lieutenant Thomas Massie and two naval acquaintances to kidnap Joe Kahahawai, one of the Hawaiians. They interrogated Kahahawai, and someone in their group shot him dead.

During their attempt to dispose of Kahahawai's body in the ocean, they by chance became involved in a high-speed chase with the police. The police fired shots and the car was stopped near Hanauma Bay, a former volcano and now an extremely popular tourist snorkeling site. Fortescue and Lt. Massie and their two accomplices were all charged with second-degree murder. At their trial, despite being defended by the famous Clarence Darrow, the Hawaiian jury found the four guilty of manslaughter but recommended leniency. The guilty verdict created a furor on the mainland and US congressmen pressured Governor Judd to pardon the murderers.

Two weeks later, the judge sentenced the defendants to ten years' hard labor. Within minutes the four were taken to Judd's office across the road from the courthouse. Judd, concerned that if the sentences were enforced, the US Congress might further restrict Hawaii's territorial self-government, commuted all sentences to only one hour. All four defendants had to leave Hawaii and there would be no retrial of the four surviving local Hawaiians. Distorted reporting of the whole affair had an exceedingly negative effect on Hawaii's image in the mainland US.

of the Republican party controlled the territory's politics and patronage, for expedient reasons, the Japanese identified with that party and thus acquired some middle-class positions and trappings, but for the most part remained deferential and were careful not to be seen as constituting any political or social challenge.

Also in the 1930s, ships of the Japanese Imperial Navy began occasional friendly visits. They were particularly well received in the town of Hilo on the Big Island, whose ethnic population was 60 percent Japanese. But as US–Japan tensions increased, such visits ceased and mainland Americans became suspicious of Hawaii's many Japanese.

Native Hawaiians
In the mid-1850s native Hawaiians comprised about 95 percent of the population. By 1930, in a census of 368,000 people, only 6.15 percent were pure Hawaiian and 7.66 percent claimed part-Hawaiian blood. The Caucasian and Asian competitive society, which emphasized thrift, education, and social climbing, were alien to native

Hawaiians and left many of them demoralized. At the aristocratic level, however, there had been much intermarriage between Caucasians and native Hawaiians, and these people and their descendants joined the elite group.

INTER-WAR TOURISM

Besides Spreckels's efforts, Queen Lili'uokalani promoted tourism in 1892, prior to the coup. A Hawaiian Promotion Committee was created in 1902. World War I largely killed tourism, but it thrived during the "Roaring Twenties." To keep Hawaii beautiful and with amazing foresight, billboards were banned in 1927. In 1929, just prior to the Great Depression, Hawaii drew about 22,000 visitors. But it was not just tourists who travelled on the great steamships between California and Honolulu—one's family and

Honolulu, 1930s. A woman views a panorama of low-rise Honolulu from the heights of Punchbowl. In the distance a Matson liner enters Honolulu Harbor; behind it, Sand Island. To its right stand the chimneys of the powerhouse and the isolated Aloha Tower, the highest structure in the islands. Below the liner appear Ali'iolani Hale, Honolulu Hale (city hall), and 'Iolani Palace. In the middle right are the tower and roof of St. Andrew's Episcopal Cathedral. Hawaii State Archives

friends did too, and their arrival on "Boat Day" was marvelous, as Peggy Hicock Hodge nostalgically explains:

> Hundreds of hot, sweaty bodies of excited people on the second floor of the pier squirming in position to say aloha. Everybody was meeting somebody—like a huge reunion of the whole town—relatives, friends, businessmen, old teachers, classmates.... [T]he Royal Hawaiian Band... blared with brass and woodwinds and

Worshipping at Shirley's Temple,
1935

In the 1930s, while the United States and the world were experiencing the worst economic depression in history, while Hitler was seizing Germany and the militarists were taking Japan, a tiny Hollywood film star brought relief and immense pleasure to filmgoers almost everywhere films were shown. Her ever-smiling face, shining in wholesome, light-hearted, cleverly crafted films, helped them forget their troubles. She was Shirley Temple, born April 23, 1928. In the days before television, she was a megastar before that term had been invented, and her face was one of the two or three most famous in the world.

This dimpled, singing, tap-dancing darling with golden ringlets (gold only on the billboards, not in the black and white movies) had already made many hit films before 1934 when she starred in *Bright Eyes*, noted for her delectable song "On the Good Ship Lollipop," her most famous. She was given a special academy award for this role.

Now it was Hawaii's turn to share her celluloid success. With her parents (her mother was the passionately dedicated force guiding her career), she arrived in Honolulu on July 29, 1935, on the luxury Matson liner *Lurline*. The newspaper *Star-Bulletin* headlined "Depression is ended." Duke Kahanamoku, sheriff of Honolulu, welcomed her, as did the captain of Pearl Harbor Navy Yard and 10,000 cheering grown-ups and children who thronged Pier 11 to sinking point. Shirley immediately thrilled them with a dockside rendition of "On the Good Ship Lollipop." She met the governor, Joseph B. Poindexter, in 'Iolani Palace and repeated the song. Cameramen, reporters, and crowds followed her trail everywhere. A Shirley Temple non-alcoholic cocktail was concocted at the Royal Hawaiian Hotel, Waikiki. She was on the front pages of the papers every day for three weeks.

Before the end of the 1930s, Temple was the most successful performer in the world. She made later visits to the islands, but the one in 1935 was her greatest.

steel guitars the nostalgic songs everyone knew—
"Akaka Falls" with the tremulous falsetto voice of Lena
Machado, "Hawaii's songbird," reaching to the rooftops
of the rusted, weathered corrugated ceiling and beyond;
"The Song of the Islands," that left you "chicken-
skinned" and teary-eyed.... Eager voices cried out for
friends and relatives aboard. An electrifying tremor
passed through the crowd when the band finally surged
into the martial strains of "Hawaii Ponoi," our anthem,
followed by a lively hula with everyone swaying and
clapping in rhythmic beat.... Bells clanged, whistles
blared.... Off [the passengers] came, waving and
shouting to the crowds below who greeted their loved
ones with embraces and leis.

Naturally there was a decline in tourists in the early 1930s,
but as the economy improved, special efforts went into
developing tourism and attracting conventions. Beginning

*Opened in 1901, the Moana Hotel was Waikiki's first major modern hotel,
though there had been large hotels in downtown Honolulu in the second
half of the 1800s.* Hawaii State Archives

in 1935, the Hawaii Tourist Bureau paid for a radio program "Hawaii Calls." Normally broadcast short wave from the *lanai* (veranda) of the Moana Hotel and produced by Webley Edwards, the show was heard on the mainland and carried by networks in Australia and Canada. Short wave took it to the world, and it received fan mail from as far away as Britain and South Africa. Almost all island entertainers were featured, many going on to be well known, such as Lena Machado, Alfred Apaka, Nina Keali'iwahamana, Haunani Kahalewai, Pua Almeida, Harry Owens, Sol Bright, Al Kealoha Perry, Benny Kalima, Danny Kaleikini, Palani Vaughn, Bill Kaiwa, and more. Many of them, aware of their massive radio audience, were inspired to write songs that the world now associates with Hawaii. Radio's significance in alerting the world to the existence of Hawaii can hardly be exaggerated.

In the same year, Pan Am began mail flights from the mainland to Honolulu in its famous "Clipper" seaplanes or flying boats. Passenger flights to Honolulu were inaugurated

This is Pan American Airlines' 74-passenger (sleeping berths for 36) Boeing 319 Cal. Clipper seaplane/flying boat, floating near Ford Island Seaplane Base in Pearl Harbo its first flight in 1939 from San Francisco to Honolulu. From Honolulu it flew via N Island and Wake Island to Manila, refueling at each stop. The largest commercial pla

from San Francisco in 1936 and from Auckland, New Zealand, in 1939, but these had little tourist impact.

Tourists were mostly wealthy people who travelled on the luxurious and leisurely Matson liners, the first and most famous of which was the *Malolo*. The line constructed the first hotels in Waikiki to provide proper accommodation, equally expensive. The prince of these was the pink stucco *Royal Hawaiian*, completed in 1927, which still exudes chic and cachet. However, because it was constructed on a former swamp and so close to the beach, the builders had some problems with subsidence. To provide more land for hotels and businesses, reclamation of water-logged Waikiki began from 1921 to 1929 with the Ala Wai Canal. Soon famous film stars such as Mary Pickford, Douglas Fairbanks, and the superb child star Shirley Temple, as well as plutocrats such as the Rockefeller family, were arriving.

By 1940, with growing likelihood of war, Matson's liners became carriers of military personnel. Economically, military spending would soon take the place of tourism.

produced prior to the Jumbo, only twelve of the luxurious and safe 319s were built. Crusing speed was 183 mph (www.flyingclippers.com/B314.htm) Hawaii State Archives

Hawaii Begins the Chinese Revolution

An elegant statue of Sun Yat-Sen stands in the northwest corner of Chinatown in North Beretania Street near Nu'uanu Stream. Hawaii has been called the "Cradle of the Chinese Revolution," for it was in Honolulu that Sun Yat-Sen established the first Chinese revolutionary body of the twentieth century, the Hsing Chung Hui (Revive China Society). In 1905 it became the strong political party Deng Meng Hui (Alliance/Sworn-Together Society). And it was in Honolulu that Sun and perhaps a hundred other Chinese first vowed to bring down the Manchu Dynasty.

Nine uprisings later, in 1911, Sun Yat-Sen's Deng Meng Hui overthrew the decayed Manchus and developed into the powerful Guomindang (or Kuomintang—the Nationalist Party). The very first of these uprisings in Guangzhou (Canton) was funded with about $6,000, mostly Hawaiian-Chinese money. As Sun writes in his autobiography, "I advocated for many months, and very few people responded." It was mainly Chinese-Hawaiian relatives and friends who contributed substantially.

Each member of Hsing Chung Hui paid $5 as membership, and stock was sold at $10 a share, to be repaid as $100 after the proposed revolution had succeeded. Later uprisings, which required much larger funds, still found Hawaiian support but raised most of the money in Hong Kong, Japan, Europe, Canada, and the United States.

Still, it all began in Honolulu. In fact, one can probably argue that without Chinese-Hawaiian money, there would have been no Sun Yat Sen/Deng Meng Hui Revolution, no Guomindang, and so no Mao in 1949 either.

Nevertheless, in 1941, the year of Pearl Harbor, tourist numbers had again increased to 32,000 and the hotel industry struggled to keep pace.

WAR PREPARATIONS; SOME JAPANESE DEPART

In September 1940, with the war in Europe and China worsening, the US Congress introduced the draft that required every male between 18 and 35 to register for compulsory military service, and in November Franklin D. Roosevelt was elected to an unprecedented third term as president.

From early 1940 to mid-1941, the area and facilities at Pearl Harbor were greatly expanded as was the civilian workforce needed for construction. Soon the Navy Yard was able to manufacture steel casings of almost any size. Military preparations at Schofield Barracks and elsewhere paralleled these developments, and Honolulu became a boom town.

In February 1941, Admiral Husband E. Kimmel was made commander of the naval district at Pearl Harbor and of the whole Pacific fleet. He replaced Admiral James O. Richardson, who had been dismissed after claiming that the facilities at Pearl Harbor were inadequate, that moored ships were at risk from the air and too far from adequate military support, and that for safety the fleet should be based in California. Though in hindsight he appears to have been correct, President Roosevelt and relevant cabinet members opposed his views. Kimmel, presumably elated at his appointment, would soon come to regret it.

In April the Japanese passenger ship SS *Kamakura Maru*, carrying German and Japanese evacuees from mainland US, stopped at Honolulu to transport about 250 Hawaiian Japanese who wanted "to return home."

Ordinary activities and simple pleasures remained important. In September 1941, Clark Gable and Vivienne Leigh's classic romantic epic *Gone with the Wind* was showing at local cinemas, as were the escapades of Bob Hope, Bing Crosby, and Dorothy Lamour in *The Road to Zanzibar*.

Events more serious than anything shown in Hollywood's celluloid fantasies were about to unfold. A year earlier, the top secret code of the Japanese diplomatic corps had been deciphered. A handful of chief intelligence officers in Washington had been monitoring Japanese diplomatic correspondence around the world. The consensus among the elite military and the cabinet was that Japan would attack the United States and the British Empire and Commonwealth late in 1941.

10

PEARL HARBOR AND WORLD WAR II

CONSIDERABLE FORESIGHT IN PRE-WAR PREPARATION

Two days after the Japanese had devastatingly attacked the US naval base of Pearl Harbor and other service installations on Oahu, the secretary of the Territorial Medical Association received an urgent radiogram from Washington. The US Office of Civil Defense advised his members to take "immediate action" to establish medical field units, train volunteers, and so forth. Fortunately for Hawaii, all this and much more had been organized months and in some cases more than a year earlier.

Being geographically closer to Japan and having a large proportion of residents of Japanese ancestry, people in Hawaii were more aware of the world situation and more realistic than many in the mainland US. There were, however, some who held the attitude that "it can't happen here." So preparing Honolulu was not easy.

In May 1940, members of the Hawaiian chapter of the American Red Cross who had been active in arranging "Bundles for Britain" (the British had already been at war with Nazi Germany for nine months) decided it would be sensible to plan for an emergency at home. They began by preparing large numbers of bandages. To their dismay, they found that supplies of cotton cloth were inadequate and only one pair of bandage scissors could be bought in all Honolulu.

Still, preparation steadily progressed. In June (19 months before the attack), doctors and nurses began first-aid classes for volunteers in the throne room of 'Iolani Palace. Within a few months, 50,000 surgical dressings were ready. They also established a blood plasma bank. Schools were surveyed to be used as first aid stations. Civilian police volunteers were trained. Plantations organized provisional police forces, produced defense plans, and paid for firefighting equipment and the construction of plantation hospitals. They also allowed the Army to use their lands. Business houses donated ambulances. The Honolulu Medical Preparedness Committee had mobilized 3,000 volunteers by June 1941 to render emergency help.

In May, supported by all the relevant civilian and territorial government bodies, a crucial bill for $8,415,000 to fund preparations such as first-aid stations, more firefighters, and so on went before the Territorial Legislature. To people's disgust, it failed to pass the lower house—blocked apparently by personal animosities. A special session of the legislature passed the bill in September.

Large numbers of workers were arriving in Hawaii for war preparation and many had union experience on the US west coast. Union membership had reached about 10,000 early in 1941, and in June 1941 the ILWU and Castle & Cooke Terminals signed Hawaii's first written wharf workers union contract. The agreement was propitious because it allowed peace on the wharves at this crucial moment.

There were practice "black-outs." People stocked emergency foods. The Hawaiian Pineapple Co. constructed a half-million dollar warehouse of canned foodstuffs. The Army spent some $750,000 on a great underground warehouse to provide Oahuans with three months of normal food supplies. (This was a huge amount, because in 1941 lamb and steak cost about 35 cents per pound and grapefruit were about 12 cents each.) The common view that the people of the territory were taken by surprise when war broke out is quite false.

On November 27, the US government and military leaders decided to take all aircraft carriers to sea and move half the Army planes from Pearl Harbor. A dispatch went out to all commanders in the Pacific: "This dispatch is to be considered a war warning. An aggressive move by Japan is expected within the next few days. This will probably be an amphibious expedition against either the Philippines, the Thai or Kra Peninsulas, or possibly Borneo." The military was also warned to beware of local Japanese saboteurs in Oahu. On November 30 and again on the day before the attack, Frank Knox, the secretary of the Navy, announced that "The Navy is ready to meet any threat." Given that so many communications between Tokyo and the Japanese Consulate in Honolulu relating to US naval movements had been decoded, whether Pearl Harbor should have been given more warning by the government remains a controversy.

PEARL HARBOR, OTHER BASES ATTACKED

Twenty-nine year old Takeo Yoshikawa (a.k.a. Morimura Tadasi) spied on Pearl Harbor and Honolulu for eight months before the attack and provided the Japanese military with crucial information. No one took particular notice of him because the population held so many Japanese. Some days he wore the clothes of a sugarcane worker when he climbed to Aiea Heights above Pearl Harbor to spy on ship and plane movements. From ideal Aiea, the naval base and Honolulu lay spread before him like a model. He discovered that warships were generally home during weekends, that warplanes were parked at nearby Hickham Field, and that planes rarely patrolled north of Oahu. Other days he wore a business suit and worked as a secretary at the Japanese Consulate on the Pali Highway, where it still stands. After the United States declared war and because they possessed diplomatic immunity, Takeo and the entire consulate staff were shipped back to Japan—and great honor.

It took the six-aircraft carrier force of the Japanese eleven days to sail the 4,000 mi from Yokohama, via a rendezvous in the far north Kuril Islands, to within about 200 mi of Honolulu. A few days after the carriers, 27 submarines departed, all with seaplanes for reconnaissance, and on five, a midget submarine. The midget subs were to sneak into Pearl Harbor to launch torpedoes after the air attack had begun. The large submarines were to wait beyond the harbor to torpedo fleeing US ships.

At 6 AM on December 7, 1941, led by Commander Mitsuo Fuchida, the first wave of 43 Zero fighters, 49 high-level bombers, 51 dive bombers, and 40 torpedo bombers took off to attack. The planes carried no parachutes. The Zero was at that date far superior to the standard American fighter, the P-40.

Honolulu and Pearl Harbor stand on the south coast of Oahu. In the north, two inexperienced American privates

Useless Advice from Washington

At 1:20 PM on December 9, 1941, some fifty-three hours after the Japanese attack, the secretary of the Hawaiian Medical Association received the following urgent radiogram from Washington:

> US OFFICE OF CIVIL DEFENSE
> WASHINGTON, DC, US GOVERNMENT
> December 9, 2:32 PM
>
> HAWAII TERRITORIAL MEDICAL ASSOCIATION
>
> OFFICE OF CIVILIAN DEFENSE REQUESTS YOU. URGE ALL HOSPITALS TO ESTABLISH IMMEDIATELY EMERGENCY MEDICAL FIELD UNITS IN ACCORDANCE WITH PLANS OUTLINED IN MEDICAL DIVISION BULLETINS NUMBER ONE AND TWO AND DRILL WEEKLY. WHERE NECESSARY RESERVE FIELD UNITS SHOULD BE ORGANIZED WITH MEDICAL, NURSING AND TRAINED VOLUNTARY PERSONNEL DERIVED FROM THE COMMUNITY. URGE IMMEDIATE ACTION.
>
> GEORGE BAEHR, MD, CHIEF MEDICAL OFFICER

Though the Hawaiians had already done all this and much more months previously, they replied unemotionally that they were already very active and medical matters were being attended to. Never again did they receive a communication from Dr. Baehr.

J. L. Lockhard and G. L. Elliott, who operated the primitive radar on the 4 to 7 AM shift, reported to their base that they were registering incoming planes. The enlisted man whom they spoke to could not find an officer (it was breakfast time). Finally he (and unfair fate) found Lieutenant K. Tyler, who was not on the base staff at all but merely a pilot whose superior had advised him to learn a little about the general radar system. Tyler knew the US carrier fleet was maneuvering out at sea and that American B-17 bombers were also arriving that day, and he assumed the planes on the radar were from one or the other: "So I thought about it for a moment and said, 'Well don't worry about it,' and went back awaiting the hour until the next relief."

To protect against sabotage, the US planes were neatly lined up outside their hangars. They became simple targets for the Japanese. Only eighteen American planes were able to take off.

All told, 21 ships were sunk or badly damaged, 328 planes were destroyed or made unusable, 2,403 military personnel were killed and 1,178 wounded, and 69 civilians killed. The greatest destruction was to the battleship *USS Arizona*. A 1,760-pound armor-piercing bomb dropped by a high-altitude bomber penetrated its decks. The explosion in the forward magazine ignited over a million pounds of gunpowder, producing a huge fireball. Some 1,177 men were dead or entombed. Hickam Field, Wheeler Field, Ewa Marine Corps Air Station, Bellows Field, and Kane'ohe Naval Air Station were also attacked.

Fortunately for the United States, the attackers destroyed only a small section of the Navy Yard and dozens of fuel tanks were undamaged. Even more fortunately, all of the Pacific Fleet's aircraft carriers were at sea. Their escape would soon prove crucial.

In the disarray during the attack, many of the shells fired by the US anti-aircraft batteries were badly fused or not fused at all and so failed to explode in the air, and on missing their targets they fell in various parts of Honolulu and Pearl Harbor where they exploded on impact. At least forty landed in the built-up area. One scored a direct hit on a parked car in Channel Street near Honolulu Harbor. Another blew a massive hole in the front garden of the governor's residence in Washington Place. Locals assumed these were deliberate Japanese bombs—a double error because the attackers intended to destroy military targets, not civilian ones.

December 7 and 8 were frenetic. Dr. Ralph Cloward, for instance, was the only neurosurgeon in the islands. He worked in a 250-bed hospital, but had to deal with about 1,500 wounded with head injuries, most of them lying on stretchers in the grass, and choose whom to treat—no point in operating on a man with part of his head blown away. He did not return home until December 10, after having performed 42 head operations.

Hawaii's Wartime Experiences

Blame

President Roosevelt and Knox, secretary of the Navy, obviously wanted to avoid blame. Knox arrived in Honolulu on December 11. Within days he had returned to Washington and presented his report. It (erroneously) accused the local Japanese of conspiracy, together with inadequate fighter planes and anti-aircraft guns.

Soon after, Roosevelt appointed a five-man commission of inquiry led by Justice Owen J. Roberts to determine who was responsible and to recommend action. Even this commission was unaware of everything the government had known prior to the attack. The Roberts Commission was not a normal court of law and the two military leaders in Honolulu, Lieutenant-General Walter E. Short and Admiral Husband E. Kimmel, were interrogated but not allowed to confront other witnesses. Most of Kimmel's staff was now at sea, which made his defense difficult. After further deliberations in Washington, the commission reported. It too blamed (incorrectly) aid given by local Japanese. And as the Roosevelt Administration desired, after further deliberations in Washington the commission fully exonerated the secretaries of state, war, Navy (Knox), and the Army and Navy chiefs of staff, and by implication Roosevelt. However, somebody's head had to fall, and of course Kimmel and Short were blamed and retired. Kimmel was replaced by Admiral Chester E. Nimitz, Short by Lieutenant-General Delos C. Emmons.

By May 1946, there had been nine more investigations. Administration and military made mutual recriminations. Much remained in doubt. How could Short be so blameworthy, given the false intelligence he had received?

Preparations Against Invasion

For months after the attack, Hawaiians and the military were concerned there would be another attack or invasion. In fact, on December 9 the staff of Admiral Yamamoto began to prepare for just such an attack. Three Japanese divisions went into training and various plans were made to control the territory. In Japan throughout 1942, there was widespread discussion of an invasion of Hawaii.

The "Battle" of Niihau Island

Naval airman Shigenori Nishikaichi was in the second wave of Japanese planes attacking Oahu but was hit and rapidly lost gasoline. Over isolated Niihau, he was forced to land in a rough field and knocked unconscious.

The few hundred farmers who lived on Niihau were all employed by the owner of the whole island, Aylmer Robinson, who had recently moved to nearby Kauai. Most of the farmers were unaware of the increasing tension between the United States and Japan. One of the few who were aware was 29-year-old Howard Kaleohano, who saw the crash, dragged the pilot from the plane, and took and hid his papers and pistol.

When the Niihauans heard about the attack, they imprisoned the pilot. A local Japanese couple born in Hawaii, the Haradas, helped him escape, tried to get his papers back, and prepared him to leave the island on a Japanese submarine supposed to rendezvous off the coast. For two days the pilot and the two Japanese terrorized the islanders to find the papers.

Realizing that they had to get the news to Kauai, Kaleohano and five other men left at night and rowed the 20 mi to Waimea, Kauai, against stiff headwinds. An expedition to rescue the islanders and capture the pilot and conspirators was mounted, but by the time the troops from Kauai arrived, the "battle" was over.

This is what happened: Failing to find the papers, the Japanese threatened to kill hostages and burned Kaleohano's home on Wednesday morning. They also set the plane ablaze. A well-built, powerful sheep farmer named Ben Kanahele, his wife Ella, and another woman became hungry and were sneaking back into the village to get food when they were caught by the pilot and Mr. Harada. Soon afterwards, captives and captors were all standing on a slope near a small stone wall. At that point, Harada decided the task was hopeless and unbuttoned his shirt to commit ritual suicide, reaching for the shotgun the pilot was holding. The pilot, momentarily distracted, was attacked by Ben and his wife. The pilot fired three shots that hit Ben in the left chest, left hip, and penis. Ben went berserk. As he had done with thousands of sheep, the powerful Ben grabbed the small pilot by the neck and a leg, lifted him in the air, and (unlike with sheep) smashed him against the stone wall. Ella bashed the head of the pilot with a rock, and with a hidden knife Ben cut his throat. In despair Harada grabbed the shotgun, fired it into his abdomen, and crumpled in a dying heap. Ben survived and he and Howard Kaleohano received decorations for bravery.

Civilians on the Big Island, who called their voluntary organization the Hilo Minutemen, do their duty by laying barbed wire to hinder the expected Japanese invasion in 1941. Hawaii State Archives.

Japanese submarines patrolled the islands from December to the end of January 1942, sinking six ships. Submarines also shelled the harbors of Hilo on the Big Island, Kahului on Maui, and the harbor at Lihu'e on Kauai, causing minor damage. On March 4, 1942, two amphibious planes from Japanese submarines flew reconnaissance missions over Oahu and dropped their two bombs.

All important buildings in Hawaii were camouflaged, including Honolulu's famous Aloha Tower, then the tallest structure in the territory. Women who had formerly woven leis for the necks of tourists were persuaded to weave camouflage nets, though camouflage itself received some skepticism. Beaches were strung with barbed wire to prevent Japanese landings. "But they left us a puka to walk through to swim on Waikiki," wrote a young woman in January 1942.

To forestall misuse of US currency should Hawaii be captured, all paper money in the territory was recalled and burned in the crematorium of Oahu Cemetery or in a sugar plantation furnace. Replacement notes had the word "HAWAII" superimposed—useful nowhere but on the islands.

As in World War I, gardens sprouted. The swathes of magnificent dahlias in the grounds of Queen's Hospital were uprooted by the kitchen staff to be replaced with eggplant, lettuce, carrots, sweet potatoes, and onions.

The US victory at the Battle of Midway in June 1942 was the crucial Pacific naval battle. From that date, Hawaii was never seriously threatened and became a staging area for forward operations.

Martial Law

Lieutenant General Short warned Governor Joseph Poindexter that he expected a Japanese invasion within a day, helped by supposed local saboteurs, and that martial law was essential. At 3 PM, after consulting with President Roosevelt, Poindexter—with extreme reluctance and bullied into so-doing—declared the Territory of Hawaii under martial law and Short assumed control. Some 370 Japanese, 98 Germans, and 14 Italians were arrested to prevent aid to the enemy. Garner Anthony, then territory attorney general, wrote after the war that the military controlled everything except taxation, including "regulation

Daniel K. Inouye

In August 1959 the House of Representatives was strangely quiet. The new young member from Hawaii walked into the well of the House and faced the speaker, Sam Rayburn.

"Raise your right hand and repeat after me," the speaker instructed.

For an instant the House held its collective breath because the new member did not raise his right hand. He raised his left—for he had no right arm. It had been mangled and amputated fighting the Germans in Italy. Despite this deviation, Congressman Daniel K. Inouye was the first member elected from Hawaii and also the first member of Congress of Japanese descent.

Born in 1924, Inouye was a member of the famous World War II 442nd Regimental Combat Team from 1944 to 1947. Soon promoted to sergeant, he fought for three months in the tough Rome–Arno campaign. In one of the most bloody encounters of the war, fall 1944 found him in the mountains of eastern France helping rescue a Texas battalion, "the Lost Battalion," surrounded by the enemy. There he won a Bronze Star and a commission on the battlefield as second lieutenant. Back in Italy in the final months of the war, he was shot through the abdomen while assaulting a strongly defended hill. He continued to fight, advancing alone against a machine gun position and tossing two devastating hand grenades before a German grenade shattered his right arm. He used his left arm to throw his final grenade and fire his machine gun before being put out of action by a bullet in his leg. A cluster of bravery awards including a Distinguished Service Cross and 20 months of military hospitals followed.

After World War II, he took advantage of the GI Bill to take degrees at the Universities of Hawaii and George Washington. Within a few years, he had been elected to the territory's House, Senate, the US House of Representatives in Washington DC, and in 1962 the US Senate, and was re-elected another seven times.

In 1968 while young people rioted outside, Inouye delivered the keynote address at the Democratic National Convention in Chicago, appealing for racial tolerance and democratic change. In the 1970s he set a high standard as a member of the Senate and party committees. In 1988 he was instrumental in the passing of the crucial Native Hawaiian Education and Health Care Acts.

Inouye has helped shape defense policies and worked hard to improve the armed forces and their quality of life. He has continued to champion the interests of the people of Hawaii. In 1992 he jointly introduced Congress's Apology Resolution to native Hawaiians. In 1993, crowning the efforts of others, he helped return to state control the devastated target practice island of Kahoolawe. In the late 1990s and early 2000s, he received a plethora of honors for his continuing distinguished service, including the Medal of Honor—America's highest military award—and the Grand Cordon of the Order of the Rising Sun from the government of Japan.

of traffic... liquor... censorship of the press... freezing of wages and employment... the removal of keys from parked cars... registration of females over sixteen... chlorination of water..."

Poindexter believed martial law would be temporary, but it remained for almost three years, long after it was necessary. Blackouts, curfews, frozen wages, rationing, and endless regulations were soon normal in this previously "laid-back" tropical Eden. Strikes were illegal too, so the ILWU agreement was now redundant. Large numbers of buildings were confiscated. The huge campus of Punahou School, for instance, was taken on December 8 by the Corps of Engineers, and kept for the duration of the war.

Whatever the problem, minor or major, the military instituted another "general order." The military judges in the provost court always interpreted the order in the military's favor, even convicting people for infringing the "spirit" of the order rather than the order as stated! In 1942 alone, some 22,000 people came before the main Honolulu military court—and only 359 were declared innocent. As the war retreated farther from Hawaii's shores, civilians became tired of military attitudes. Despite the fact that the new governor complained in Washington and some functions were returned to civil bodies, the military stubbornly kept what it could. Most of it was illegal: After the war, the US Supreme Court found unambiguously that the civil courts should never have been supplanted by military tribunals.

Hawaii's Japanese: A Complex Issue

To the military command who believed the reports about Hawaiian Japanese cooperation with the enemy, the fact that Hawaii held about 160,000 people of Japanese descent (almost 40 percent of the population) looked at first like a nightmare. Initial ideas of interning them all in western states were soon rejected. First, under war conditions, it would have been impossible to transport so many people. Second, Americans of Japanese ancestry were actually indispensable in the whole cross-section of Hawaii's labor force. Still, about 480 were interned.

Those with strongest pro-Japanese feelings were *issei*, people who had arrived directly from Japan. The most dedicatedly Japanese of them had returned to Japan prior to

Must-See Sites: Oahu
Outside Downtown Honolulu

Waikiki Beach

Waikiki is a tourist shopper's paradise and is probably Hawaii's best known area—famous for its ambiance, not its looks. At the intersection of Kalakaua and Kuhio Avenues stands King Kalakaua's statue. Stretching from the Hilton Hawaiian Village to Kapi'olani Park, a number of adjoining beaches with various names form the beach at Waikiki, one of the most famous single stretches of sand in the world; in the Kuhio Beach section stands the statue to the marvelous surfer Duke Kahanamoku. Abutting the beach are three famous hotels, Halekulani, Royal Hawaiian, and Moana, attractions in themselves.

US Army Museum

In Fort DeRussy, off Kalia Road and near Hilton Hawaiian village, the US Army Museum is settled in a massive 1911 bunker of 22 ft (7 m) thick walls on the beach side, with displays and weapons of ancient Hawaii and US wars. It also holds a bookstore.

Diamond Head Monument and Park

So called because sailors thought they had discovered diamonds (actually calcite), this famous 760 ft (234 m) high volcanic peak with flat crater was once the site of a military fortification. Starting on the crater floor and partly through a tunnel, a three-quarter mile trail leads to the rim, which provides a 360° panorama on a clear day to Maui and Molokai.

National Memorial Cemetery of the Pacific

Just north of downtown in Punchbowl Crater, a former site of human sacrifices, is this national cemetery. Here some 40,000 veterans and members of their families are buried. The 112 ac site has flat white headstones placed level with the green grass and a striking cream stone memorial.

Bishop Museum

A mile or so from downtown in suburban Kalihi stands Hawaii's greatest museum, Bishop Museum. It was founded in 1889 by Charles Reed Bishop as a memorial to his late wife Princess Bernice Pauahi Bishop. At first the museum was a repository for the royal possessions of this direct descendant of King Kamehameha the Great and her relatives Queen Emma and Princess Ruth. The heart of the museum is the Hawaiian Hall, with a grand staircase, railings, and display cases of magnificent Hawaiian *koa* hardwood. Today, as the Hawaii State Museum of Natural and Cultural History, it houses millions of items that tell the history of Hawaii and Polynesia: feather and wooden images of the god Ku, Prince Kuhio's racing canoe, the skeleton of a huge sperm whale, artifacts from Hawaii's various immigrant groups, superb feather capes, and an unmatched

Hawaiian Hall is the oldest and chief building of Bishop Museum, which stands in suburban Kalihi. The Museum pursues a famous research tradition and preserves millions of items from the history and culture of Hawaii and Polynesia. Bishop Museum

collection of rare plant and animal specimens. Here are the *Watumull Planetarium* and *Shop Pacifica* offering books and gifts, regular hula and Hawaiian craft demonstrations, special exhibits, and lessons in hula and lei-making. Bishop Museum promotes and pursues Polynesian and Hawaiian ethnographic research and has nurtured world-famous researchers such as New Zealand Maori Sir Peter Buck and American Kenneth P. Emory.

Queen Emma Summer Palace

The Queen Emma Summer Palace lies on the Pali Highway a few miles north of downtown Honolulu. Built in the 1840s, the palace was used by Queen Emma and Kamehameha IV as a hill retreat. An intriguing combination of Greek revival and Hawaiian, it was willed to Emma in 1850 by her uncle, John Young's son. Set in a cool tree-filled oasis with mango trees planted at her wedding in 1856, now about 100 ft high, the palace houses many royal artifacts. The Daughters of Hawaii saved the building from demolition in 1913.

Nuʻuanu Pali Lookout

Just off the main Pali Highway, this flat area on top of a ridge in the Koʻolau Mountains provides a superb green view over northern and eastern Oahu. Here in the 1795 Battle of Nuʻuanu Pali, Kamehameha I defeated the remnants of the Oahuan armies, who either were pushed or jumped to their deaths over the *pali* (cliff). Careful not to be blown off by the howling winds, visitors can peer over the cliff and ponder the warriors' fate.

Pearl Harbor Naval Base
About 10 mi west of downtown stands this great US naval base, and there are three sections open to visitors.

The *USS Arizona* Memorial, visited by over 1,500,000 annually, has a visitors' center. The documentary film and boat ride to the memorial are free. Built in 1962, the white, clean-lined 184 ft memorial sits above the sunken *Arizona* without touching it. Here 1,177 men are entombed, and oil still seeps from the wreck.

Bowfin Park is a moored World War II submarine, and the Pacific Submarine Museum traces the historical evolution of such ships. From May 1943, the *Bowfin* sank 44 enemy ships. The park holds many examples of torpedoes and missiles and even a Japanese suicide torpedo.

In 1998 the decommissioned *USS Missouri* was brought to Ford Island for the *Battleship Missouri* Memorial. The 887 ft long ship launched near the war's end served as flagship for the fierce, bloody battles of Iwo Jima and Okinawa. The place where the Japanese signed their surrender on September 2, 1945, is marked on its foredeck. In telling historical juxtaposition, the *Missouri* is moored merely a few hundred yards from *Arizona*. Visit www.ussmissouri.com for more information.

The National Korean War Musuem
Just east of Schofield Barracks and about 20 road miles north of Honolulu, this is the nation's only Korean War Museum. Built and staffed mostly by volunteers, it holds 38 themed galleries, filling its 1940s World War II Quonset Hut, and is still expanding. Visit www.nkwm.org for more information.

Byodo-In Temple
About two miles north of Kaneʻohe on the windward coast, this termite-proof concrete replica of a 900-year-old Kyoto temple is hidden in the verdant Valley of Temples (a nondenominational cemetery). The site and its surrounding fluted green mountain walls are simply exquisite. A large reflecting lake, tinkling waterfalls, a 7 ton bronze bell, and a beautifully crafted 9 ft (3 m) golden Buddha complete the effect.

North Shore Surfing Waves
Centered on Waimea and the site of international competitions, the world's best waves for surfing arrive here in mid-winter. The area includes Sunset Beach, Rocky Point, Banzai Pipeline, Waimea Bay, Chun's Reef, Haleʻiwa, and Avalanche. Just inland from Waimea, there is excellent viewing from the 250 ft Puʻuomahuka Heiau State Monument.

the war, but thousands who remained expected or hoped that Japan would win. Some 248 Hawaiian Japanese (not consular personnel) were also repatriated to Japan during the war. But attitudes varied immensely.

Notably, the majority of *nisei*—people of Japanese descent born in North America—were pro-American. After Pearl Harbor, many young male *nisei* wanted to enlist. Because of security concerns and contemporary prejudices, they were rejected. *Nisei* in the ROTC were also discharged. Such was the concern about a Japanese invasion that even Americans of Japanese ancestry in the National Guard (who by law could not be discharged) were transported from the islands to Wisconsin. There they were renamed the 100th Infantry. At last in January 1943, *nisei* were able to join up—to fight in North Africa and Europe. About 9,000 volunteered in the first month, some 3,000 of whom were selected and became the 442nd Infantry. Others became translators in the Pacific.

Following the liberation of Rome, the two units were amalgamated, fighting in the difficult north Italy campaign. So determined were these *nisei* to demonstrate their loyalty that their casualty rates were three times the normal. The 100th and the 442nd became the two most decorated units in US military history: They returned home as heroes.

Hawaii as a Staging Area

Some 43,000 soldiers at the time of Pearl Harbor increased to the all-time high of 253,000 in June of 1945, as an invasion of Japan became increasingly likely. Naval strength went from about 6,000 to 137,000 at the end of 1944, and marines from 7,500 to 116,000 in August 1945, the final month of the war. Thousands of acres of land were taken over by the forces for barracks, tent-grounds, warehouses, machine shops, ammunition dumps, and other facilities.

Tenacious Japanese resistance in the Pacific's tropical islands brought the need for a jungle warfare training facility at Schofield Barracks. The Hawaiian Islands, with their rugged terrain and warm climate, were ideal. It was no game—men were killed in training. Oahu and other islands were also the scene of training for crucial amphibious landings. When the invasion of Japan looked inevitable, instructors in a special village the troops called

Armed forces personnel cling to every available vantage point of the USS Missouri, *moored 18 miles out in Tokyo Bay. On September 2, 1945, on the open deck, the Japanese delegation officially surrendered to General Douglas MacArthur.*
The Army Signal Corps Collection in the US National Archives

"Little Tokyo" taught house to house fighting.

All five of the largest airports were extended. The military constructed major roads, such as the Nimitz Highway on Oahu from the airport to downtown and Saddle Road, passing between the two great volcanoes, to link the two sides of the Big Island. (The first attempt to construct a road, from Kona to Hilo, began in 1849 and continued for years until Mauna Loa erupted and lava covered most of it.) From before the war, the uninhabited island of Kahoolawe and some sections of Molokai had become places for target practice and this intensified. WACS (Women's Army Corps) arrived in 1944 to work in administration and transportation.

Honolulu became a hothouse of service men on "R & R"—centered on Hotel Street, a few blocks in from Honolulu Harbor. Entertainers and Hollywood stars such as Bob Hope and Betty Hutton were brought out to amuse the troops. The US Navy took over the famous pink Royal Hawaiian Hotel on Waikiki for recreation. Because there were many isolated units far from the "bright lights," the USO (United Services Organization) organized travelling troupes and shows, many based on home-grown hula dancers. But even Honolulu proved inadequate. With less than 200,000 residents (many had left for the mainland), it was really still only a town, and the influx of tens of thousands of service personnel to the island overwhelmed its facilities. As one writer put it, hoping to find the romance and the exotic charm of Hawaii, often all the men found were thousands of other guys wandering around looking for the same thing.

JAPANESE–HAWAIIAN REACTIONS TO THE END OF THE WAR

Hawaiians were as astonished as the rest of the world when the war ended suddenly with the dropping of the atomic bombs. Japanese defeat was a shock to thousands of Hawaiian Japanese *issei* who assumed Japan would win. Few *issei* took part in US victory celebrations. Many even psychologically refused to accept the fact of Japan's defeat, living on rumors and illusion—the United States was trying to hide the fact that Japan had won; the Japanese fleet lay off Pearl Harbor waiting to enter when the mines were cleared, etc. After all, such *issei* had been born in Japan and many remained Japanese, not American citizens. After the Pearl Harbor attack, a departing Japanese pilot crash-landed in tiny Niihau, the farthest main island, and a local Japanese *nisei* couple supported him and helped him terrorize the Niihauans.

But for the *nisei,* the war had clarified attitudes very differently. Their American identity came to the fore. Early in the war, they emphasized the term "AJA" (Americans of Japanese Ancestry), rather than *nisei,* and they became determined that after the war they would play their role as full citizens. After the war, some returned to their former jobs; others became executives in Big Five companies. Of those officers and enlisted men of Japanese ancestry who stayed in the armed forces, most were assigned to the Allied Occupation Force in Japan where they acted as translators. Some went into politics.

11

STATEHOOD AND ECONOMIC CHANGE

A NEW REGIME: POLITICS AND LABOR

Rise of the Democrats

After the war, trends such as increasing unionization and racial intermarriage continued. The war had also changed Hawaiians in ways unexpected. Though the business oligarchy did not yet know it, the war had brought a broader democracy to the islands. Japanese-Hawaiians who had fought in the 100th and 442nd Infantries were never going to accept second-class citizenship again, nor were Filipino, Chinese, or other veterans belonging to ethnic minorities. Many veterans became politically active. As one returning *nisei* put it in the *Hawaii Times* in November 1945: "We have helped win the war on the battlefront but we have not yet won the war on the homefront. We shall have won only when we attain those things for which our country is dedicated, namely, equality of opportunity and the dignity of man."

Many took the opportunity provided by the "GI Bill of Rights" (the Servicemen's Readjustment Act) of 1944 to continue their education or training. They attended college to study law, medicine, teaching, engineering. The most famous was Daniel K. Inouye, an able and ambitious young *nisei*. He studied law and became a power in the ever more significant Democratic Party and the first person of Japanese extraction to be elected to Congress. Other veterans entered politics too, such as the native Hawaiian Daniel Akaka, who also became a senator. He had been with the Army Corps of Engineers on the island of Saipan when the B-29 bomber *Enola Gay* took off to drop its atomic bomb on Hiroshima. Soon the children of the plantations would be voted into key political positions.

Meanwhile there had been a struggle for control of the Hawaiian Democratic Party. There were two key players, both Jacks. One was Jack Hall, whom we have already met as head of the ILWU, and the unions remained his stronghold. The other was Jack Burns, a detective in the Honolulu Police Department. Burns rose through the party ranks, championing the ordinary worker. He forged strong links in the Japanese and Chinese communities, and his career prospered as these groups became politically influential. He helped men like Inouye and Patsy Mink to rise in the party, strove to limit the power of Hall and the ILWU, and created a solid power base for himself. In 1948 he was elected Hawaiian delegate to the US Congress.

At the 1948 Democratic State Convention, Burns and Hall both sought leadership of the Democrats, but finding they marshaled about the same amount of support decided to cooperate, at least until the 1952 convention. Burns won party control, but Hall remained the predominant force in organized labor. The story of Hall and Burns is important, because in 1954 the now united Democrats were able to defeat the Republicans for the first time and, reversing the previous political party history of Hawaii, began the Democrat and labor union control of the islands that would extend into the new millennium. (They still had some struggles: Governor Samuel W. King used his veto seventy-one times during the first legislative session alone. As one political scientist put it, "Never had a governor so completely demolished a legislative program.")

Soon the Democrats were winning overwhelming majorities in both the state legislature and senate. They lost the governorship only twice. The first elected governor was a Republican, William F. Quinn. Then from 1962 until 2002, Washington Place, the governor's mansion, was occupied by Democrats. Linda C. Lingle, the first female governor, would recover it for the Republicans in that year.

Labor Unions Become Powerful
In 1945 Hawaii passed the Employment Relations Act. This strengthened the ILWU's unionization of plantation sugar and pineapple workers, and a little more than a year after the war's end, about 21,000 plantation laborers came out on strike. The first of the Big Five to agree to union demands was Castle & Cooke.

In 1949 Jack Hall marshaled the dock workers in an economically devastating and bitter strike that lasted 178 days and deeply divided the community. Though both sides suffered, the union eventually claimed victory. Unionism had "arrived" and though he had not won control of the Democratic Party, Hall was a figure of very great power.

The Cold War had begun, and increasingly America's political leaders were involved in a profound struggle against the spread of communism. Since the collapse of the USSR in 1991, much new Soviet evidence has become available and it is now clear that Moscow gave direct orders to US Communists and funded the American Communist Party with many millions of dollars. Governor Ingram M. Stainback, Delegate Joseph R. Farrington, and other community leaders were deeply concerned about Communist infiltration of Hawaiian organizations, though the degree of Communist influence in the 1949 strike and which union leaders supported Communism have always been hotly debated topics.

The US Congress soon became involved in exposing alleged Communists. Jack Hall was one of many individuals brought before the House Committee on Un-American Activities that travelled to Hawaii in 1950 to investigate Communist influence and activity aimed at the violent overthrow of the US government. Hall and 38 others pleaded the Fifth Amendment. Many at the time believed this action to be tantamount to admitting guilt. Despite determined union support, he and six others ("the Hawaii Seven") were sentenced to several years in jail. Complex appeals and legal maneuvers continued to keep them free, and in 1958, based on a US Supreme Court ruling, a superior court reversed their sentences. But the whole episode affected their standing in the community—the fate of many others during this time. In the years after the war, often the only lawyer willing to defend a laborer or union opposing an employer in a Hawaiian court was the innovative and spirited Harriet Bouslog, who struggled for fair labor laws and wages. During the "Hawaii Seven" trial, she and mainland lawyers served as counsel for Hall and others.

In 1958 Hall led another strike of plantation workers, resulting in higher wages. Instead of the political power of the Republican Party and Big Five, there had evolved an overwhelmingly Democratic administration and legislature in league with the unions. Old-fashioned business paternalism had been replaced by modern bureaucratic populism.

DESIRE FOR STATEHOOD

So it was the Democrats who now led Hawaii's bid for statehood. For many US presidents and legislators, Hawaii's large non-white majority was always the great argument against statehood. Segregation-minded Southern Democrats were opposed to accepting another state that would have a majority of non-whites. Congressional investigating committees continually recommended "further study" of the issue, and opponents on the mainland regularly managed to find new reasons for rejection. In 1931, for instance, Delegate Victor K. Houston introduced a Hawaiian statehood bill in Congress. A month later the Hawaiian Massie rape case exploded onto the front pages and the bill had no chance (see pages 226–227). In 1950 the outbreak of the Korean War stalled proceedings. In 1953 a statehood bill passed the House; in the Senate, its opponents used procedural technicalities to block its progress. At home, many native Hawaiians preferred second-class territorial status quo to closer integration. Some people wanted a "Commonwealth" on the lines of the US agreement with Puerto Rico.

Despite endless rebuffs, from the 1930s the Hawaiian delegates to the US House of Representatives fought continually for statehood. Hawaii established a Statehood Commission to pressure Washington and marshal favorable facts. By the early 1950s, the following were typical supporting arguments: Though Hawaii had no say in how its federal taxation was spent, it paid more than nine other states; with about 500,000 people, it was larger than four current states: Delaware, Montana, Wyoming, and Vermont; except for Oklahoma, its population was larger than that of any other territory at the time it had been granted statehood; 90 percent of residents were US citizens.

By the 1950s, Alaska was also asking to become a state, and in time the two territories joined ranks. Finally early in 1959, the United States House and Senate passed statehood

In 1958 Hawaii dispatched a strong delegation to Washington DC to lobby for statehood. Pictured left to right are former governor Oren E. Long, former delegate to US Congress (and wife of a former delegate) Elizabeth P. Farrington, Gov. William F. Quinn, former governor and former delegate to US Congress Samuel Wilder King, and Lorrin P. Thurston, son of the coup leader, publisher of the Honolulu Advertiser, *and chairman of the Hawaii Statehood Commission. Their goal was achieved in 1959.* Hawaii State Archives

bills and President Dwight Eisenhower, a longtime supporter, signed the bill. Hawaiian citizens now had to ratify the acts. They agreed by a majority of about seventeen to one. Only tiny Niihau, with its native Hawaiian population, rejected the act. Of the 1,800,000 ac the federal government had acquired at annexation, it returned to Hawaiian control all except 432,000, which it retained for national parks and the military.

Hawaii was now the fiftieth state and the US flag reflected the fact in an additional star. There was an almost immediate economic boost, and steady growth would continue until the boom in the late 1980s and the bust in the 1990s.

Duke Kahanamoku: Swimmer, Star, Surfer, and Sheriff

Native Hawaiian Duke Kahanamoku (named because of a visit by the Duke of Edinburgh) was a Waikiki beach boy, surfing and Olympic swimming champion, Hollywood star, sheriff of Honolulu, and a great ambassador for Hawaii.

He rose to prominence in a swim in Honolulu Harbor for which he was timed at breaking the world 100 meters freestyle record by 4.6 seconds. The American Amateur Athletic Union refused to accept the time, declaring, "No one swims that fast!" People had to believe when, a year later, Kahanamoku won the 100 meters freestyle gold medal at the 1912 Stockholm Olympics—and more gold medals at the 1920 and 1924 Olympics. (There were no Olympics in 1916 because of World War I.) He also evolved a new style, the flutter kick, which largely replaced the scissors kick.

In the 1920s and '30s, the Olympian became an actor. He appeared in about thirty Hollywood films with the likes of Ronald Coleman, Dorothy Lamour, and John Wayne. In 1925 he spectacularly rescued eight men from drowning off Newport Beach.

Back home he was elected sheriff of Honolulu twelve times until 1961 and from then became the paid official welcomer, greeting thousands of visitors to Waikiki and Honolulu, including some of the stars he used to work with.

As a sort of ambassador at large, Kahanamoku travelled to mainland US, Europe, Australia, New Zealand, and elsewhere to teach surfing, and his legacy is acknowledged everywhere surfers congregate. He is also remembered for his exemplary sportsmanship and humility. The stretch of sand near the Hilton Hawaiian Village is named after him. Here his extended family once lived. When in 1968 he died at the age of 77 from a heart attack, more than 10,000 attended his Waikiki funeral, scattering his ashes from outrigger canoes in the surf.

Near Kalakaua Avenue close to the Moana Surfrider Hotel is the larger-than-life statue of Duke Kahanamoku by Honolulu sculptor Jan Fisher. It is rarely free of leis.

Growth of Tourism

The superb climate and scenery provided natural foundations for the extraordinary growth of tourism, which boomed as the sugar industry proportionately declined.

New Developments and Millions of Japanese Visitors

Post-war, middle-class tourists became most common. Among the first were servicemen who had tasted a little of Hawaii during the war and wanted to test it fully in peacetime. The booming US economy of the 1950s and '60s put surplus income in the hands of increasing numbers of people, and Hawaiian tourism benefited. Some 40,000 tourists in 1950 became 175,000 by 1959. That was the year jet travel from the mainland was introduced. Days on Matson liners were converted into mere hours in planes. Jet planes became larger and faster and—coupled with the burgeoning building of special resorts, the first being at Ka'anapali on the West Maui coast—brought a massive 500 percent increase by 1968 with some 1,200,000 travellers. From 1969 the 747 jumbos continued this trend.

The boost created tens of thousands of jobs in construction, cement-making, architecture, city and/or county councils, and to service tourism and hotels, and the unions ensured that most were well-paid. In the 1970s, Honolulu began to grow quickly, with the IBM building, the East-West Center at the university, the huge Ala Moana shopping center, the Ilikai Hotel in Waikiki, the Kahala Hilton near Diamond Head, Castle Memorial Hospital on the windward side of the range, and so on, along with the arrival of mainland supermarket chains. As in American cities generally, it became a car culture. Whatever their status, most people wore similar tropical clothing, so it was one's car that defined one's economic, cultural, and ethnic status. Bus travel carried social negatives; the rich drove expensive British or European cars; the US military preferred American automobiles; the middle-class Americans, the Japanese, and Chinese bought Japanese vehicles; the native Hawaiians, Pacific Islanders generally, and the Filipinos liked small trucks with four-wheel drive.

In time, new entrepreneurial ideas found scope: entertaining tourists at luau, flying them from one island to another or to several islands in a day, taking them to watch moving lava, guiding them on bicycles down the road from the summit to the base of Haleakala Volcano, organizing sailing vacations, and developing specialist vacations such as visits to the many film production sites in Kauai or to a variety of golf courses or fishing spots in the various islands. Tourism became Hawaii's gods, hotels, its *heiau*, and both (mostly) blessed their people.

In the 1980s, Honolulu and Maui developed even more rapidly. As the Japanese economy inflated during the second half of the 1980s, the yen appreciated against the dollar, and suddenly Hawaii experienced huge numbers of Japanese tourists who shopped a great deal, often in Japanese-owned stores, as well as a wave of direct Japanese investment in business and prestigious residential property. In the late 1970s, Japan accounted for something like 60 percent of all foreign-owned assets in the state; by the early 1990s, this number had increased to close to 90 percent. Japanese tourists were visiting Hawaii but staying in now Japanese-owned hotels. Opposition to such Japanese control was widespread, lessened somewhat by the use of American management.

But the eviction of low-income Hawaiians from apartments in which they had lived for years fueled resentment against the Japanese tourists yet again. The mayor of Honolulu, Frank Fasi, claimed, "We don't want you and we don't need you. I don't want Honolulu to become a suburb of Tokyo." Fasi even journeyed to Tokyo to upbraid the Japanese, though not everyone agreed with his way of thinking, including the governor.

The Lanai Example

Perhaps the most unexpected change concerned the island of Lanai. For close to seventy years, nearly all the 2,000-odd laborers, mostly of Filipino or Japanese extraction, worked for the Hawaiian Pineapple Co./Castle & Cooke Inc., who owned most of the island.

In 1987 the energetic Californian entrepreneur David Murdock, who realized that cheap labor in the Philippines and Central America was challenging the Hawaiian pineapple industry, took over Castle & Cooke. His solution was an extraordinary conception—no less than a reorientation of the total life and economy of Lanai. In effect, the

The Puka (Tunnel) through the Pali, 1852–1957

At least as early as 1852, people had suggested that a tunnel should be cut through the *pali* (cliff) of the Koʻolau Mountains north of Honolulu to improve communication between the Nuʻuanu Valley and the fertile north side of Oahu. *The Polynesian* wrote in 1852, "Oahu residents *will never be satisfied* until a tunnel is dug through the Pali suitable for the passage of carts and wagons." They must have been dissatisfied for at least a century.

Hawaii's economy could certainly not afford a tunnel in the 1850s, so the people of the town had to content themselves with improvement of the age-old trails to the top of the *pali* and stop there. By the early '40s, there existed a precipitous trail carved down the windward face and only used by the hardiest souls, with a rope. Otherwise one had to go round via the coast. Government and business money paid to cut a slightly improved trail down the windward side in 1845, along which farmers began carting produce to the capital. In 1862 this was improved to a narrow road to accommodate horse-drawn traffic.

Under the young local engineer "Johnny" Wilson in 1897, this carriage road across the Pali was widened and "straightened" with the use of dynamite and covered with asphalt, but it still included many curves, most famously an S-bend on the Honolulu side and an 180-degree hairpin turn on the windward side. Further widening occurred after 1900 to make way for the new-fangled automobiles and trucks. The road was still "chicken-skin" time, as Hawaiians say. The adventure writer Jack London commented that on his drive they were "fairly hanging to a stark wall for the best part of two miles."

By 1931 about 2,000 vehicles were using the Pali Road daily. Various plans for construction were frustrated by the Depression and World War II. Hoping for the fruition of such plans, in 1947 Andy Cummings and Hilo Hattie (Clare Inter) wrote a hit *hapa haole* (half-foreign) hula song, *When They Build the Puka in the Pali*. Construction actually commenced in the mid-1950s. One traffic tunnel was opened in May 1957 (though drivers often ignored the one-way traffic schedule) and the two tunnels in August 1961. Today visitors can see the windward portals of the Pali Tunnels from the Pali Lookout. The old Pali Trail is still usable by cycle and foot but not vehicular traffic.

whole of the island's 140 sq mi (363 sq km) would become a huge hotel, its grounds, its golf courses (striking and emerald green like most Hawaiian courses), and its support system. Small farms grew organic food for hotel tables, forests became a site for guests to hunt deer, visitors used the dirt roads for their rented jeeps.

The only town, Lanai City, was tidied a little and public facilities provided but left essentially the same. Murdock conceived two distinctly different grand hotels. Skilled tradespeople and artists of the town were hired to help paint the art and decorate the new hotels.

Historically as spectacular as the hotels was the fact that the island's young people began to return to live on Lanai—they would not have come to plant, pick, and pack pineapples but willingly became part of this visionary enterprise. An aging population was rejuvenated.

Recession and its Results

Almost every Hawaiian resident had a job; property values soared; wages, salaries, and investment incomes increased; and more hotels and resorts were built. By the early 1990s, there had been another 600 percent tourist increase with numbers over 7 million, now including more than 2 million from Japan, and tourist income was adding more than $10 billion a year to the economy. Meanwhile, the legislature used the prosperity to load local business with new taxes and union-sponsored regulations such as universal health care for employees.

Japan's economic "bubble" burst in the early 1990s. The 1991 Gulf War also scared away tourists and the mainland went into recession, and as a result the Hawaiian economy suffered. Mainland tourist bookings declined and Japanese bookings fell even more. Throughout the 1990s, Japan's financial stagnation caused the sale of prestigious Japanese-owned resorts, hotels, and golf clubs at much reduced prices. The taxes and regulations now became job-killers, and newspaper headlines blared, "Welfare cases growing by 20%," "Island business failures hit record." Between statehood in 1959 and the year 1990, Hawaii's economy had doubled every 14 years. The rate of expansion during the 1990s was so negligible that it looked like it would be 2080 before the economy had doubled again. When the tourist industry and businesses contracted, everyone in Hawaii was affected.

James Michener, Novelist of Hawaii

For over fifty years James A. Michener was a best-selling writer, with many tens of millions of copies of his books sold—books that diverted and informed, and sometimes misinformed, his readers on their subjects. He also gave tens of millions to charity.

After a tough childhood, Michener studied literature as a scholarship student at Swarthmore, taught in schools and universities, then worked as an editor in New York City. His Quaker pacifism was overcome by service as a naval officer in World War II. Shore duty in the Solomon Islands provided him with the material for his first book, the moderately successful *Tales of the South Pacific* (1947). This won a Pulitzer prize, spectacularly notifying the literary world of his presence. He gained fame and financial independence with the Rogers and Hammerstein Broadway musical version of the book, the hit *South Pacific*, which ran for years and later became a film. Later in his life, he donated his collection of Japanese *ukiyo-e* (Edo Period popular art) to the Honolulu Academy of Arts.

With his most ambitious novel, the 937-page *Hawaii*, he perfected a literary formula, a way of writing about some region of the world that contemporary readers were suddenly interested in. Interweaving the lives, tribulations, and achievements of a number of key families through many generations, he presented history as an epic story.

For much of the period between 1949 and the publication of *Hawaii* in 1960 and after, Michener lived in Honolulu and became seriously involved in the push for statehood. He researched the book for four years and wrote it in three. The book was made into a film in 1966 and translated into thirty-two languages.

Because it allowed him to follow *Hawaii* with many other books—*The Source* (Israel), *Alaska*, and so forth—this technique was his strength. It was his weakness as well, for its very success encouraged him to overuse it. *Hawaii* was in the stores at the time when people became aware of the new state. It is also credited with strongly encouraging the growth of tourism.

Programs that were believed to help tourism were popular, though sometimes such help could negatively affect other parts of the economy. While the hotel industry benefited from 1990s hotel tax exemptions, the tax payer— i.e., other businesses and the ordinary person—paid for the maintenance of streets used by hotel guests, the education of the children of hotel employees, the state-financed courts used by hotel management to secure property rights, and so on. Government eventually realized that tourist promotion dollars must be spent selectively and in 1998 adopted the policy that not the taxpayer but those who benefited from generic promotion must pay its costs.

Given its limited land, in Hawaii hotel and condominium expansion can have problematic side effects. About 60 percent of land is still privately owned, and much of that by large groups such as the Bishop Estate. Development has been influenced by groups of investors called *hui*. Some *hui*, often Chinese-controlled, withheld land from development in order to increase its value. Home ownership became impossible for ordinary workers, and many people who had lived in the same neighborhood for decades, even generations, were dispossessed. Most affected were the native Hawaiians. Many were unable to afford any kind of accommodation and lived in shacks on beaches. The arrest of such people became a state-wide scandal.

After the terrorist attacks on September 11, 2001, there was an immediate drop in tourism, with the resulting loss of tens of thousands of Hawaiian jobs, though it settled at around 80 percent of year 2000 levels.

From the 1990s, in search of jobs and less expensive places to live, substantial numbers of Hawaiian residents moved to the mainland. By 2005 tens of thousands had gone to live in another but diametrically different tourist mecca: Las Vegas, Nevada. Originally they had been attracted there on vacation—the equivalent of a quarter of the population of the state, a state where gambling is illegal, travelled each year to Las Vegas. Hawaii's ubiquitous ABC convenience-cum-drugstores have now opened three outlets in that city. Hawaiian and Aloha Airlines continually increase their services from Honolulu to Vegas, and many Hawaiians call Vegas the "Ninth Island."

Diversification of Agriculture

Decline of Sugar and Pineapples

The period when the Democratic Party took over from the Republicans as the dominant force in Hawaiian politics coincided with the beginning of the decline of the great Hawaiian economic mainstays, the employers of the large majority of union members, and the sources of most Democratic votes: the sugar and pineapple industries.

Part of the economic success of sugar and pineapples in Hawaii rested on the low wages of the workers. When the ILWU and other unions became powerful, profit margins declined. A changing world economy and competition from countries with cheaper labor meant that by the 1990s, plantations and mills were closing at depressing rates—by 1998 every sugar mill on the Big Island had closed. It was a sign of the times when some of the sugar and pineapple farms and factories remained operating because of their connection to tourism.

Diversification: Coffee, Papayas, Macadamias

A wider range of products is now coming from Hawaiian fields and forests. Hawaiian farmers produce more than forty different commercial crops. In the last three decades, there has been a shift to smaller, but more numerous farms. There were about 5,400 farms in 2005. Pineapples remain Hawaii's largest crop (about a third of agricultural production), followed closely by greenhouse/nursery products, then sugarcane (about a sixth). Increasingly successful major crops of recent decades have been macadamia nuts, coffee, papaya, and seeds—though all but seeds have had a long presence in the islands.

Seedlings of macadamia trees were brought to Hawaii from eastern Australia in 1881, but all early farming attempts failed. Twenty years of research at the University of Hawaii during the 1930s and '40s radically improved the quality, and when large investors such as Castle & Cooke and C. Brewer entered the market in the 1950s, commercial sales became substantial. From the 1970s, macadamia production continually increased, mostly on the Big Island, and Hawaii has a significant percent of the world total.

Coffee had been grown as early as 1817 and in the 1820s was produced in the Manoa Valley, now suburban Honolulu,

Moon Over Hawaii

On July 24, 1969, the space capsule *Columbia* from the
Apollo 11 moon mission splashed down about 812 mi
(1,307 km) southwest of Honolulu, returning the three
astronauts Neil. A. Armstrong, Edwin E. "Buzz" Aldrin, and
Michael Collins safely to Earth. Armstrong and Aldrin had
been the first men to walk the moon's surface.

Wearing isolation garments in case they were bringing
home unknown moon bacteria, they were lifted from the
water by the waiting Navy helicopter and transported to the
USS Hornet. On ship and shore they stayed in quarantine
for three weeks.

History books often ignore the role Hawaii played in the
mission, for they merely mention the splashdown, and then
the story shifts to Houston. Always omitted are the multitudes
of at least 25,000 people who welcomed the astronauts at
Pearl Harbor and stood cheering and waving along the road
to neighboring Hickham Airforce Base. (Here a plaque
celebrates the first place they touched earth's soil after the
mission.) The Hawaiians lining the route were trying to see
these men who had achieved this great feat of modern
exploration.

The astronauts first sight of ordinary earth was Ford
Island in Pearl Harbor, where they peered from their 35 ft
biologically protected trailer at the crowds outside. At Ford
Island, they had showers and a physical examination, but
debriefing occurred at Houston.

Bureaucracy always has its way. Amazingly, the three
astronauts had to be cleared through US customs and
immigration. They completed the forms during quarantine.
According to Aldrin in their written answers to questions where
they had been, they said that their Flight Number 11 had
departed Cape Kennedy, stopped en route on the moon, and
returned them to Honolulu. Items acquired on the way were
"moon rock and moon dust samples—manifests enclosed."

and grew on all main islands. But fluctuating prices, plant
diseases, and Latin American competition restricted or
caused all early efforts to fail. Due mainly to the specially
suitable district of Kona on the west coast of the Big Island,

coffee was at last cultivated successfully. Kona has rich volcanic soil, a cooler altitude at 1,200 ft and above, and the protection of Mauna Kea and Mauna Loa from the northeast trade winds. There is sun in the morning and clouds in the afternoons at that altitude to bring adequate gentle rainfall. But the success of the industry may owe as much to the workers as to the weather—from the beginning of the twentieth century, the large plantations began to give way to small farms worked tenaciously by families. Many were Japanese immigrants who rejected the harsh plantation work. The parents and grandparents of Hawaiian astronaut Elison Onizuka were such coffee farmers. The industry again faced problems in the 1970s and '80s, but the renewed popularity of coffee drinking in the United States in the '90s brought prosperity. In fact, Kona coffee is unique and has found a niche in the world market.

Prior to the mid-1950s, most papayas were produced in backyards or on family farms in Oahu. Pushed out by the growth of Honolulu and other towns, major production transferred in the 1960s to the Puna District, the eastern volcanic apex of the Big Island. Jet transport to the mainland opened a market. Then the deadly ringspot virus hit. By 1997, with production down to 60 percent, the papaya industry looked doomed. Thanks to grower-financed research at Cornell and the University of Hawaii, within four years the use of resistant genetically improved varieties had returned production to original levels.

One of the most exciting of recent intentions is to develop a bamboo industry, again in the Puna District of the Big Island. Bamboo, really a large grass, is one of the most easily sustainable and environmentally positive crops on earth, per unit of weight stronger than steel and easily harvested.

Hawaii has long had a reputation for top quality, fresh deep-sea fish, and these are in high demand on the mainland and internationally. To distinguish these fish, wholesalers and retailers worldwide use Hawaiian names, e.g., *ono* instead of wahoo, *mahimahi* instead of dolphin fish, and *ahi* instead of yellowfin tuna. High-tech aquaculture also began in the early 1960s, producing sumptuous quantities of fish, shrimp, lobster, abalone, and seaweed, as well as more exotic items such as giant clams and seahorses.

Ellison S. Onizuka, Astronaut (1946–86)

Ellison Onizuka, who was both the first astronaut of Asian extraction and the first from Hawaii, wanted to be an astronaut from when he was a small boy, but he told no one: "I just kept quiet and read all I could about the space program." His second generation Hawaiian-Japanese family would not have understood, nor would his neighbors in tiny Keopu in the north Kona coffee-growing district of the Big Island. They scarcely knew what an engineer was. Now the Center for International Astronomy on the Big Island is named after him.

Ellison Onizuka entered active duty with the United States Air Force in January 1970 after receiving his commission at the University of Colorado through the four-year ROTC program.

As an aerospace flight test engineer and test pilot, Onizuka worked at the Sacramento Air Logistics Center at McClellan Air Force Base and the USAF Test Pilot School and Air Force Flight Test Center at Edwards Air Force Base, both in California. He logged more than 1,700 hours flying time and won many outstanding commendations.

Chosen from thousands, he completed a one-year NASA training and evaluation period in 1978 and 1979. Subsequently he worked on orbiter test and checkout teams and launch support crews at the Kennedy Space Center and numerous other technical assignments.

His first space flight was as a mission specialist on the *Discovery* shuttle flight STS 51-C, which had been delayed several times, the first Department of Defense space shuttle mission. Launched from the Kennedy Space Center in Florida in January 1985, *Discovery* made 48 orbits of the Earth before landing. With the completion of this flight, Onizuka logged a total of 74 hours in space.

Onizuka was a mission specialist on STS 51-L, which left the Kennedy Space Center at 11:38:00 EST on January 28, 1986. Among the six other crew was the elementary school teacher Sharon Christa McAuliffe. They all died instantly when *Challenger* exploded one minute and thirteen seconds after launch.

A short time before the disaster, Onizuka had been asked what his long-term plans were. He replied, "To fly as long and as many times as I can."

The Military

Hawaii remains the United States' most militarized state. The five services still control about 250,000 ac or about 6 percent of the state. With Pearl Harbor and neighboring Hickham Air Force Base, the Army's Schofield Barracks in mid-island, Kaneʻohe Bay Marine Corps Base on the northeast coast, the US Coast Guard's 14th District Base on Sand Island in Honolulu Harbor, the huge coral-pink Tripler Army Medical Center on the slopes of Moanalua Ridge overlooking northwest Honolulu, and more than a hundred other sites and installations—from radar stations on the Koʻolau Range to Fort DeRussy Beach, which abuts Waikiki Beach—the military control about a quarter of the island of Oahu. Oahu is the center for military activities from California through Australia to the Middle East and East Africa. As it was on December 7, 1941, Pearl Harbor is still home to the Pacific fleet. With around 45,000 servicemen and servicewomen with some 50,000 dependents and employing about 19,000 civilians, military spending in Hawaii can reach around $3 billion a year. Hawaii had come a long way from Pearl Harbor when Japanese-Hawaiian General Eric Ken Shinseki, born on Kauai, was appointed the 34th Chief of Staff of the entire United States Army in June 1999.

Businesspeople and state politicians of all parties support the military presence, and the Hawaii Chamber of Commerce lobbies in Washington to maximize this presence. Military reductions in the early 2000s were disappointing for Hawaii. Socially, military personnel tend to keep to themselves, so despite such a large enclave, tensions between military and locals are minimal.

During the Korean War (1950–1953), US forces once again made Hawaii a staging ground. Hawaiians volunteered, and about 4,000 were drafted, almost twice the national average. Some 456 people from Hawaii died in the war; more than 900 were wounded—Tripler Army Medical Center became enormously busy, and Pearl Harbor expanded facilities. The connection has continued. Today over 17,000 Korean War veterans live in Hawaii, and the nation's first and only Korean War Museum stands in Wahiawa, just east of Schofield Barracks. The director says veterans of the war "walk around looking at displays with this kind of time-warp stare.... It is a temple as much as a museum."

The effects of the Vietnam War (1957–1975) were similar to those of the Korean War, though they lasted much longer and were much more socially divisive, though less so than on the mainland. Some 277 Hawaiians were killed and about twice as many wounded. Again Tripler received thousands. In both wars, industry lost skilled tradesmen to war work, mainland defense workers arrived in large numbers, and Hawaiian labor also went overseas to work for the military in places like Guam and Okinawa. Several thousand non-Communist Vietnamese fled to Hawaii after the war.

New Governors Reflect Ethnic Makeup

Since the mid-1970s, incumbents of the governor's office have at last reflected Hawaii's demographic makeup. George Ariyoshi, 1974–86, was the first governor of Japanese ethnicity; John Waiheʻe, 1986–94, was the first native Hawaiian; Benjamin Cayetano, 1994–2002, was the first Filipino-American; Linda Lingle, elected in 2002, was the first of Jewish faith. She is also became the first woman to lead  Hawaii in the almost 110 years since Queen Liliʻuokalani was deposed and is the first Republican governor since 1962.

Lingle was elected to Maui County Council in 1980 and later became mayor of that county for two very successful four-year terms—the first woman in that office and the youngest ever. Travel magazines began calling Maui "Best Island in the World"—as the airport proudly proclaimed. With Hawaii's economy now booming (2005 was a record tourism year), Lingle has proved to be a popular governor, despite being a Republican in a largely Democratic state. (At the time of writing, the house had a four to one Democratic majority, the senate five to one.) As in other similarly divided states, what will be interesting to watch in Hawaii is whether a Republican governor and her Democratic colleagues can work together for the good of the state—as they have done to a considerable degree since 2002.

Jaws—the Wave

Imagine skiing down the face of a five-story building travelling forwards at 25 mph, changing its face with shifts and chops and all the time trying to crush you. That's a weak description of riding a surfboard down "Jaws."

Jaws is the name the elite and most fearless of Hawaiian surfers give to the massive waves that form off the north shore of Maui, a little east of Ho'okipa Beach where the Peahi Valley meets the ocean. Here, not far from Maui's main urban area of Kahului-Wailuku, a spur of ancient reef pokes out underwater from the shore with a deep-water channel on each side. It catches the fast-moving waves coming from the northwest Pacific, suddenly forcing them from deep water into shallow. They immediately rear up into huge walls of water, with white heads like a thousand running, roaring Tyrannosaurus Rex. Only in the last 20 years have men dared to challenge Jaws's power.

Riding Jaws lasts about 17 to 22 seconds, but surfers prepare for at least 24 hours. The key to surfing Jaws is to first surf the weather reports of the University of Hawaii online to see if any storms have moved in from the coasts of Japan and northeast Russia toward the Aleutians. When such storms produce winds that flow consistently in the same direction for hundreds of miles, they create large swells that race across the North Pacific. Some 390 mi northwest of Maui, they pass the National Weather Service buoy No. 51001, which measures their height and speed about twelve hours before they reach the beach. Fifteen- to twenty-foot waves at the buoy become true monsters when they hit the spur of reef. When Jaws is small, it is 20 ft (6 m). At its best (or worst), it can have a face of 60–70 ft (18–21 m). As one newcomer put it, "When I thought I should have been nearly at the bottom of the face I realized I was not even halfway down."

Too powerful for the conventional approach of paddling, Jaws requires a combination of surfing and windsurfing techniques and equipment: the board must have footstraps, and surfers are towed into the swell by a jet ski before letting go of the towrope and beginning the ride down and across the face. If after riding Jaws surfers reach the calm channel, they are towed out to the commencement area by the jet ski to begin again. If they are dragged under by Jaws, they have to be rescued in the few seconds between waves.

The General Economy

For 200 years, Hawaii has been an "export/service" dominated economy led by sandalwood, whaling, sugar and pineapples, the military, and now the last of these, tourism. Each has been encouraged by the region's natural resources: naturally growing sandalwood; whales in the millions of square miles of surrounding ocean; the natural harbors of Honolulu and Lahaina; warm-temperate climate, ample water supply, and fertile soils for sugar and pineapples; a strategic position for the military; and for the tourists, an ideal climate and an endless variety of picturesque scenery, from snowcapped volcanoes and black volcanic wastelands to lush green valleys, as well as beautiful beaches and massive surfing waves.

Historically, emphasis on these "natural" industries has made sound economic sense. In fact, since the mid-1970s Hawaii's level of exports (most being of course to the mainland) has been about five times that of the United States as a whole. On the other hand, as the 1980s and 1990s once again showed, such historical dependence on the outside world makes Hawaii's now highly regulated economy more vulnerable to events beyond its control. Hawaii needs sustainable, multi-crop agriculture to protect against the vulnerability of tourism, and that appears to be the trend.

Must-See Sites: Lanai

The smallest of the inhabited islands, Lanai was probably first settled in the 1400s and remained a fief of Maui's chiefs. Caught up in the expansionist wars of the late 1700s, it was ravaged in 1778 by Kalaniopu'u of the Big Island and population declined to a few hundred by the late 1800s. In the third quarter of that century, Mormons, led by the enigmatic Walter Murray Gibson, attempted to establish a colony. Several efforts at growing sugarcane and raising cattle failed, though the ranch manager George Munroe introduced the moisture-gathering Cook Island pines, now so common. From the 1920s, pineapples became the mainstay until tourism took over in the 1980s.

Lanai City

In the central uplands with its many Cook Island pines and its elongated central Dole Park, little Lanai City lolls languidly and contentedly in a pre-World War II time warp. It was built by Dole's pineapple company in the 1920s and is still the only town on the island. As in the 1920s, houses are left unlocked, and people have plentiful time to chat. There are tiny wooden general stores and souvenir and art shops and the modest shingle-roofed Lanai Hotel in town. Just outside Lanai City and pleasantly cool at 1,600 ft (493 m) is the superb Lodge at Koele, set in a pine forest like some mighty late-1800s European hunting lodge. Nearby is one end of the pine-studded Munroe Trail, which allows one to drive along the island's volcanic mountain spine. The trail's highest point is Lana'ihale, at 3,370 ft (1,020 m), giving splendid views of the other islands.

Palawai Basin, and Coasts

To the south, the great bare, flat, shallow Palawai Basin, a remnant of an extinct volcano, gives some idea of the mighty pineapple plantation that once filled it. On the south coast, like a vast stuccoed villa on the Riviera lies the splendid Manele Bay Hotel, commanding an ocean view above the fine beach of Hulopo'e Bay (which like all Hawaiian beaches is public) and the remains of an ancient village. Nearby, a little off the coast, is the great legend-shrouded Sweetheart or Pu'u Pehe Rock.

Enjoy the dirt roads, the single gas station, the native Hawaiian village ruins, the isolated beaches—like the northern Shipwreck Beach with its decaying World War II Liberty Ship offshore (shown below)—and the almost palpable peacefulness.

12

Native Sovereignty?

Encouraged by the struggle for civil rights in the mainland US in the 1960s, a native Hawaiian renaissance was beginning to take place by the 1970s. Many issues merged to create national feeling: the re-emergence of long-distance ocean voyaging; desire to recover the island of Kahoolawe; opposition to continuing commercial take-overs of land and the movement to protect ancient sites; revival of traditional hula; and an interest in the Hawaiian language. And in 1993, on the 100th anniversary of the coup against the monarchy, the US Congress and President Clinton apologized for the acts of their predecessors. As part of all these and developing from them, there arose the demand for some kind of returned Hawaiian sovereignty.

Issues that Moved Native Hawaiians

Navigation

When Hawaiians no longer navigated the far ocean, their early knowledge of navigation methods was lost. Its recovery is an exciting story. The resurrection of Hawaiian navigation methods was part of a larger movement that occurred in the Pacific and Polynesia generally, stimulated by a book by New Zealand pioneer David Lewis, *We the Navigators*, published by the University of Hawaii Press in 1972. Lewis was devoted to the rediscovery, preservation, and propagation of the ancient Polynesian methods of navigation.

For many years, the University of Hawaii anthro-pologist Ben Finney had opposed the view that Polynesian colonization was accidental. He was determined to prove that, using traditional methods of navigation, ancient Hawaiian double canoes could deliberately sail vast distances across the Pacific. In 1974–75, joined by Thomas Holmes and artist Herb Kane, he established the

Polynesian Voyaging Society. The society constructed a voyaging canoe in the ancient style. Its name was *Hokule'a*, the Hawaiian name of the star Arcturus.

In 1976, navigated by Mau Piailug from Satawal in the Caroline Islands in Micronesia (where knowledge of the ancient methods had been tenuously preserved), and monitored by David Lewis, *Hokule'a* sailed from Honolulu to Papeete Tahiti. Mau Piailug navigated by the ancient methods, guided by the sun, star patterns, winds, waves, currents, flights of birds, color of water, the appearance of clouds, and other natural phenomena. This was the first Polynesian double canoe deep ocean voyage in perhaps 500 years.

Hokule'a then returned north in the total control of a Polynesian crew, though this time using navigation instruments. Near the end of his book, *Hokule'a: The Way to Tahiti*, Finney writes:

> Our efforts... had turned the tide against those who claimed that traditional canoes and navigation methods were not good enough to have allowed the ancient Polynesians to set out purposefully to explore and settle their island world... [our] voyage to Tahiti had rescued the ancient Polynesians from their damnation as mere "accidental voyagers" and put them back in their rightful place among the most daring and resourceful voyagers the world has ever seen.

Against better judgment, besides the men Finney wanted, six native Hawaiians were accepted as crew because of the insistence of certain board members of the Polynesian Voyaging Society. The worry was that these men had no experience in the self-discipline necessary for a long voyage on a tiny crowded craft. In fact, four absolutely refused to share in ship-board duties or learn navigation from Mau Piailug. Had their behavior sabotaged the expedition, it would have been tragic, for its success has come to have immense significance for the rebirth of a confident native Hawaiian self-image. After the voyage, all crew members were reconciled, and they and volunteers of different ethnicities have for many years worked together to develop the Polynesian voyaging traditions they all admire and cherish.

Since that time *Hokule'a* has made many successful

Ben R. Finney, Voyaging Pioneer

Convinced that early Polynesian settlement was deliberate, Ben Finney first thought of building a voyaging canoe and sailing it to Tahiti while a student at the University of Hawaii. In the mid-1960s at the University of California at Santa Barbara, he and his students built *Nalehia* ("The Skilled Ones," named for the graceful gliding of her twin hulls), a 40 ft (12 m) replica double canoe that provided basic information for the historic 1976 voyage.

After working in the Navy and steel and aerospace industries, Finney received anthropology degrees from the Universities of Hawaii (1959) and Harvard (1964) and taught in California and Australia before joining the faculty at the University of Hawaii in 1970, where he has worked in anthropology ever since. His fieldwork has taken him through Polynesia and New Guinea in Melanesia, as well as to the NASA Johnson Space Center and Zvezdnyy Gorodok (Star City), an hour's drive east of Moscow. In 1973 he founded the Polynesian Voyaging Society and was its first president.

His initiative and perseverance were crucial in getting the canoe *Hokule'a* ("Star of Joy") built, and he sailed on its first famous long-distance voyage to Tahiti in 1976, writing about the voyage in his fascinating book, *Hokule'a: the Way to Tahiti*. He was aboard the *Hokule'a* voyages to New Zealand in 1985, to Rarotonga in the Cook Islands in 1992, and to the Marquesas in 1995 in the support vessel. Also in 1995 he was present at and documented the great assemblage of canoes and the subsequent ceremonies at the holy island of Raiatea in the Society Islands, after which he sailed with the fleet back to Hawaii.

Finney has continued to test and reconstruct Polynesian voyaging canoes for long voyages to help solve questions of early Hawaiian and Polynesian history. More recently working at NASA and elsewhere, he has evolved an anthropological approach to the exploration and hoped-for colonization of space. He is also interested in SETI (the search for extraterrestrial intelligence) and the revival of ancient cultures.

voyages from Hawaii to Tahiti, the Cook Islands, and even New Zealand. By 2004 the double canoe had been navigated by nature across more than 100,000 mi of the Pacific.

Hawai-iloa, a second canoe named after a mythological discoverer of Hawaii and built with materials more like those of the early voyagers, was completed by the 1990s. In 1995 *Hawai-iloa* and five other reconstructed canoes sailed north from the high, serrated Marquesas across the Equator to Hawaii to commemorate the original discovery of Hawaii and to celebrate the 1970s revival of long-distance voyaging.

It is now common for native Hawaiians who have learned the ancient methods of traditional navigation to take groups of young men and women to sea, where they learn the discipline, attitudes, and cooperation of ancient seafaring.

In May and June 2004, *Hokule'a* sailed to the ancient islands that stretch 1,200 mi to the northwest of Kauai, probably the first double canoe, traditionally navigated voyage there in several centuries. The voyage was made in cooperation with various private and government agencies and schools; the aim of the Polynesian Voyaging Society was to contrast the northwest chain's relatively pristine environmental condition with that of the inhabited main islands and thus to increase environmental awareness among Hawaii's young people. Master navigators Nainoa Thompson and Bruce Blankenfeld also examined the skill of the most recent of the navigator candidates.

Kahoolawe, the Sacred and Shelled Island

For decades after World War II, native Hawaiians were unhappy because the US military continued to use the 45 sq mi uninhabited island of Kahoolawe, just south of Maui, as a firing range and training area, off-limits to civilians. Kahoolawe had traditionally been of religious significance and held sites of archaeological interest.

In the 1970s, native Hawaiian activists began to make sneak runs, paddling ashore at night to annoy the Navy. The thrill of the undertaking and their unquestioned moral certainty were an irresistible combination. To everyone's dismay, one night two popular activists, George Helm and Kimo Mitchell, paddled on their surfboards to the island and disappeared without a trace.

Decades of protests, including occupations of the

island, ended in 1994 when it was agreed it would be returned to the state of Hawaii as a reservation for Hawaiian culture. A rehabilitation program began to remove unexploded ordinance and debris, restore *heiau* and ancient houses, and reintroduce native plants attacked by a huge feral goat population. Sites are now on the US National Register of Historic Places. The Navy did not formally hand over the island until November 2003.

In April 2004 the Navy removed its last barge full of debris in its unprecedented $460 million cleanup of something like 84.5 percent of the island, though significant quantities of ordnance remain in completely inaccessible areas. The rains of winter 2005–06 brought huge areas of green plants across the reviving island. As activists have wryly noted, that some ordnance remains is actually an insurance against commercial development. One observed, "It provides an ironic sense of protection.... It's never going to be safe for hotel or golf course development."

Loss of Land and Ancient Hawaiian Sites

Increasing tourism and new residents brought a need for new hotel and house construction. Windward Oahu was soon being developed. In 1970 Henry J. Kaiser planned to build expensive houses in the Kalama Valley. But pig farmers and mixed farmers of native Hawaiian and Asian extraction already lived there. They would have to be evicted, their way of life destroyed for wealthy newcomers. The organization Kokua Kalama formed to oppose the development. Some members were arrested for trespassing, but the evictions succeeded and the houses were built. What happened in the Kalama Valley spurred native Hawaiians and their supporters in the wider community to action.

For much of the twentieth century, when business premises or hotels were constructed, remains of ancient culture in the area were generally ignored. The so-called Battle of the Bones began in the mid-1980s with the decision to construct the Ritz-Carlton Kapalua at Honokahua, Maui. The company wanted to build the hotel right on top of an ancient burial ground of perhaps 2,000 graves dating from the 800s to the mid-1800s. By then native Hawaiians were no longer accepting such actions, and their protests stopped the proposal. After a year of negotiating, the chain agreed to

Erected in 1990 on the 100th anniversary of Duke Kahanamoku's birth, the popular bronze statue of Hawaii's superb swimmer and surfing ambassador stands on Kuhio Beach, facing Kalakaua Avenue, Waikiki. Some critics say the real Duke would never have stood with his back to the ocean. Maria G. Figueroa

locate the hotel back from the beach, thus preserving the ground, which was reconsecrated by a *kahuna*. The most important result of the Ritz-Carlton imbroglio was legislation that prevents construction from desecrating ancient historical sites. For example, the Manele Bay Hotel on Lanai was built inland from the beach, thus preserving the remains of a unique, ancient Hawaiian fishing village. Recently, some large hotels and resorts have begun to employ "cultural advisers" to inform staff and guests of the significance of things native to Hawaii.

A multiplicity of activities and demonstrations has

continued. A massive 1993 gathering of thousands protested at 'Iolani Palace for four days against the overthrow of the Hawaiian kingdom a hundred years earlier, and both cool and fiery speeches called the native community to action; the palace was draped in black bunting and then-Governor John Waihe'e, a native Hawaiian, gave orders that only the Hawaiian flag, not the American, must fly over state government buildings during that period. In 1997, legislation was proposed that would have restricted access to undeveloped private land by those gathering plants for traditional Hawaiian medicines. In response, protesters gathered in the atrium of the capitol for twenty-three hours of drumming, successfully preventing the bill's passage. Protests in the form of motorcades, as at Kahului airport on Maui in 2001, have tried to prevent such things as legal challenges to the legitimacy of the Office of Hawaiian Affairs and Hawaiian homesteads. Patient but persistent community pressure in 2004 in several parts of the islands and especially in the Big Island were aimed at reviving the frustratingly stalled program to protect ancient Hawaiian burial sites.

Ill-conceived action can also harm the native cause. One such action was the attempt to stop the construction of geothermal wells in Kilauea Volcano "to prevent desecration of the volcano goddess, Pele." This protest was medieval and retrograde, the geological equivalent of wanting to reinstate religious *kapu* to stop women from eating bananas or the medical equivalent of reintroducing human sacrifice to end an epidemic. (Later attempts to halt the project because of the emission of gases dangerous to the health of local people were a very different matter.)

Hula

There is something quintessentially Hawaiian about the hula, and modern native Hawaiians see it as crucial to their cultural identity. Though acknowledging its significance for tourism, native Hawaiians see much tourist hula as kitch, and have sought to rescue the more serious aspects of the art. A number of well-attended festivals bring many *hula halau* together to compete. Among these is the usually sold-out, week-long, gloriously colorful Merrie Monarch Festival in Hilo on the Big Island (named for King Kalakaua).

Hula is now a living, evolving core Hawaiian activity and is spreading outside Hawaii's borders. There are hula schools in more than thirty US states and at least six other countries. At time of writing, for instance, there were dozens of hula schools in the San Francisco Bay area alone. The annual World Invitational Hula Festival at the Waikiki Shell in Honolulu is evidence of this expansion.

Renewal of Language

As with hula, so with language: In large part, a language defines a cultural or ethnic group. Nineteenth-century political and economic developments established English as the dominant language of the kingdom. There was some opposition to private Japanese-language afterschool programs. But at no time in Hawaii's history have Japanese, Chinese, or other languages ever been illegal and, despite common claims to the contrary, neither has the Hawaiian language. Eventually English became the medium of instruction in all government-funded schools and most parents saw the necessity of English for fitting into the social and economic system. Hawaiian was slowly dying out.

Paralleling Polynesian language developments elsewhere, there has been a resurgence of interest in preserving the Hawaiian language since the late 1970s. The state has helped, with special efforts by the Department of Education. There is a multitude of immersion programs in both private and public schools in which classes are conducted entirely in Hawaiian. At university level, courses have burgeoned, and the first all-Hawaiian language college exists in Hilo. Since 1978 Hawaii has been, with English, one of the two official languages of the state.

The 1993 Apology Resolution

High-octane fuel added to the sovereignty fire in 1993. In October and November that year, the US Senate and House passed United States Public Law 103–150, the "Apology Resolution," which acknowledged the 100th anniversary of the January 17, 1893, overthrow of the kingdom of Hawaii and offered an apology to native Hawaiians on behalf of the United States. It was signed by President Clinton on November 23. Hawaiian Senator Daniel K. Inouye introduced the resolution, stressing that "It's just a simple

Courting Dance of Lanai Lizards, 2004

This charming essay by Joana Varawa appeared in the *Lana'i Times* on July 15, 2004, a fine example of modern Hawaiian writing:

Male calls me out to the verandah to see something. I am tired and grouchy, want only to sleep. He comes in and says, "Joana, the Jackson is doing this." And he imitates the lizard's slow motion, very slowly up one leg, the front leg, and very slowly forward and then down, with a little sideways jerk. And he says, "And the girl is doing this." And he dances from side to side, swaying in a slow sweet shuffle, and says, "The boy goes like this" and so slowly reaches out his arm from his side and paws me. "They are holding hands," he tells me. "Come outside and look." And I go outside and peer into the tangled vine and see nothing but leaves and branches.

"There. There." I peer and peer and finally make out the dark mottled body of the female. She is almost black around her head, shoulders, belly, and back, then becomes a mottled, spotted black and green, so that her body dissolves in the middle into shadows and spots. The male is fierce bright green, his long tail curved around a branch. It is the first thing I see, that bright green succulent coil, and then almost without believing that anything could be so brilliant, I make out the long body of the male laid along the branch. His head is adorned with spiky horns, one longer than the other and his brilliant green eye is centered with a round black dot, that swivels around, almost popping out of his head. He lumbers along the branch so slowly it seems he hasn't moved, but he has, and the female sways from side to side, tossing her body left and right, very visible and fey. He finally reaches her and very slowly reaches for her, and she takes his hand. It is clearly a hand, and clasps it. Male says, "Look look, they are holding hands" and they *are* holding hands.

I try taking a picture and nothing happens. I take several and become frustrated, missing the slow dancing Jacksons as I try to photograph them. But Male is watching intently and is beside himself with happiness. "They are holding hands," he says, "look, she is reaching for him, she is touching him."

It is dark now, and later drops of rain cool the air. The moon is coming, the sky is grey and white and swirling in the wind, and I wonder if the Jacksons are together, and if they are holding hands.

resolution of apology." Nevertheless, the apology has been used as a justification for action and native Hawaiians have derived much political capital from it. Some key clauses are:

> Whereas, from 1826 until 1893, the United States recognized the independence of the Kingdom of Hawaii, extended full and complete diplomatic recognition to the Hawaiian Government, and entered into treaties and conventions with the Hawaiian monarchs to govern commerce and navigation....
>
> Whereas, without the active support and intervention by the United States diplomatic and military representatives, the insurrection against the Government of Queen Lili'uokalani would have failed for lack of popular support and insufficient arms;
>
> Whereas, the indigenous Hawaiian people never directly relinquished their claims to their inherent sovereignty as a people... either through their monarchy or through a plebiscite or referendum;
>
> Whereas the Republic of Hawaii [i.e., the settlers' oligarchy] also ceded [to the United States] 1,800,000 acres of crown, government and public lands of the Kingdom of Hawaii, without the consent of or compensation to the Native Hawaiian people of Hawaii or their sovereign government;
>
> [the Congress] expresses its commitment to acknowledge the ramifications of the overthrow of the Kingdom of Hawaii, in order to provide a proper foundation for reconciliation between the United States and the Native Hawaiian people.

WHAT KIND OF SOVEREIGNTY?

On July 31 each year, drawing an analogy between 1843 and the present time, native Hawaiians gather in the park of Thomas Square, Honolulu, to celebrate the anniversary of the British restoration of Hawaiian sovereignty by Admiral Sir Richard Thomas. At the 2004 ceremony one participant said, "The importance of this ceremony is that it represents the continuity of our people [and our] responsibility to provide... for the restoration of our government." Another declared, "We are recalling the historical event that

This bronze statue of Kamehameha in helmet and feather cloak was unveiled by King Kalakaua in May 1883, in the tiny town of Kapa'au, the district of Kamehameha's birth. It had for a time been lost at sea near the Falkland Islands in 1880. Its better-known duplicate stands in front of Ali'iolani Hale in Honolulu. Hector L. Torres and Catherine Metz

occurred right here in 1843 and applying it today. We're calling upon the United States government to withdraw from its illegal occupation of our Homelands."

As Governor Linda Lingle said about Hawaiian sovereignty in January 2003 soon after being elected, "This is an historical issue, based on a relationship between an independent government and the United States of America, and what has happened since and the steps that we need to take to make things right."

But what is to be done to "make things right"? One sees a bumper sticker in Hawaii which reads: "GOT KOKO?" meaning "Do you have Hawaiian blood?" This is a shortcut statement for a matter of immense complexity.

It is not even clear how many different sovereignty groups there are, because they tend to split into factions—Nation of Hawaii (oldest and largest), both Kingdoms of Hawaii (there are two), the Hawaiian Kingdom, Reinstated Hawaii Kingdom, and so forth. A working estimate identifies about 10 groups whose total membership is perhaps 50,000 out of the approximately 250,000 people in the islands who claim to be part-Hawaiian, "native Hawaiian," or "Hawaiian." An early group formed in 1972 was Aboriginal Lands of Hawaiian Ancestry (ALOHA). In 1978 an Office of Hawaiian Affairs (OHA) was set up to protect and help native Hawaiians (with loans for instance), the environment, and OHA assets, but some have opposed its actions as being too connected to the state government. Several attempts have been made to gain consensus, and in 1987 a constitutional convention for a Hawaiian nation was called, at which a constitution was drafted, and even a president of Ka Lahui Hawai'i ("The Hawaiian Nation") was chosen. But at a later election in 1999, split by partisan issues, only 9 percent of eligible native Hawaiians voted. Difficulties continue to arise over alleged control by the state government and over tactics and strategies and who should be allowed to vote.

What is advocated runs a whole gamut. One group argues that the Bayonet Constitution of 1887 is the appropriate one. In 1998 another group crowned a Hawaiian monarch at 'Iolani Palace in Honolulu: his Royal Highness, Akahi Nui, great-grandnephew of Queen Lili'uokalani.

Individual sovereignty activists also vary widely in approach and temperament. There is the much-publicized tenured professor at the University of Hawaii, Manoa, Dr. Haunani-Kay Trask (born in California), who has said she hates *haoles* (Caucasians). In her speech at the 1993 centenary of the overthrow of the monarchy, she howled, "I am NOT an American, I am NOT an American, I will DIE before I am an American...." As Kenneth R. Conklin, another University of Hawaii professor, says on his website: "She speaks and writes with a fiery passion that intimidates opponents and often frightens even her allies." Though her tactics offend many, she has considerable support, and anyone who has read the native Hawaiian history in this book will understand some of the reasons for her emphatic discontent.

Dr. Noa Emmett Aluli, executive director of Molokai General Hospital, uses different tactics, working within the system getting better medical treatment for native Hawaiians and encouraging traditional medicine; wanting native Hawaiians to adopt a healthy diet and lifestyle; pushing for the wider utilization of Hawaiian Home Lands; calmly but with determination achieving on many fronts. Aluli never uses angry rhetoric, never attacks an opponent or raises his voice, and is not anti-white American or anti- any ethnic group, but simply pro-native Hawaiian.

It is important to point out that many native Hawaiians are not sovereignty activists. While they want to preserve and extend native Hawaiian culture and the welfare of native Hawaiians, they are content to be American citizens and do not want separatism.

Nationhood within the United States

The most canvassed model of sovereignty is nationhood within the United States, the "Nation within a Nation" approach, supported by sovereignty activists like Dr. Aluli. This idea is also widely supported among the general Hawaiian population as a solution to sovereignty pressures. There are ample precedents, with more than 300 recognized "nations" within US territorial limits, made up of Native Americans (American Indians), Aleuts (on the Aleutian Islands, part of Alaska) and Inuits (Eskimos) in Alaska. This model is popular because it is the least contentious and racially divisive and because many people believe that US history shows that secession will never be allowed.

Though not independence, this model allows much autonomy: a specified territory to control, the right to determine the preferred type of government, within certain limits the right to police and administer justice, immigration control, and the right to charter businesses. As has happened in the Native American "nations," this model creates a good groundwork for preserving the minority culture. In the case of Native Americans, there have, however, been problems with this model, such as unsuitable constitutions drafted by the US Department of the Interior, inadequate mechanisms for resolving conflict, steady erosion of sovereignty by federal

Old Mores Linger

Many of the old Hawaiian ways of life still linger, but they acquire modern forms. Here is an account of the complex social relationships in Keʻanae, a native Hawaiian district midway along the rugged Hana Coast of northeast Maui. The residents maintain irrigated taro fields first cultivated more than 500 years ago:

> Keʻanae is perceived by islanders and tourists alike as a traditional Hawaiian place. Village residents identify themselves as people engaged in farming and fishing, descendants of the Hawaiian commoners…. [V]illagers still grow taro, but today the Polynesian staple is grown primarily for the market. Most of Keʻanae's taro is destined for Honolulu supermarkets in the form of factory-ground poi, the starchy paste that once formed the bulk of the Hawaiian diet. No one in Keʻanae subsists solely by farming and fishing. Taro marketing, wage labor, pensions, and social security link the community to the outside economy. Several men commute daily to work in construction or road labor while their wives and children maintain the taro patches. Except for retired residents, all but one of the adult males in the village held [wage-paying jobs] at the time of [this report]; only one householder was a full-time taro grower….
>
> In Keʻanae, almost anyone with part-Hawaiian ancestry may be called Hawaiian if he or she acts Hawaiian. Acting Hawaiian is primarily a measure of participation in symmetrical, in-kind exchanges… "In Keʻanae you *give*, don't sell." A taro farmer always tries to muster unpaid labor from within the family to harvest for the weekly market order. Growers who successfully manipulate family ties may even prevail upon younger relatives to drive in from outside for the occasion, rather than pay non-relatives….
>
> One party may strive to indebt the other, prompting an anxious overcompensation by the unwilling participant. Outside the sphere of kinship, relationships tend to cycle between amity and avoidance in response to perceived inequities in exchange. The terms of exchange inside are goods and work; primarily foodstuffs, but also transportation, hospitality, taro shoots for planting, and various other small services and favors…. Some goods are higher than others in their compensatory value and in their power to obligate the recipient to make a return gift…. Accepting hospitality for a night is more portentous than dropping in to "talk story" for an afternoon. Certain commodities are appropriate to particular situations, but the rules may be manipulated to create indebtedness….

Accepting poi—symbolically the stuff of life—from anyone but a close relative would be shameful. For fear of incurring indebtedness, elderly people and those with no patches open, are confronted with the irony of living in a community known as "the taro place" and having to buy poi at the supermarket in town.

Pork is the highest food gift. The main course at a luau, the Hawaiian feast, is always *kalua* pig, cooked in an underground oven… the guests are expected to consume much and to carry away the balance when they leave. The luau foods then become the stuff of many future in-kind exchanges… superficially, the material circumstances of life are much the same for all Keʻanae households as the result of a more or less conscious effort not to appear more prosperous than one's neighbor. Violating the egalitarian ethic usually leads to a breach of communication, mutual avoidance, "talk stink" (censorious gossip) and accusations of social climbing—"acting high." Acting high can mean entertaining *haoles* [whites/foreigners] in one's home… or trying to create indebtedness by giving too much in exchange.

—*Jocelyn Linnekin, "Inside, Outside: A Hawaiian Community in the World-System," in* Clio in Oceania, *edited by Aletta Biersack,* © *Smithsonian Institution Press, Washington DC, 1991*

courts, corruption of ruling bodies, huge sums spent on lobbying Congress, and that millions of dollars in revenue from casinos somehow bypasses many of the people, who still live in poverty. Ideally the Hawaiian nation would learn from and so be able to avoid such negative features. Indeed, Native American nations are now addressing these very problems.

Native Hawaiians who prefer this model ask for the return of the Ceded Lands (Crown and Government Lands ceded to the United States by the republic at annexation), which include, for instance, substantial sections of the Waiʻanae area on the west coast of Oahu. To make for larger contiguous areas, there might be exchange of Ceded Land in some areas for US land in others.

More Specific Sovereignty

Some argue that sovereignty should be more complete. After all, before the coup Hawaii was an independent nation, recognized as such by not just the United States but by other great powers such as Britain, Japan, and France. Such was never the case with the Native American lands.

A precedent might be that of the Iroquois, who have their own passports and a recognized status at the United Nations, separate from that of the United States. Another precedent might be the Commonwealth of Puerto Rico, which as an "Associated State" of the United States has its own taxation system, its own team at the Olympic Games and in other sporting competitions, but does not control immigration. Presumably native Hawaiians would choose to amalgamate preferred aspects of such models.

Total Independence

This approach calls for absolute separation. Though it is extreme, its supporters range across the whole spectrum of native Hawaiian life. Some advocates want the return of whole islands to the independent Hawaiian nation, Kahoolawe certainly. (In fact, Kahoolawe is already acknowledged as significantly native and would come under general native control even in the plan for nationhood within the United States.) Details are debated; some independence groups argue for complete sovereignty but inclusive government with naturalization and citizenship open to all races. As the leader of Reinstated Hawaiian Kingdom puts it: "We're for full independence, with the Americans as allies."

GENERAL ISSUES AND THE AKAKA BILL

Within the wider Hawaiian community there exists a lot of goodwill toward the idea of some native Hawaiian sovereignty, as evidenced by the Native Hawaiian Reorganization Act of 2005 (S. 147), often called the Akaka Bill after its chief sponsor, Senator Daniel Akaka, the first native Hawaiian in the Senate, with eight co-sponsors, many from other states. The Akaka Bill would give native Hawaiians the same rights as Native Americans, Aleuts, and Inuits, and a nation within the United States. For six long years, the OHA, Hawaii's governors, and all the Hawaiian delegation (both Republicans and Democrats) have pursued such federal recognition of native Hawaiians, but have encountered congressional delays and challenges

Viewed from the roadside lookout, Ke'anae ("the mullet") Peninsula, formed by a lava flow from Haleakala, is seen protruding from the north shore of Maui. In fields that glint like mirrors, taro, the native Hawaiian staple for making poi, has been grown here for more than 500 years. Taro was brought to Hawaii by the Tahitian conquerors. Hawaii Visitors and Convention Bureau and Ron Dahlquist

of various sorts, the most recent being postponement to allow for legislation to mitigate the effects of Hurricane Katrina in late 2005.

As already shown, native Hawaiian status has been recognized at state level, and native Hawaiians participate in many state and federal programs, such as renewal of the Hawaiian language. But all political movements invite reaction, and in recent years the courts have heard claims that such special entitlements are unconstitutional because they are racially discriminatory. The first, in the year 2000, achieved a rejection of OHA rules that prevented non-native Hawaiians from voting in OHA elections. The Department of Hawaiian Home Lands (DHHL) has been similarly challenged, as well as the Kamehameha Schools, over their race-based admissions for native Hawaiian children (which had been accepted as appropriate since 1887). If passed, by giving federal status to special arrangements for native Hawaiians, the Akaka Bill would make it possible to circumvent these challenges.

Whatever the degree of Hawaiian sovereignty, it is assumed the inhabitants would continue to respect and make use of the ideals and institutions of liberty and democracy that in general US law protects. (There were none of these in ancient Hawaii, though individual rights were recognized during the kingdom from the 1830s.) Hawaiian culture, as rejuvenated today, would also be free of the religious and social repression known under the old social hierarchies.

Another fact about the movement for sovereignty should be remembered. Because it is occurring in a modern Western democracy, Hawaiian activists are not in danger of being killed for their political views. This situation remains in great contrast to equivalent political activism in most of the rest of the world. Since the early 1990s, for instance, the Chechens have died in the hundreds of thousands in their struggle to be free from Russia, which conquered their country in the early 1800s.

Chronology of Major Events

BCE

c. 1300   Last eruption of Mauna Kea on Big Island.

CE

c. 350   First Polynesian settlers from the Marquesas (some estimates earlier).

c. 1200   Second wave of settlers from Tahiti, become *ali'i* (chiefs).

1758   Kamehameha the Great born in North Kohala on the Big Island.

1778   First recorded European encounter; English Captain James Cook arrives, names archipelago Sandwich Islands after British lord.

1779   Cook killed in dispute with Hawaiians at Kealakekua.

1782   Kamehameha inherits power in the northern part of Big Island, begins conquest of other islands.

c. 1790   Most recent eruption of Haleakala Volcano on Maui.

1791   Pu'ukohola Heiau completed; Kamehameha controls all Hawaii Island.

1792/93   Captain William Brown first European to see Honolulu Harbor.

1794   Big Island is made a protectorate of Great Britain by Vancouver (never ratified by Britain).

1795   Kamehameha defeats chief of Oahu at Battle of Nu'uanu; only Kauai and Niihau outside his rule.

1801   Last eruption of Hualalai Volcano near Kailua-Kona, Big Island.

1803   John Young imports first horse.

1804   Kamehameha's invasion of Kauai postponed by plague.

1810   Kamehameha unifies Hawaiian islands through treaty with King of Kauai.

1810/20s   Sandalwood trade.

1814   Parker begins cattle industry on Big Island.

1815   Attempt by German G. A. Scheffer of Russian American Co. to take control in Hawaii.

1816   Honolulu Fort constructed.

1819   King Kamehameha dies; Liholiho takes throne as Kamehameha II (1819–1824).

1819   Liholiho and Ka'ahumanu destroy *kapu* (taboo) system; first whale caught off Hawaii by US ship; beginning of 50 years of whaling industry.

1820   First Protestant missionaries led by Bingham and Thurston from New England.

1823   Kamehameha II travels to Britain, dies of measles.

1825   Boy King Kauikeaouli ascends throne as Kamehameha III.

1834	Honolulu Police established by King Kamehameha III.
1832	Death of Ka'ahumanu; Kamehameha III for a time abolishes mission edicts.
1836	First newspaper in English published, *The Sandwich Island Gazette*.
1837	Hilo tsunami.
1838	Commencement of construction of Kawaiahao Church.
1839	Kamehameha III promulgates the Declaration of Rights and religious toleration.
1840	Kamehameha III promulgates first constitution.
1840s	Whaling at its zenith.
1842	First house of representatives elected.
1843	Unauthorized, Lord George Paulet annexes Hawaii, disavowed by Britain.
1843	Great Britain and France agree Sandwich Islands are an independent state.
1848	Kamehameha III authorizes Great *Mahele*, beginning land alienation to foreigners.
1849	French admiral De Tromelin destroys Honolulu fort, terrifies town.
1849–51	California gold rush brings boom to Hawaii agriculture.
1850	United States and the kingdom of Hawaii ratify treaty of friendship, commerce, and navigation.
1852	First Chinese contract sugar workers; new constitution.
1853	Smallpox epidemic kills thousands, mostly native Hawaiians.
1854	Kamehameha III dies; Alexander Liholiho takes throne as Kamehameha IV.
1858	C. R. Bishop and W. A. Aldrich begin Bishop Bank, predecessor of First Hawaiian Bank.
1859	Honolulu Gas Company established.
1860	Queen's Hospital, project of Kamehameha IV and Queen Emma, is begun.
1863	Elizabeth Sinclair purchases Niihau Island from King Kamehameha IV for $10,000.
1863	Kamehameha IV dies; Prince Lot ascends throne as Kamehameha V.
1864	Kamehameha V promulgates royal-based constitution.
1868	First Japanese contract plantation workers arrive.
1873	William C. Lunalilo elected king; mutiny of palace troops.
1874	King Lunalilo dies; David Kalakaua elected king.
1876	United States and Hawaii reciprocity treaty allows sugar into United States duty free.
1878	Lydia Kamaka'eha (later Queen Lili'uokalani) writes "Aloha 'Oe"; first telephone on Hawaii; first Portuguese arrive from the Azores.
1881	William H. Purvis introduces macadamia nuts.

1882   'Iolani Palace completed.

1884   Bernice Pauahi Bishop dies; Bishop Estate created, including establishment of Kamehameha Schools; United States extends 1875 reciprocity treaty for seven years in return for exclusive right to Pearl Harbor as naval base.

1887   King David Kalakaua forced to accept Bayonet Constitution.

1888   R.Wilcox leads unsuccessful revolt against Bayonet Constitution.

1889   Father Damien dies in Molokai leper colony.

1889   R. Wilcox leads second unsuccessful revolt against Bayonet Constitution.

1889   First artesian well drilled in Ewa plain, Maui, for commercial sugar and pineapple.

1891   King Kalakaua dies in San Francisco; Queen Lili'uokalani enthroned.

1893   Monarchy overthrown with complicity of US Consul and marines; provisional government under Dole declared, requests annexation by the US

1894   Republic of Hawaii declared with Dole as President (July 4).

1895   Revolt against Republic of Hawaii crushed; Queen Lili'uokalani forced to abdicate.

1898   Spanish-American War; Hawaii annexed as territory; Ceded Lands go to federal government; Dole appointed territorial governor

1900   Great Chinatown fire; first workers arrive from Puerto Rico.

1901   Foundation Hawaiian Pineapple Company.

1901   Honolulu Rapid Transit electric streetcars.

1902   First Korean workers arrive; Prince Jonah elected delegate; entrance to Pearl Harbor improved.

1903   Tourism committee formed.

1904   Counties created.

1905   First workers from the Philippines.

1907   College of Agriculture and Mechanic Arts established, now University of Hawaii.

1908   First mayor of City and County of Honolulu.

1909   Japanese workers on strike in sugar plantations.

1910   First plane flight in Hawaii.

1914   Hawaiians of British extraction go to World War I; German ships seek safety in Honolulu.

1917   United States declares war on Germany; German ships/ assets seized.

1920   Hawaiian Homes Commission Act; National Parks on Big Island (now Volcanoes National Park) and Maui

	(now Haleakala); Japanese workers strike.
1924	Violence in Kauai strike; sixteen workers, four police killed; Japanese immigration prohibited.
1927	Billboards prohibited.
1930s	Great Depression.
1935	Pan American Airways begin "China Clipper" seaplanes via Hawaii to Far East.
1935	"Hawaii Calls" radio program; Pan Am Clippers make airmail flights.
1940–41	Pearl Harbor improved; Kauai dock strike.
1941	Japan attacks Pearl Harbor; United States declares war; martial law established.
1944	Servicemen's Readjustment Act.
1945	Martial law ends; war ends; U.N. founded—Hawaii listed as non-self-governing territory.
1946	Tsunami hits Hilo.
1946	"Great Sugar Strike" on 33 plantations.
1950	Congressional investigations into Hawaiian Communist influence.
1952	First TV station.
1955	Pineapple cultivation at peak, 76,700 ac.
1959	Hawaii becomes 50th state; first jet service.
1960	First season Hawaii Opera Theater.
1968	ILWU pineapple workers strike for 61 days.
1974	9,000 ILWU sugar, pineapple workers strike for 21 days.
1976	Hokule'a, imitation double canoe, recreates voyage to Tahiti.
1978	Office of Hawaiian Affairs (OHA) set up.
1980s	Japanese tourism & investment boom; beginning of native Hawaiian activism & moves for Hawaiian sovereignty.
1983	Beginning of continuing series of eruptions of Kilauea Volcano, Big Island.
1990s	Last large-scale closing of sugar plantations and mills; economy in doldrums.
1992	Dole Co. shuts down last pineapple cannery.
1992	Hurricane Iniki hits Kauai.
1993	Congress passes the "Apology Resolution."
2000	US Supreme Court decides OHA elections violate 15th Amendment.
2002	First female governor, Linda Lingle, elected, first Republican since 1962.
2003	Challenges to native Hawaiian affirmative action; Kahoolawe handed over to state by Navy.
2005	Akaka Bill seeks native Hawaiian parity with Native American tribes.

Cultural Highlights

Bishop Museum
This is Hawaii's premier cultural icon. See sidebar, page 246.

HEIAU
Hawaiian *heiau* (temples) are "must-sees," such as ancient Mo'okini Heiau in North Kohala, and Kamehameha's marvelous restored Pu'ukohola Hieau in South Kohala, both on the Big Island. See sidebars.

Hawaiian Historical Society
Founded in 1892, the society is dedicated to preserving historical materials of Hawaii and the Pacific region and to publishing scholarly research on Hawaiian and Pacific history. Queen Lili'uokalani was among the first members and Charles Reed Bishop the first president. The society presents historical lectures and programs, free to the public. Its library provides a rich research collection of printed and manuscript material for use by members, scholars, historians, history buffs, serious students, and others in the community. Its publications include books emphasizing original sources, a papers series published between 1892 and 1940, *Annual Reports,* and *The Hawaiian Journal of History.* The latter, first published in 1967, is a readable first-rate source devoted to original articles on the history of Hawaii, Polynesia, and the Pacific. See www.hawaiianhistory.org/index.html.

Theater, Opera, Music
Honolulu's spectacular **Neal S. Blaisdell Center** has been in operation since 1964 (www.blaisdellcenter.com). Its concert hall hosts performances of the **Hawaii Opera Theater**, the state's resident company that had its first season in 1960, as well as the big Broadway and West End musicals. Here too Oahu's main concerts, both master works and "pops," are staged by the Honolulu Symphony, first organized in 1902. Samuel Wong conducted the classics for nine seasons until 2005, presenting innovative East–West concerts. Matt Catingub, pops conductor since 1998, has included many major mainland performers in the program, their enticement being his composition of the orchestra arrangements. The **Hawaii Youth Symphony Association** also performs, drawing upon student musicians from all the islands. Visiting mainland and foreign ballet companies dance here. The center is conveniently located in downtown at the foot of Punchbowl, accessible to Waikiki hotels and shopping centers, and stands on the historic site

of the former Ward Estate known as "Old Plantation," acquired by the city and county of Honolulu in 1958. The many artesian springs have been changed into the tranquil tropical fish ponds that surround the arena and exhibition hall. The sweeping lawns and coconut tree groves have existed since the 1800s. Facilities are ideal for cultural attractions, community shows, trade shows, pop concerts, and general entertainment.

Manoa Valley Theater in Manoa, **Diamond Head Theater** at the foot of Diamond Head (Hawaii's oldest theater company, 1915), and **Kumu Kahua Theater** are all semi-professional local companies. The latter has a 100-seat theater in the historical former King Kamehameha V Post Office (1871) and performs plays about Hawaii by Hawaiian playwrights.

Hawaii Ballet Theater (the state's oldest troupe), **Hawaii State Ballet** (1983), and **Ballet Hawaii** (1976) maintain high standards, using innovative Hawaiian conceptions.

The **Hawaii Theater building** (1922) in the center of downtown is itself a cultural gem. It closed in 1984, but determined theater enthusiasts bought it from the Bishop Estate and with $33 million restored it to its original glory and reopened it in 1996. Its stylish interior has marble floors, Shakespearean bar reliefs, and trompe l'oeil mosaics. The 30-foot *Glorification of the Drama*, an eye-catching mural of muse-like figures by Lionel Walden, graces the proscenium arch. Now the theater is a popular prime downtown attraction with top mainland, overseas, and local dance, music, and theater performances.

The **Honolulu Dance Theater,** which plays mainly at the Hawaii Theater, blends dance and theater to produce a unique local mix. The company's 2004 production of Tchaikovsky's "Nutcracker," for instance, became the "Hawaiian Nutcracker Ballet"; Princess Kauilani and Prince Kawananakoa were featured in principal roles and the Christmas party was held at 'Iolani Palace (including hula). A fantasy "Land of the Rainbow" had dancing geckos, peacocks, surfers, and pineapples. There were no mice and soldiers, but instead wild boars and ancient Hawaiian warriors. There were also *menehune*, who danced with ukuleles or played surfers—but no snowflakes!

The **Maui Arts and Cultural Center** in Kahului has two theaters used by Maui's theater groups. The lovingly restored Spanish Mission style **'Iao Theater** (1928) in Wailuku also hosts productions.

Royal Hawaiian Band

King Kamehameha III formally organized the Royal Hawaiian Band in 1836, the first brass band in the Pacific. In 1872, following the request of King Kamehameha V to the Prussian government to help improve the band's standards, Heinrich Wilhelm Berger arrived in Honolulu. With Berger as bandmaster, modern Hawaiian music began. Giving heed to the polestars of Hawaiian life—respect for *ali'i* (chiefs/leaders) and *aloha'aina* (love of the land)—he quickly gained favor and served until 1915. The band became a focus and venue for the expression of Hawaiian music. During that time Berger conducted thousands of concerts, arranged about 1,000 Western and 200 Hawaiian melodies, and wrote hundreds of compositions, many becoming some of Hawaii's best-loved songs. He instructed the royal family and enthused and taught several generations of musicians.

The former bandmaster, Hawaii-born Aaron David Mahi served from 1981 to 2005 and, like Berger, crossed easily between the musical worlds of Hawaii and the West. Mahi noted that "In Hawaiian music, the most important aspect is the *mele* (words). The Western approach of developing the melodic line can actually enhance or reinforce the *mele*...." Along with classical music, marches, polkas, schottisches, and waltzes, the band plays famous songs of Hawaii in their traditional Berger arrangements: "Aloha 'Oe," "Hawaii Pono'i," and "Hilo March." An agency of the city and county of Honolulu, the band plays every Friday at 'Iolani Palace from noon for an hour, every Sunday and several other days at various venues, and many special events each year. It often travels overseas and in 1988 played a sold-out performance at Carnegie Hall.

New Musical Instruments, Royal Contributions, and Modern Performers

Hearing Hawaiian music is hearing its history. The guitar first arrived either with the whalers and traders or the *paniolos* (cowboys). In time Hawaiians loosened or "slacked" their strings, tuning in any way they wished, and slack key is now iconically Hawaiian. In 1878 from the Azores, the Portuguese plantation workers brought their small *braquino* and *rajao*, which somehow metamorphosed into the utterly Hawaiian ukulele ("jumping flea" in Hawaiian).

The origins of the Hawaiian steel guitar may never be known, though many attribute it to late 1887 and Joseph Kekuku. A schoolboy at the recently opened Kamehameha Schools, over a period of time Kekuku is supposed to have used the school workshop to turn out a steel bar to slide along the gut strings, to fix steel strings, then to raise them so they wouldn't hit the frets.

He later toured the United States, popularizing the Hawaiian steel guitar, until his death in 1932. Others claim Gabriel Davion, an Indian sailor, and James Hoa, a Hawaiian "of Portuguese ancestry," as originators around 1885. Sol Hoopii (1902–53) was perhaps the most famous Hawaiian steel guitarist. Despite the fact that the steel guitar has been adopted by other music, such as country and western, there remains an identifiably Hawaiian sound and style of playing.

King David Kalakaua and his sister Queen Lili'uokalani were two of the most talented and prolific composers in island history. King Kalakaua loved hula, encouraged the steel guitar and ukulele, had his own musical group, and promoted Hawaiian music as a matter of national pride. With Heinrich Berger, he co-composed Hawaii's national anthem *Hawaii Pono'i*, which is still sung at gatherings and games. The queen was an even more gifted musician and wrote about 150 pieces, the most famous the wistful, ever-popular "Aloha 'Oe" ("Farewell to Thee"). Many, including one of Hawaii's greatest present-day song-writers, Dennis Kamakahi, acknowledge the inspiration of the queen's compositions.

In 1915 a group of Hawaiian musicians, dancers, and singers were a sensation at the San Francisco Pacific International Exposition, and their hula music swept North America and after World War I, Europe, and was taken up by Tin Pan Alley. By the 1930s, genuine and *hapa-haole* (half-foreign) hula music were accepted as typically Hawaiian both in the islands and overseas, stimulated by the radio program *Hawaii Calls*. Hollywood adopted it too, and until the 1960s there was a golden age of Hawaiian music. Rock killed Hawaiian music for a decade or more until the Hawaiian cultural renaissance, when new rhythms, instruments, and electronics seized the imagination of the young and returned them to their musical heritage.

The most influential Hawaiian slack key guitarist ever was Philip "Gabby" Pahinui (1921–80) with his expressive vocals and soulful falsetto. The modern slack key period began around 1946, when he made his first recording. Gabby was a prime influence in keeping slack key guitar from dying out in Hawaii, and his many special techniques helped it to become more accepted as a solo instrument.

New generations of Hawaiian entertainers have continued to emerge. Given all the talented performers and writers in the last three decades, it is invidious to provide names, but representative of a multitude are: guitarist Keola Beamer; musician and entertainer Don Ho; the velvet voice and playing of the mighty Israel Kamakawiwo'ole (Iz); Keali'i Reichel; Robert Cazimero; the three ladies of Na Leo Pilimehana; Moe Keale; and recently

Amy Hanaiali'i Gilliom with her spectacular falsetto. More native Hawaiians now know their language well and express themselves poetically in it, which is an important reason their music is flourishing. Hawaiians of all ethnicities have continued to blend popular Western music genres and the rhythms of immigrant groups with traditional Hawaiian to form unique mixtures: Music is ubiquitous in Hawaii, a gift from the gods.

ARTIFACTS AND ART

The **Honolulu Academy of Arts** opened in 1927 and was the inspiration of philanthropist Anna Rice Cooke. This striking, airy gallery where "east meets west" near Thomas Square in downtown Honolulu displays a permanent collection of Pacific, American, Asian, African, and European art. The Pacific is well represented with Hawaiian (feather leis, tapa beaters, koawood calabashes, poi pounders), New Guinean, and Micronesian artifacts, illustrations of Hawaii by artists such as John Webber and James Clevely of the Cook expedition, nineteenth-century scenes, and the works of twentieth-century Hawaiian artists such as Huc Luquiens and John M. Kelly. The Asian exhibits are outstanding with Chinese bronzes and jades, Korean ceramics, Indian miniatures, and the James A. Michener collection of Edo Period popular Japanese art. Americans such as Winslow Homer and Mary Cassatt and the Samuel H. Kress Collection of European Renaissance masters and moderns such as Van Gogh, Monet, and Picasso are featured.

As there exist six main islands of the archipelago, it can be suggested there are six main twentieth- and twenty-first-century Hawaiian masters. Trained in England, Madge Tennant (died 1972) said she envisioned the Hawaiian rulers as having descended from gods of heroic proportion, intelligent and brave, bearing a strong affinity to the Greeks in their legends and persons. Her portraits of Hawaiians that reflect this viewpoint are mainly displayed at the Tennant Art Foundation on Punchbowl. Tadashi Sato (1923–2005), born on Maui and inspired by nature, produced superb murals and mosaics, such as the 30 ft wide blue and gray *Aquarius* of the State Capitol concourse and the 60 ft *Portals of Immortality* in Lahaina. Jean Charlot, who arrived in 1939 after perfecting his technique in Mexico, became famous for his frescoes and his art criticism until his death in 1979. Many of his murals and sculptures can be seen in the Jean Charlot Collection at the University of Hawaii, Manoa, Honolulu. John M. Kelly (died 1962) who arrived in 1923 to stay a year but just stayed, produced technically superb, painstakingly detailed etchings and color engravings, most now at the Honolulu Academy of Arts. The *Honolulu Star* called him the artist who probably did more than any other to acquaint the world with Hawaii's Polynesian and Asian faces, moods, and characters. Huc Luquiens (1881–1961) was a master of drypoint etching and produced unique island landscapes. Trained in Chicago and since returning to his father's islands in 1970 at age 40, Herb Kane has produced a unique body of stylish, colorful paintings and murals, inspired by Hawaiian history and myth and the life of Kamehameha I. Many grace the walls of museums and public places. His much-reproduced *Battle of Nu'uanu Pali* is in the possession of the Kamehameha Schools/Bishop Estate; *Kamehameha at Kamakahonu* is in the King Kamehameha Hotel Kailu-Kona, the Big Island; *The Battle of the Red-Mouthed Gun* is at the Army Museum Fort DeRusy, Honolulu; and a series of fourteen paintings of Polynesian canoes is owned by Hawaii's State Foundation on Culture and the Arts.

Books

A number of Hawaiian authors have preserved priceless aspects of their culture:

Barrere, Dorothy B., Mary K. Pukui, and Marion Kelly. *Hula: Historical Perspectives*. Honolulu: Department of Anthropology, Bishop Museum, 1909/1980. Famous scholarly essays on ancient Hawaii's most important art form; uses early eyewitness accounts.

Bushnell, O. A. *Ka'a'awa. A Novel about Hawaii in the 1850s*. Honolulu: University of Hawaii Press, 1980. In this compassionate novel, Hiram Nihoa, the native narrator and *kahuna*, travels Oahu describing the scenes and the people he loves; in contrast the story is taken up by Saul Bristol, a disillusioned New Englander with the eyes of a newcomer. There are striking descriptions of the influenza and smallpox epidemics and a culture under siege. (Bushnell is generally recognized as Hawaii's premier novelist.)

Bushnell, O. A. *Molokai*. Tulsa, OK: The World Publishing Co., 1963. Movingly describes life in the leper colony at Kalaupapa. One of the classic pieces of fiction by a Hawaiian.

Finney, Ben and James D. Houston. *Surfing, a History of the Ancient Hawaiian Sport*. San Francisco: Pomegranate Books, 1966/1996. First book to chart surfing's Hawaiian and Polynesian origins. Little-known early etchings and old photographs.

Holmes, Tommy. *The Hawaiian Canoe*. Honolulu: Editions Ltd, 1981. Compendious, strikingly illustrated coffee-table presentation of traditions and techniques involved in building and navigating canoes, from the ancient Polynesians to the present day, by a co-founder of the Polynesian Voyaging Society.

Ii, John P. *Fragments of Hawaiian History*. Honolulu: Bishop Museum Press, 1963. Unique recollections of pre-missionary era by the intelligent nineteenth-century chronicler.

Kalakaua, King David. *The Legends and Myths of Hawaii*. Honolulu: Mutual Publishing, 1888/1990. Hawaii's last king draws on his Victorian education and his deep and caring knowledge of the oral tradition.

Lili'uokalani. *Hawaii's Story by Hawaii's Queen*. Honolulu: Mutual Publishing, 1897/1992. Fascinating autobiography of the aristocratic life of the last monarch of Hawaii also gives her account of how her kingdom was taken away.

Malo, David. *Hawaiian Antiquities*. Honolulu: Bishop Museum Press, 1951. Nineteenth-century survey of culture and society, written by a native Hawaiian brought up at the court of Kuakini on the Big Island. Christian perspective, and, with Ii, the most accurate account of pre-contact.

FILMS

There have been multitudes of films made in Hawaii to take advantage of the scenery and that is their only interest as Hawaiiana. Spectacular Kauai is most preferred, and tours of its film locations can now be taken. The best films are made about Hawaii rather than merely in it. Here is a sample:

James Jones's bestseller became *From Here to Eternity*, filmed in Oahu with top stars Bert Lancaster and Deborah Kerr (1953).

In the years of the first great increase in tourism after the introduction of jet travel, Elvis Presley and Angela Lansbury captured the essence of tourist kitch in *Blue Hawaii* (1961), filmed on Oahu and Kauai (like the modern economy, Elvis prefers tourism to pineapples). This was the first of his Hawaiian trilogy; Elvis's films continued with the growth of tourism.

In 1966 the film of Michener's bestseller *Hawaii* encapsulated a crucial period in Hawaii's history, with Max Von Sydow as missionary and Julie Andrews as his wife.

Filmed on Oahu, *Tora Tora Tora* (1970), with top US and Japanese actors, imaginatively portrays Pearl Harbor from both sides.

An example of a few films that have probed Hawaiian life was *Picture Bride* (1993), starring Yuki Kudoh and a cameo role for the great Toshiro Mifune. Filmed in Oahu, it shows the difficulties of life for a nineteenth-century mail-order Japanese bride.

In 2003, *The Ride*, Hawaiian director Nathan Kurosawa's film with Sean Kaawa and Mary Paalani, depicted the great Duke Kahanamoku as both surfer and man. Filmed in various locations, it makes use of pidgin and employs local music and musicians.

EVENTS

Hawaii's most prestigious, most popular hula gathering—the classic Merrie Monarch Festival—is a colorful, dynamic week-long hula feast in Hilo, the Big Island, honoring King David Kalakaua, first held in 1950. Festivities start on Easter Sunday. On Wednesday there is an exhibition hula night at the stadium, Thursday night the solo competition, and Friday and Saturday are for group ancient and modern hula, with a parade on Saturday morning. For information and ticket inquiries contact: Merrie Monarch Festival, c/o Hawaii Naniola Resort, 93 Banyan Drive, Hilo, HI 96720 (www.volcanogallery.com/MerryMonarch.htm). DVDs are available.

From mid-September to late October, Hawaii's Aloha Festivals, the largest statewide festivals, and the islands' main cultural events—music, dance, history—are intended to preserve the heritage and are held consecutively for a week in each of the six main islands. (www.alohafestivals.com)

Windsurfing Ho'okipa Beach, Maui. Hawaii Visitors and Convention Bureau and Rob Dahlquist

Special Events

Hawaii celebrates all the US public holidays plus many holidays and events of its own. New Year's Eve is especially lively.

January

Opening of legislature: State Capitol in downtown Honolulu, third Wednesday. Impressive ceremony, leis, Hawaiian activities.

Punahou School Carnival: One of Hawaii's most famous schools holds its large popular fair early in the month.

February or March

Mauna Kea Ski Meet & Hawaii Ski Cup: International event on state's highest mountain. Dates depend upon amount of snow.

March

Kuhio Day (March 26): The state honors popular Prince Jonah Kuhio, Congressional delegate and son of Queen Lili'uokalani. Celebrations, parades, memorial services at Nu'uanu Royal Mausoleum and Kawaiaha'o Church.

Lahaina Whalefest (early March): With lectures, dives, and more, the Whalefest celebrates this key creature of Hawaiian nineteenth-century history, which now has a safe home in Maui's coastal waters.

Haleakala Run to the Sun: The grueling and amazing 36 mi (58 km) race from sea-level to the volcano's 10,000 ft summit has been held annually since 1980.

April

International Pro Board Windsurfing Competition (early April): A ten-day tournament at the home of windsurfing, Ho'okipa Beach, North Shore, Maui.

May

Lei Day (May 1): People wear special leis and bright Hawaiian clothing. Kapi'olani Park has concerts, parades, sunset hula. Schoolchildren throughout the islands perform.

June

Kamehameha Day (June 11): First celebrated in 1872, this official state holiday honors the unifier of the islands. It is marked with a colorful parade (the first in 1916) from downtown Honolulu to the Waikiki Shell parking lot in Kapi'olani Park, where there are stalls, hula, and exhibits. Highlights are spectacular floats, the Royal Hawaiian Band, and a Hawaiian special—the traditional lady Pa'u Riders in their magnificent full-length horse-covering skirts, or *pa'u*, which allow them to straddle their horses and still look supremely elegant. Neal S. Blaisdell Center holds a hula competition. Other islands also enthusiastically celebrate the day. This is also a good time for a visit to large Kapi'olani Park in Honolulu.

July

Prince Lot Hula Festival held at Moanalua Gardens Honolulu (third saturday): Local hula schools honor the prince (later Kamehameha V) with ancient and modern hula.

August

Pu'uhonua O Honaunau Festival: National Historical Park, a former place of refuge, south of Kailua-Kona on the Big Island. Important native Hawaiian cultural gathering.

September

Hana Relay Run: This annual 52 mi (84 km) six-person race, first held in 1971, navigates 617 curves and 56 bridges through spectacular green coastal scenery from Kahului Airport to the venerable native Hawaiian town of Hana.

Outrigger Canoe Race (late September): This race from Molokai to Oahu continues to expand and, despite Hawaiian domination, draws competitors from across the world—more than a hundred in 2005.

Maui Marathon: Right from the starting ceremony, runners experience Hawaiian culture as, in the pre-dawn darkness lit by tiki torches, they receive a Hawaiian blessing and are honored by hula dancers and blown conch shells. From Queen Ka'ahumanu Center in Kahului through the central valley, with hula dancers at locations along the course, the run passes through historic Lahaina and finishes at prosperous Whalers Village in Ka'anapali Resort.

October

Halloween Party: Lahaina on Maui holds the state's largest.

November

The Hawaii International Film Festival: Featured at various cinemas on Oahu in the first week of November, then on to the "neighbor islands."

NOVEMBER THROUGH FEBRUARY

Surfing Contests: Throughout these months, surfing reigns on Oahu's north shore. Dates are decided by the condition of the surf, with day-to-day announcements. *Triple Crown of Surfing*, the world's greatest surfing contest, occurs in late November to mid-December at the spectacular Banzai Pipeline and Sunset Beach near Waimea, and at Ali'i Beach Park in Hale'iwa.

The Grand Slam of Golf (Thanksgiving week): This tournament has the toughest qualification in the world. At Po'ipu Bay Golf Course, on a magnificent rolling plateau high above the ocean at Kauai's southernmost point, the winners of the Masters, US Open, British Open, and PGA Golf Championships compete for a $1,000,000 prize.

DECEMBER

Pearl Harbor Day (December 7): Memorial service at the *USS Arizona* Memorial.

Honolulu City Lights: A feature of the Christmas festive season. Honolulu Hale (City Hall) has spectacular trees.

The Honolulu Boy Choir: Performs each year at Honolulu's Ala Moana Center to begin the season.

Contact Information

The Hawaii Visitors and Convention Bureau is a quality organization that provides help and information on almost everything Hawaiian, with premises in all the main islands. (www.gohawaii.com) Many events are listed at calendar.gohawaii.com.

The Hawaii Museums Association lists information on some 97 museums throughout the islands (www.hawaiimuseums.org).

Hawaii's two main English daily newspapers, both published in Honolulu, have sites at www.starbulletin.com and www.honoluluadvertiser.com.

The main alternative weekly is *Honolulu Weekly* (www.honoluluweekly.com).

Ecotourism

For information, contact the Hawaiian Ecotourism Association, P.O. Box 6143, Honolulu, HI 96822, www.hawaiiecotourism.org. You can also visit www.alternative-hawaii.com and gohawaii.about.com/cs/ecotourism.

National Wildlife Refuges

See www.fws.gov/pacific/pacificislands/wnwr/nwrindex.html.

Hawaii State Parks

Visit www.state.hi.us/dlnr/dsp/dsp.html.

Hawaiian Affairs & Native Sovereignty Organizations

The government-funded Office of Hawaiian Affairs (OHA) works toward better living conditions for native Hawaiians. It is located at 711 Kapi'olani Boulevard, Suite 500, Honolulu, HI 96813, or visit www.oha.org.

You can also visit the following websites for the various sovereignty groups: Nation of Hawaii at www.hawaii-nation.org; Reinstated Hawaiian Government at www.reinstated.org; Kingdom of Hawaii at www.freehawaii.org; Kingdom of Hawaii at www.pixi.com/~kingdom (there are two); The Hawaiian Kingdom at www.hawaiiankingdom.org.

Sources and Further Reading

The State Foundation of Culture and the Arts has a calendar of events at www.state.hi.us/sfca/culturecalendar.html or at www.hawaii.gov/sfca/.

Language

The are many sources for keeping abreast of what is new in Hawaiian language learning, such as the Hawaiian Language website at http://hawaiianlanguage.com. There are also online dictionaries. Coconut Boyz Cyber Hawaiian Online uses the dictionary by Pukui and Elbert as a reference (see listing, next page), with some 5,000 entries. The Hawaiian Language Center (Hale Kuamoʻo) at the University of Hawaii at Hilo also has an online dictionary, Mamaka Kaiao, that forms a supplement to Pukui and Elbert. Sound files with native speakers have helped the learning of pronunciation. A good example is Native Tongue, www.aloha-hawaii.com/hawaii/native+tongue or www.aloha-hawaii.com/hawaii/native+tongue.

Although hundreds of books have been written about everything Hawaiian, most can be found in bookstores only on the islands. Hawaiian public libraries are well stocked. Most allow visitors to borrow. Oahu, Maui, the Big Island, and Kauai all have good bookstores in the largest towns. The bookstore at the University of Hawaii, Manoa Campus, Honolulu, is probably the best source of all.

The University of Hawaii Press publishes a wide variety of materials on Hawaii and the Pacific. It has a long list for purchase by mail at www.uhpress.hawaii.edu/ (2840 Kolowalu Street, Honolulu, HI 96822).

Bishop Museum Press (1525 Bernice Street, Honolulu, HI 96817), Hawaii's oldest book publisher and one of the first scholarly publishers in the western hemisphere, publishes scholarly books and monographs on Hawaii and the Pacific. See www.bishop.hawaii.org/ bishop/press.

The Bess Press (3563 Harding Avenue, Honolulu, HI 96816), specializes in books on Hawaii and the Pacific Islands. See www.besspress.com.

Reference

Atlas of Hawaii. Honolulu: The University of Hawaii Press, 1998. This 333-page resource from the geography department is replete with maps and tabulations and amazing computer graphics.

Chapin, Helen G. *Guide to Newspapers of Hawaii, 1834–2000*. Honolulu: Hawaiian Historical Society, 2000. Complete reference to Hawaii's newspapers. About 1,250 different newspapers in at least twelve languages were printed in Hawaii. Each listing is annotated, with category, place of publication, frequency and dates, publishers and editors, and abbreviations of sources that list the paper and locations where the paper may be seen in hardcopy or on microfilm.

Forbes, David W. *Treasures of Hawaiian History. From the Collection of the Hawaiian Historical Society*. Honolulu: Hawaiian Historical Society, 1992. This catalog describes books, documents, manuscripts, photographs, maps, and memorabilia in the collection of the society. Prepared in connection with an exhibition presented by the society in 1992 to mark the centennial of its founding. Many black-and-white and color photographs.

Kilolani Mitchell, Donald D. *Resource Units in Hawaiian Culture*. Honolulu: Kamehameha Schools Press, 2001. Though produced for schools, this is a marvelous general resource.

McDonald, Marie A. and Paul R. Weissich, with photos by Jean Cote. *Na Lei Makamae: The Treasured Lei*. Honolulu: University of Hawaii Press, 2003. Following Samuel Kamakau, Abraham Fornander, and others, the authors reveal the significance of making and wearing lei and their role in Hawaiian ritual and dance.

Kawena Pukui, Mary, Samuel H. Elbert, and Esther T. Mookini. *Place Names of Hawaii*. Honolulu: University of Hawaii Press, 1974. Explains the meaning and context of more than 4,000 names.

Kawena Pukui, Mary, and Samuel H. Elbert. *The Hawaiian Dictionary*. Honolulu: University of Hawaii Press, 1957/1996. This is the most authoritative work, with 30,000 entries, Hawaiian–English and English–Hawaiian. There is also a smaller, 10,000-entry version.

Cook, Chris, photos by David Boynton. *The Kauai Movie Book* (Mutual Publishing with Wilcox Hospital Foundation & Kauai Film Commission), 1996. This coffee-table book covers everything from blockbusters like *South Pacific* to documentaries, foreign films, and surfing movies, showing the movie sites during filming and as they look today, as well as directors, stars, and the locals.

FICTION AND TRAVELLERS' TALES
Bird, Isabella. *The Hawaiian Archipelago: Six Months Among the Palm Groves, Coral Reefs, and Volcanoes of the Sandwich Islands*.

London: John Murray, 1875. Fascinating adventures and crisp social observations of an Englishwoman in 1870s, with time spent on all the major islands and a chilly expedition up Mauna Loa.

Day, A. Grove, and Carl Stroven (eds.). *A Hawaiian Reader* and *The Spell of Hawaii* (Mutual Publishing, 2 vols). Lively paperback anthologies of writings on Hawaii, including pieces by Mark Twain, Jack London, Isabella Bird, and Robert Louis Stevenson.

Harstad, Cheryl A. and James R. *Island Fire: An Anthology of Literature from Hawaii.* Honolulu: University of Hawaii Press, 2002. Vignettes of life in the islands by many of the best modern resident writers.

Michener, James. *Hawaii.* New York: Random House, 1959. Multi-generational blockbuster novel; believable, some inaccuracies; helped promote Hawaiian tourism.

Stevenson, Robert Louis. *Travels in Hawaii.* Edited by A. Grove Day. Honolulu: University of Hawaii Press, 1991. About the Scottish novelist's months in Hawaii in the late nineteenth century; includes experiences with the royals, a moving account of his visit to leper colony on Molokai, and the famous "Open Letter" in defense of Father Damien.

Theroux, Paul. *Hotel Honolulu.* New York: Houghton Mifflin, 2001. The book's narrator, a resting writer managing the hotel, offers privileged glimpses into the myriad strange stories of guests and staff, unfolding in the rooms of this middle-income hotel.

Tregaskis, Richard. *The Warrior King.* Honolulu: Falmouth Press, 1973. Fictionalized, readable biography of Kamehameha I, greatest figure in Hawaiian history.

Twain, Mark. *Letters from Hawaii.* Edited by A. Grove Day. Honolulu: University of Hawaii Press, 1966. Entertaining, youthful, and opinionated accounts of nineteenth-century Hawaii, with enthusiastic descriptions of the volcanoes of Maui and the Big Island.

Autobiography/Biography

Adler, Jacob. *The Fantastic Life of Walter M. Gibson, Hawaii's Minister of Everything.* Honolulu: University of Hawaii Press, 1986. Life of adventurer, financier, purchaser of Lanai, favorite of native Hawaiian voters, scourge of the missionary-settler party.

Armstrong, William. *Around the World with a King*. Cambridge, England: Cambridge University Press, 1904. Readable autobiographical account of world trip of King David Kalakaua.

Beaglehole, J. C. *The Life of Captain James Cook*. London/Stanford CA: A & C. Black/Stanford University Press, 1974/1998. Culmination of life's work; masterful account of this greatest of all explorer-seamen, by the doyen of Pacific historians.

Boelen, Captain Jacobus. *A Merchant's Perspective: Captain Jacobus Boelen's Narrative of His Visit to Hawaii in 1828*. Honolulu: Hawaiian Historical Society, 1988. The only Dutch account of a voyage to the Hawaiian Islands in the early nineteenth-century. Portrays the last days of the sandalwood trade and the important role of the sea-captain merchant in the early period of relations with foreigners. Contrasts the conditions of the lives of *ali'i* and commoners and describes Honolulu as a port town.

Bingham, Hiram. *A Residence of Twenty-one Years in the Sandwich Islands*. New York: Praeger Publishers,1847/1969. Fascinating revelation of attitudes of this pertinacious Congregational missionary leader.

Cahill, Emmett. *The Life and Times of John Young*. Aiea, Hawaii: Island Heritage Publishing, 1999. Illustrated biography of one of the most amazing figures of early modern era, an Englishman, Kamehameha the Great's most trusted adviser.

Daws, Gavan. *Holy Man: Father Damien of Molokai*. Honolulu: University of Hawaii Press, 1970. Best biography of nineteenth-century Belgian priest who ministered to the lepers.

Hall, Sandra Kimberley. *Duke: A Great Hawaiian*. Honolulu: Bess Press, 2000. Photo-filled tribute to this unique Olympic swimmer, surfer, and sheriff of Honolulu.

Kerlviet, Melinda Tria. *Unbending Cane: Pablo Manlapit, a Filipino Labor Leader in Hawaii*. Honolulu: University of Hawaii Press, 2002. Account of controversial 1920s plantation labor leader who challenged the might of sugar barons.

Kraus, Bob. *Keneti: South Seas Adventures of Kennety Emory*. Honolulu: University of Hawaii Press, 1988. Story of the long life of the great Bishop Museum ethnologist-archaeologist who died in 1992 and proposed the now-accepted theory of Polynesian origins.

Melville, Herman. *Typee*. New York: The Heritage Press, 1846/1963. Much set in the Marquesas Islands, but with aspects of his time in Hawaii; Melville's marvelous experiences in the South Seas inspired later writers such as London and Stevenson.

Ledyard, John. *John Ledyard's Journal of Captain Cook's Last Voyage*. Edited by James K Mumford. Corvallis, Oregon: Oregon State University Press, 1963. Report of Ledyard's adventures as the sole American in Cook's crew.

Thurston, Lorrin A. *Memoirs of the Hawaiian Revolution*. Edited by Andrew Farrell. Honolulu: Honolulu Advertiser Publishing Co., 1936. The key instigator of the coup d'etat recalls the eventful days.

de Varigny, Charles. *Fourteen Years in the Sandwich Islands 1855–1863*. Translated by A. L. Korn. Honolulu: University Press of Hawaii 1864/1981. Perceptive account by sophisticated Frenchman who became a Hawaiian government minister; report of 1868 Mauna Loa eruption.

History

Beekman, Allan. *The Niihau Incident*. Honolulu: Heritage Press of the Pacific, 1982. Only detailed account of terrorizing of Niihau by crashed Japanese pilot in days after Pearl Harbor.

Campbell, I. C. *Worlds Apart: A History of the Pacific Islands*. Christchurch, New Zealand: University of Canterbury Press, 2003. Up-to-date, scholarly but readable history that puts Hawaii in its wider context. (Largely rewritten version of his earlier *A History of the Pacific Islands*.)

Coffman, Tom. *The Island Edge of America: A Political History of Hawaii*. Honolulu: University of Hawaii Press, 2003. A political narrative of twentieth-century Hawaii from annexation to the present that links the multicultural and transnational forces that shaped the islands.

Cowan Smith, Virginia & Bonnie Domrose Stone. *Aloha Cowboy*. Honolulu: University of Hawaii Press, 1998. Illustrated story of 180 years of *paniolos* (cowboys) in Hawaii.

Daws, Gavan. *Shoal of Time*. Honolulu: University of Hawaii Press, 1968. Lengthy, authoritative history of the Hawaiian Islands, from European contact to statehood in 1959.

Dougherty, Michael. *To Steal a Kingdom: Probing Hawaiian History*. Waimanalo, Hawaii: Island Style Press, 1992. Moving revisionist history, which uses their own words to distinguish or damn famous figures of the nineteenth century, from Bingham and Judd to Melville and Lili'uokalani. Argues that official Hawaiian history writing has been biased by controlling families.

Dye, Bob, ed. *Hawaii Chronicles*. Honolulu: University of Hawaii Press, 1996. Little-known stories of outstanding people and places from the Manila galleons to Pearl Harbor; from the pages of *Honolulu Magazine*.

_____. *Hawaii Chronicles II*. Honolulu: University of Hawaii Press, 2000. Accounts of artists, writers, politicians, local heroes, sovereignty activists since World War II; from the pages of *Honolulu Magazine*.

_____. *Hawaii Chronicles III*. Honolulu: University of Hawaii Press, 2000. Reports of Hawaiians who lived through World War II; from the pages of *Honolulu Magazine*.

Grimshaw, Patricia. *Paths of Duty: American Missionary Wives in the Nineteenth Century*. Honolulu: University of Hawaii Press, 1989. Hard times for women in Hawaiian and other islands.

Takaki, Ronald. *Pau Hana: Plantation Life and Labor in Hawaii, 1835–1920*. Honolulu: University of Hawaii Press, 1983. Scholarly work that reads like a novel about the oppressive conditions on Hawaiian plantations.

Kamakau, Samuel M. *The People of Old*. (3 vols). Honolulu: Bishop Museum Press, 1992. Anecdotal essays, originally written in Hawaiian in newspapers in 1860s. Fascinating nuggets of information on Hawaiian oral traditions; some claims unconvincing.

Kuykendall, R. S. *The Hawaiian Kingdom* (3 vols.) Honolulu: 1938, 1953, 1957. Major attempt to tell the whole story in massive detail.

Stephan, John J. *Hawaii under the Rising Sun: Japan's Plans for Conquest after Pearl Harbor*. Honolulu: University of Hawaii Press, 2001. Revealing; much important though little-known evidence.

Valeri, Valerio. *Kingship and Sacrifice: Ritual and Society in Ancient Hawaii*. Chicago: University of Chicago Press, 1985. Academic analysis of the role of human sacrifice in establishing the chief's power.

West, Rodney T. *Honolulu Prepares for Japan's Attack*. Honolulu, 1992/2002. Informative short book with many little-known details.

SOVEREIGNTY

Dudley, Michael Kioni, and Keoni Kealoha Agard. *A Call for Hawaiian Sovereignty*. Waipahu, Hawaii: Na Kane O Ka Malo Press, 1993. Readable short book on the Hawaiian sovereignty movement from a native Hawaiian viewpoint.

Twigg-Smith, Thurston. *Hawaiian Sovereignty: Do the Facts Matter?* Honolulu: Goodale Publishing, 1998. Grandson of the coup leader rebuts the sovereignty activists.

Trask, Haunani Kay. *From a Native Daughter: Colonialism and Sovereignty in Hawaii*. Honolulu: University of Hawaii Press, 1999. Aggressive contribution to the sovereignty debate from one of Hawaii's best-known activists.

NAVIGATION, NATURE, & SCIENCE

Carlquist, Sherwin. *Hawaii: A Natural History*. New York: Doubleday. Good reference on flora and fauna.

Chauvin, Michael. *Hokuloa: The British 1874 Transit of Venus Expedition to Hawaii*. Honolulu: Bishop Museum Press, 2004. Amazing story of Hawaii–British connection, political maneuvering, and heroism in pursuit of measuring the "astronomical unit," the distance between the earth and the sun, the key astronomical measurement of the nineteenth-century. (And they found time to erect the memorial obelisk to Cook in Kealakekua Bay!)

Dudley, N. S. C., and M. Lee. *Tsunami*. Honolulu: University of Hawaii Press, 1998. Up-to-date, comprehensive volume on the destructive phenomenon once called "tidal waves," with much on Hawaii.

Finney, Ben. *Hokule'a: The Way to Tahiti*. New York: Dodd, Mead & Co., 1979. Gripping story of the double canoe's construction, preparation, and first eventful voyage to Tahiti by the initiator of the Polynesian Voyaging Society. Describes tensions and difficulties and in passing reveals much about native Hawaiians.

Macdonald, Gordon A., Agatin A. Abbott and Frank L. Peterson. *Volcanoes in the Sea: The Geology of Hawaii*. Honolulu: University of Hawaii Press, 1992. A marvelous geological tour. Clearly written.

Rhoads, Samuel. *The Sky Tonight: A Guided Tour of the Stars over Hawaii*. Honolulu: Bishop Museum Press, 1993. Four pages per month of star charts. Very practical.

Staples, George W., and Derral R. Herbst. *A Tropical Garden Flora: Plants Cultivated in the Hawaiian Islands and Other Tropical Places*. Honolulu: Bishop Museum Press, 2005. High standard manual describing more than 2,100 species.

Hula, Royal Hawaiian Shopping Center, Waikiki. Maria G. Figueroa

Mo'okini Heiau
(Massive early *heiau* circa 800)

Hawi
(old sugar town)

Kapa'au
(statue of Kameh

Area of King Kamehameha's birth
in North Kohala, 1758

Kohala Mountains

Lapakahi State Historical Park
(Ruins of large fishing
village, flourished 1300s to 1800s)

Kawaihae
(Site of Kamehmeha's murder of
Keoua, 1791; cattle exports from 1830s)

Pu'ukohola Heiau National
Historic Site (1972)
(Kamehameha's Heiau to Ku
[1791], Keoua sacrificed here)

Waimea

● **Parker Ra**
(1847)

Mauna Ke
(last eruptio
circa 1300 E

Puako Petroglyphs
(circa 1200s–1800s)

KAILUA-KONA

▲ **Hualalai**
(last eruption 1800–1801)

Captain Cook
(Kona Historical Society,
building 1875, Museum 1976)

Captain Cook Monument
(1874)

Kealakekua Bay
(Cook's arrival and death 1779)

▲ **Mauna Loa**
(last eruption 1984)

Pu'uhonua O Honaunau
National Historical Park
(Refuge from circa 1550 to
early 1800s; Park 1961)

Kona Coffee
plantations from 1870s
small farms from early 1900s.

1   0   5   10 KILOMETERS

2   1/2   0   10 MILES

SCALE: .1" = APPROX. 0.39 MILE

South Point
(First Polynesian settlen
circa 350 CE; ancient fis

83)

of the Red-Mouthed Gun (1790)

'o Valley (spiritual heartland, settled circa 1000)

Honoka'a (old sugar town)

Using massive amounts of water, this was the greatest sugar cane growing and refining region from 1880s. Last mill closed 1996.

Hamakua Coast

Mauna Kea Observatories:
Univ. of Hawaii Telescopes 1968/70
W.M. Keck Observatories (Univ of Cal/Caltec)1992/96
Submillimeter Array (Smithsonian/Taiwan) 2002, etc.

Onizuka Centre for International Astronomy

HILO

(settled circa 1100 & missionaries 1822)
Tsunamis 1837, 1946, 1960
Capital of Hawaii County 1905
Lynn Museum and Mission House (building 1839, museum 1931); Hilo "Massacre" 1938

d   (1942)

Historical Map of The Big Island

aiian Volcano
rvatory & Jaggar
useum (1912)

Volcano Village

Chain of Craters Road

Kilauea Volcano
(erupting since 1983)

K'au Desert Footprints
(of Keoua's warriors)

Lo'ihi Seamount
(3180 feet below sea level and rising to break the surface in 100,000 CE)